Stages and Playgoers:
From Guild Plays to Shakespeare

Stages and Playgoers demonstrates the long, vital tradition of dialogue between stage and audience from medieval, through Tudor, to Jacobean drama. Janet Hill offers new insights into techniques of addressing playgoers from the stage and how they might have operated under particular staging conditions. Hill calls this dialogue "open address," a term that takes in a range of speeches often called "asides," "monologues," and "soliloquies." She argues that open address is a strategy that challenges playgoers, asking for answers that lie outside the stage in the playgoer/playhouse world.

The tradition of direct address has little to do with the frequently touted notion of the "fluidity of the Renaissance stage": the point is not that stage characters *can* talk to the audience but that they actually *do* reach out to the playgoers and in so doing import aspects of the audience world to the stage. These exchanges appear frequently in late medieval drama and continue to be crucial stage strategies for Shakespeare, in whose works they grow and change. By examining a native English dramatic tradition not fully explored before, Hill proposes new ways to imagine historical and contemporary performances.

Stages and Playgoers will be invaluable for students of cultural studies, medieval and Renaissance studies, theatre history, and stagecraft.

JANET HILL is assistant professor in the Department of English, Saint Mary's University.

Stages and Playgoers: From Guild Plays to Shakespeare

Janet Hill

McGill-Queen's University Press

Montreal & Kingston • London • Ithaca

© McGill-Queen's University Press 2002
ISBN 0–7735–2273–5

Legal deposit fourth quarter 2002
Bibliothèque nationale du Québec

Printed in Canada on acid-free paper

This book has been published with the help of
a grant from the Humanities and Social
Sciences Federation of Canada, using funds
provided by the Social Sciences and
Humanities Research Council of Canada.

McGill-Queen's University Press
acknowledges the financial support of the
Government of Canada through the Book
Publishing Industry Development Program
(BPIDP) for its publishing activities.
It also acknowledges the support of the
Canada Council for the Arts for
its publishing program.

National Library of Canada Cataloguing in Publication Data

Hill, Janet, 1943–
Stages and playgoers : open address from guild plays to
Shakespeare

Includes bibliographical references and index.
ISBN 0–7735–2273–5

1. Soliloquy. 2. Monologue. 3. Drama—Technique. 4. English
drama—Early modern and Elizabethan, 1500–1500—History and
criticism. 5. English drama—17th century—History and criticism.
I. Title.

PR654.H54 2002   822'.045'09031   C2001–901447–3

Typeset in 10/12 Palatino by True to Type

*In memory of Frederick and Thyrza Hill
and for Barry Fox*

Contents

Acknowledgments

My first thanks go to Anne Higgins, scholar, mentor, and friend. Her deep intelligence, humour, and real love for these plays have inspired and bolstered the writing of this book.

I am indebted to those who read and commented on the book in its early form: John Baxter, Melissa Furrow, Victor Li, all of Dalhousie University, and Robert Hanning of Columbia University. I owe particular thanks to Rachel Hands, formerly of Sheffield and Oxford universities, who offered me insights on the language of the guild plays.

I am grateful to Olga Domján for her meticulous and thoughtful reading as she prepared the book for typesetting, to two anonymous readers who offered valuable suggestions when the book was young, and to Joan McGilvray for her astute and friendly comments.

This work also depends on the warmth, patience, and support of friends: in Canada, in particular Caroline Abbott, Janet Baker, Roberta Matthews, and Gillian Maycock; in England, June Anderson's sharp intuitions about plays, staging, and space have always challenged any unquestioned notions I may have had.

I have learned much about drama and performance from the lively responses of Conrad, Imogen, Ned, and Louisa Fox.

To Barry Fox I owe more thanks than I can repay for his sensitive translations, his practical help, and most of all his capacity to listen, to understand, and to respond with unique insight.

Finally, I return to where it all began. I owe Francis Berry an inestimable debt. It is he who as poet, teacher, and friend, first led me to care deeply about drama and performance.

Despite all the help and support I have received in writing this book, all mistakes, misjudgements, or misunderstandings are wholly my own.

Terminology and Translations

TERMINOLOGY

I use the term "play" for each of the four cycles discussed. The segments that some call "pageants" or "plays" are here called "episodes."

In many cases the titles of episodes are those used in the cited source-editions. However, where a non-specialist reader may have difficulty with, for instance, *Mactacio Abel*, I give the title by which it is commonly known, in this case *The Killing of Abel*.

TRANSLATIONS

The translations by Barry Fox of medieval and early modern English extracts in this book are not word-for-word; rather, they are in the form of production scripts for a modern non-specialist audience.

Stages and Playgoers

Introduction

This book is about a stage strategy I call "open address" and how it operates in plays from late medieval drama to Jacobean Shakespeare. Let me begin with an example of what I mean by "open address." Imagine that we could travel to late medieval Yorkshire and attend a performance of a play associated with the Corpus Christi festival, Towneley's *The Killing of Abel*.[1] Its plot is based on the Bible story of Cain and Abel, two brothers who make sacrifice to God. In both the Bible and the play Abel offers God a generous sacrifice, which God accepts; Cain offers a mean one, which God rejects. Furious at God and at his brother, Cain slays Abel. God then condemns Cain to wander forever throughout the world, unable to die or to be killed by others. This plot must have been familiar to everyone watching the Towneley performances.

Appearing in the Towneley episode, but not in the Bible, is a character called Pykeharnes, Cain's servant. Also in the episode, but for obvious reasons absent from the Bible, are references by master and servant to life in late medieval Yorkshire. For instance, Cain is very much a local farmer when he grumbles about tithes exacted from him by the Church: "My farthing is in the preest hand/ Syn last time I offyrd" (104–5).[2] In addition to the allusions to local life and its concerns, there are frequent occasions when the characters talk directly to the Yorkshire crowds. Open acknowledgement of audience presence is a very prominent part of this episode: the scurrilous duo of Cain and Pykeharnes, as well as God, all speak directly to the playgoers. Here is Cain after realizing he cannot escape God's prohibition against anyone killing him:

And hardly, when I am dede,
Bery me in Gudeboure at the quarell hede;
For, may I pas this place in quarte,
Bi all men set I not a fart. (366–9)

(And, when I am dead, make sure
You bury me in Goodybower,[3] at the head of the quarry.
Oh yes, if I can get out of this place safe and sound,
I won't give a fart for anyone.)

He is enraged, and turns his anger on the audience. There is nothing universal in Cain's animosity; it is directed straight at the watching crowds. He is speaking specifically about Yorkshire, the actual place and the present time. He is scoffing at its people themselves; to Cain it is Wakefield's people who aren't worth a fart. Despite being cursed by God, he asserts pigheadedly that he'll "pas" through "*this* place" (my italics), the very ground that he and the crowds occupy at the moment of performance. He doesn't just state his intention to empty air; he *hurls* it at the audience. He demands that *they* bury him in *their* local quarry.

We cannot be sure how, year after year, different audiences responded to Cain's insults and demands. They may have yelled back abuse for abuse; they may have shifted away from him, putting ground between themselves and Cain. Perhaps, knowing the story as they did, they taunted him. We can surmise that no playgoer would have been likely to attack Cain physically, because, earlier in the play, the audience had been directly warned about God's curse on anyone who might slay the murderer.

Though we cannot know the actual responses, it is clear from his words that Cain is pushing the audience for reactions. In fact, he is trying to engage in dialogue with the playgoers, even if the audience's side of the dialogue remains implicit. His words recognize that they are there with him, a solid presence. Cain speaks *with* his audience, positioning its members openly as the other half of a conversation. Whether the audience's half of that conversation was actually silent or was voiced, Cain *in*vokes their presence and *pro*vokes their responses. Equally important, Cain summons up these responses from the playgoers' contemporary, local world. Here I return to my term: When playgoers are openly addressed, when their reality is made an integral part of the play, as in *The Killing of Abel*, then what I call "open address" is taking place.

This kind of dramatic address is very much a hallmark of medieval drama and is often referred to as "direct address." (I discuss terminology more fully later in the book.) For the moment, let me just say that "direct address" is too rigid a term for the kind of inclusive address I have in mind. It suggests a one-way dynamic, stage to audience only; I consider it vital that the audience return the stage's gaze, that they be partners in the address. Open address runs through all types of medieval plays: folk drama; morality plays, both early examples such as *The Castle of Perseverance* (about 1405–25) and later ones such as *Mankind* (about 1465–70); as well as the plays variously known as "Corpus Christi," "guild," "civic," or "mystery" plays. It is with this last genre of medieval drama that I begin my exploration of open address.

Guild plays were mounted yearly by various English towns from the late fourteenth to the mid to late sixteenth centuries. The close involvement of the audience by the stage in the drama of this period is widely recognized. Susan Bennett sums up the general view when she writes that "medieval and sixteenth-century audiences ... functioned in an active role. There was a flexibility in the relationship in stage and audience world which afforded in different ways the participation of those audiences as actors in the drama."[4] As we can see from our brief visit to Wakefield's play, Bennett's comments on "flexibility" and "audience participation" are pertinent. Her suggestion about exactly how audiences were drawn in to these plays, however, is less helpful. In chapter 1 I explain in detail that addresses in guild plays did not embroil audiences as *actors* but rather as their unchanged, everyday selves.

Like Bennett, Meg Twycross describes a tight alliance between address and audience in medieval drama:

Every character can be his own story-teller. Modern theatre, under the influence of Brecht, is partly returning to this stance: it is not as unfamiliar to us as it was a few decades ago. Medieval theatre is merely less self-conscious about it. There was no need to create the "illusion" of naturalistic theatre, the self-contained hermetically sealed world in which the characters are aware only of each other, and on which we eavesdrop. If the audience needs to know something, it is told directly. A character unselfconsciously tells the audience how he feels. He also tells you "what he is doing at the same time as he is doing it." ("Theatricality," 47)

Twycross, who has been closely involved in performance reconstructions of medieval drama, continues: "The true amount of direct address in these plays becomes apparent only when they are performed. There is no such thing as a soliloquy: the character shares his fears and distresses with the audience's willing ears" ("Theatricality,"

55). While I very much admire Twycross's work and agree with many of her conclusions about ways in which characters in medieval drama talk to their audiences, I am cautious about "discovering" medieval performance strategies from modern reconstructions. Performing medieval plays today is both important and desirable, but for the sake of the plays themselves – they're good drama. Furthermore, contemporary performances of medieval plays teach us a great deal about ourselves as audiences and players, but what we learn from them about medieval practices and responses is much more problematic.

In chapter 1, I examine the strategies used in acknowledging playgoers from medieval stages – not a new topic. What *is* innovative is my perspective on how these strategies connect audiences to the plays. To anticipate briefly my argument in chapter 1: In guild plays open address takes place on a stage where no area is ever neutral, un-temporalized or un-spatialized. The texts of these plays and evidence regarding their production techniques make it clear that the *primary* stage was the specific ground on which the drama played: the quintessentially English local town or countryside, well known to all the playgoers – their immediate space, their present time, never allegorized nor historicized. Open address imports specificity of local late medieval place and time, along with material facts of everyday contemporary life, into guild drama. As Twycross and others have observed, character-audience intimacy in the plays is linked to the medieval "movement of popular piety that sought to bring the individual into a personal relationship with Christ" ("Theatricality," 55). While this is certainly true, talking openly to playgoers is also a potent and complex aspect of drama. Open address siphons one world (the audience) into another (the play). In this book, my focus is the dramaturgical power of this kind of talk. I follow it as a stage strategy which undergoes changes as it appears in new staging systems, but which, again and again, feeding off the living presence of the playgoers, injects the drama with diverse, often conflicting and uncertain, perspectives.

Nor do I claim that recognizing open audience acknowledgement is a fresh comment on Tudor or renaissance plays, which also come under scrutiny in this book. The innovation lies in pinpointing how openly addressing playgoers from the stage may have operated *within specific staging conditions*. In chapters 2 to 4, the term "open address" takes in a range of speeches usually known by other names: "asides," "monologues," and "soliloquies." For the last of these in particular I explain my reasons for renaming the concept. In general, the purpose of placing these speeches under the umbrella of "open address" is to direct attention away from conventional assumptions about them. For now, suffice it to say that I am looking at those words meant only or primarily for audience involvement. The book's impulse is always towards how various speeches make contact with the playgoers; it looks not only at what is said, but also at what kind of exchange is set up with audiences. In each case, I attempt to show what happens to our understanding of each play if we think of the address as "conversations" with a "real" world.

As I trace shifts and continuities in techniques of audience acknowledgement, from the guild plays through Tudor drama, and from Shakespeare's early drama to his final plays, I set out on a new journey – not a straightforward path. Although the book examines open address more-or-less chronologically, I neither intend it to be a comprehensive theatre history nor set out to suggest that drama and its strategies develop in neat chronological order. It would be an impossible task to track each moment at which every play, from the medieval period to the close of Shakespeare's career, can be considered as openly talking to its audience. In his *Dramatic Texts and Records of Britain: A Chronological Topography to 1558*, Ian Lancashire cautions against holding an "'evolutionary' assumption about the growth of British drama" (ix—xxxi). He describes how various areas of fifteenth- and sixteenth-century England produced many different kinds of plays under an array of auspices. Among his examples Lancashire lists scriptural and secular plays in London and the provinces, court plays and revels, mummings and folk plays, university and school drama, travelling "noblemen's interludes" – all playing while guild plays flourished.

Just as Lancashire has shown for the types of plays, there was also overlap in the development of stage techniques. Consequently, I have chosen what seem to me the most significant examples of open address, for reasons to be explained later. I have chosen to focus on a series of moments when it seems clear and particularly interesting to me that a play addresses not just the characters on stage but also the playgoers, and that it does so in order to absorb the spectators and their world into the play. At these moments the stage is structured in such a way that while the playgoers gaze on it, the stage explicitly returns their look, embedding both character and playgoer in an "It-is-important-that-we-both-know-that-I-see-you,-and-that-I-know-that-you-see-me" situation.

Here I need to consider three questions about the reasons for my choices. First, why guild plays and not other drama of the same period? Second, why the particular selection of Tudor plays? Finally, why Shakespeare and why not some of his contemporaries?

To begin with the first question: It is well known that guild plays are not the only medieval drama to openly address audiences. Other plays (such as morality and folk plays, for the latter of which we have no medieval texts) produced during the same historical period also do so. I have chosen to focus on guild plays because of the unique character of their open address. This form of drama searches out the temporal and spatial specifics of the playgoers' lives, a particularization not characteristic of the addresses of morality drama (our other extant texts), which tend to involve audiences through universalisation and allegorisation, or of folk drama (always late texts), which ritualizes its audiences.

As for the second question, the Tudor plays I have chosen best represent shifts in how staging conditions change the way open address operates. Special attention is given to how much of the open address in this period differs from the guild plays with respect to its construction of time, space, and audience. In chapter 2, I argue that open address in these Tudor plays creates a more distant audience; the dominant staging conditions make it crucial to separate stage time and space from audience time and space. In the Tudor staging system, open address generates a disjunctive relationship that enables the play to go forward.

Finally, to answer the third question: In this book I show that Shakespeare inherited two vital traditions of audience exchange from earlier drama: the open address of guild plays, which implicates the playgoers in the play, and that of Tudor drama, which, distancing the playgoers, constructs them as audience for performance time, "for the nonce." Shakespeare had a different stage to work with than either of the earlier traditions, the public playhouse's permanent scaffold. At first, address on Shakespeare's stage seems largely to ignore the audience. Then it moves closer to guild play address, importing onto the scaffold the world of the people in the playhouse. Because it draws on the diverse physical reality in the playhouse, Shakespeare's open address refuses to allow the heroic, the singular, the romantic, to hold his stage.

I did not choose to focus on Shakespeare because I believe him to be the only renaissance playwright to address audiences openly in the public playhouses. Varying kinds and degrees of playgoer acknowledgement can be found in the plays of Greene, Marlowe, Dekker, Jonson, and many others; Middleton's plays in particular are rife with them. But investigating other early modern playwrights' uses of audience address would necessarily constitute a separate long and interesting study. Another reason for limiting this study to Shakespeare is that, as a practitioner of theatre, I noticed the multiplicity of ways in which he makes his characters' words speak directly to their audiences. Then, as a critic of drama, I felt curious about what seemed to me Shakespeare's complicated and shifting connection to older dramatic strategies. I perceived a double gap, one in theatrical and another in literary investigations. I hope this study fills it.

As you read, it will be evident that the plays are situated historically. I do not claim, however, original historical discovery as one of the achievements of this work. Throughout it I lean heavily on a range of scholarly shoulders. For instance, anyone who thinks and writes about English medieval drama cannot fail to bless the scholars who initiated the Records of Early English Drama (REED) project and those who continue the investigation. The REED volumes are rich mines of information about medieval and early modern playing conditions – allocation of parts, guild involvement, production expenses, costumes, cost of costumes and props, *inter alia*. The collected documents are compelling reading for anyone interested in early drama, offering not only concrete details but also accounts of contemporary attitudes to early dramatic production. I have used REED research extensively. However, because more historical data remain to be discovered, and much remains to be learned about how to interpret what has already been discovered, I have tried to balance caution and excitement, aware that all historical records are ongoing and that I, too, wear historical blinkers.

Further invaluable information about medieval drama may be found in William Tydeman's accounts of medieval playing, Meg Twycross's essays on early dramatic performance, and Clifford Davidson's writing on practicalities of production. The medieval section of this book dealing with the medieval period has been greatly influenced by Martin Stevens's vision of each guild play's temporal and geographical specificity, a vision that has (to my mind) rescued this form of drama time and again from being blurred into a single monolithic play.

In the section of the book dealing with early modern drama – the period until recently always, and often still designated "Tudor" – my main historical source is David Bevington. His *From "Mankind" to Marlowe*, although written as far back as 1962, remains a seminal text for anyone fascinated by these mixed and sometimes "unconsidered" plays in the English dramatic canon. More recent works have also provided evidence about this period in drama: John Coldewey, on small local productions and the practices of travelling players; Ian Lancashire, on the types of plays and where they were performed; and Robert Potter, on the dramatic structure of Tudor plays.

The third section of the book, the discussion of Shakespeare, begins with accounts of the growth of Elizabethan public playhouses, of the entrepreneurs who funded and built these theatres, and of the playing companies and audiences who occupied them. Many historians of the stage have provided me with a firm historical foundation here: Michael Hattaway, Andrew Gurr, John Orrell, Peter Thomson, R.A. Foakes, and Alan Dessen. This section owes much, too, to Paul Yachnin's *Stage-Wrights: Shakespeare, Jonson, Middleton and the Making of Theatrical Value*, an account of how the work of these dramatists is not a "mirror of [renaissance] culture" but rather "depicts the [renaissance] world in ways refracted by the interests of the playing companies and the playwrights" (xiii). I depend throughout on these critics' studies of renaissance theatre, its players and their playing techniques, various playhouses' architecture, their stages, props, and costumes, as well as the behaviour, class, attitudes, and general composition of audiences – in short, great and small details of early modern theatre life.

Another group of critics influencing the book comprises scholars and practitioners who examine the stage. Among them are J.L. Styan, with his pioneering stage-centred criticism; Bernard Beckerman and his work on theatricality; and Wolfgang Clemen and his close readings of stage address. Anne Righter's (Barton's) study of medieval and early modern drama is immensely important. I admire this work, although, as will become apparent later, I find myself disagreeing with almost every conclusion she reaches about addressing the audience. Michael Bristol has an extraordinary capacity for seeing how Bakhtin's ideas about real physical bodies matter deeply in early modern drama. Anne Higgins shows how vital it is to remember that real people watched – and had their full everyday lives implicated in – the drama of medieval streets and markets. Jan Kott's staccato pronouncements about Shakespearean drama, his visionary style, his idiosyncratic ways of imagining Shakespeare, all have the potential to animate texts for me.

Although, like Bristol and Higgins, Robert Weimann is a historian of theatre, I place him with this group of critics specifically because of his account of stage position in the English native tradition: "As long as the performance of the play is substantially enriched by the potential social significance involved in the actor-audience relationship, the full meaning of drama may be defined as an image of the impact of this relationship on the performed text" (7). Such statements about the possible links between audience space and stage space first moved me to see that medieval drama is not, as Rosemary Woolf describes it, a series of "speaking pictures" (101); instead, as Weimann has shown, it is a drama of dynamic and animated exchanges between characters and playgoers. Weimann also seems certain that both medieval and Shakespearean address have the potential to reach out and almost physically touch their audiences.

A final seminal influence has been Francis Berry, whose explorations of Shakespeare's staging continually reshape my thinking. His *Shakespearean Inset* is an early study, but it remains one of the most insightful accounts of the versatility of Shakespeare's manipulations of stage time and space.

As this book unfolds, it will become clear that I don't always agree with everything these critics say. Nevertheless, each has in some way jolted me first to consider, then to reconsider, my thinking about stage, playing space, playhouse, audience, players, address, and so on. All the critics who have most influenced the book draw on what is tangible. They have in common an insistence on the importance to drama of the physical, the concrete; of playgoers' actuality, of the presence around stages of real people living real lives.

A recent publication requires special comment here: Michael Mooney's splendid *Shakespeare's Dramatic Transactions*. This account of the significance on Shakespeare's stage of the continual interplay of locus (framed playing space) and platea (unframed playing space) has Weimann's work as its driving spirit. I single out Mooney for special attention because our critical paths run close. We are both interested in "a 'bridging across' or communicative carrying through of effect from stage to audience" (xi). Mooney argues, as I do, that Shakespeare "reached out from the hemisphere of actors to a second hemisphere – the one the spectators occupied" (xi). Our paths diverge at several crucial points, however. We see exchange of medieval drama with the audience through very different eyes. Mooney extends Weimann's argument about *Figurenposition*, the idea that characters and their relationship with their audiences are defined by where they stand physically in the stage space. For both Weimann and Mooney (as for many other critics), characters on the platea of medieval drama are on undifferentiated ground and can be understood as belonging to the world of the audience, while figures standing in and speaking from loca (e.g., structures such as Heaven or Noah's Ark) are understood as being distanced from the audience both theatrically and historically.

My fundamental point of departure from Mooney (and from Weimann) is that their arguments are based on definitions of platea and locus that I cannot share, on the conception of "neutral undifferentiated 'place' and symbolic location" (Weimann, 212; Mooney, 18). As I implied earlier, I believe that *both* locus and platea were *always* localized by the city or countryside in which they were set up. The interplay between the two is, for Weimann, the primary stage dynamic in guild plays. In chapter 1, however, I contend that this dynamic is secondary to the interplay between the stage as a whole and the world of the audience.

According to Mooney, the workings of the old stage positions, "the interplay of locus and platea," continue to be played out on the renaissance stage and have been "surprisingly undervalued as an aid to discussion of Elizabethan and Jacobean theatre" (18). Using Weimann's conception of medieval platea and locus as, respectively, undefined and defined playing spaces, Mooney claims that "from his downstage position a character could step out of the play, freeing himself from the place and the time of the action and allowing himself to comment on the events, to reveal his own feelings, or otherwise to engage the spectator's confidence" (17).

Mooney then argues that "words in a Renaissance playscript are meant to be spoken from distinct stage locations" (17). In this statement lies the nub of my second problem with his formulation. I think that Shakespeare's huge permanent scaffold and the enclosing walls of his playhouse deeply altered the way old traditions of address were played out. Characters on Shakespeare's stage, as I shall show, could and did talk openly to the playgoers, but never stepped out of the play. The nature of the new architecture enforced a profoundly altered exchange between stage and audience. It is worth mentioning, too, that I consider the use of "downstage" and "upstage" for the renaissance playhouse (terms used by both Weimann and Mooney) distracting. The terms have been coined for modern stages, and their application to renaissance drama demonstrates, however subtly, the imposition of a modern template.

This book may seem at times to tread on familiar ground or to echo ideas to which we have grown accustomed. In fact, the reverse is true; my argument challenges many familiar starting points or assumptions about ways in which medieval and early modern theatre operated. I am not writing a new history of the period, but I do take issue with some commonly held notions of staging and with many conventional ways of referring to speeches, particularly those invoking audience presence. It is because of the many preconceptions surrounding standard usages such as "soliloquy," "aside," "monologue," and "direct address" that I avoid using them. The terms themselves are innocuous; often, however, the ways and contexts in which they are employed are not. For instance, "soliloquy" is something of a misnomer; it is not always spoken *solus*, nor does it have to operate as if the speaker believes himself or herself to be unheard by anyone else. What we commonly know as "soliloquy" does not always or only confront us with a stage persona searching for an internal state or psyche, as we are so often led to assume. But I am not simply dismissing old notions, nor are my terms roses by other names. "Open address" is used in order that these speeches may be examined from a wholly fresh perspective. This book offers new and fuller thoughts about address. For instance, in discussing Hamlet's speeches as "soliloquies," Wolfgang Clemen calls them "self-interrogating"; what I want to add is that these speeches are also "audience-interrogating." Some "monologues" are in fact "dialogues" with the playgoers.

My fundamental argument is this: Stretching from medieval drama to early modern drama is a long and vital tradition of stage-audience dialogue, which I call "open address." The idea of any exchange between stage and audience brings up questions about time and space. In the auditorium or its equivalent, audiences inhabit a "here and now," the present place and time of their ordinary world; they gaze on a "there and then," the place and time of the stage. From the stage, characters move and speak within a fictional "here and now," which may or may not bear resemblances to the audience's place and time. In open address the stage looks frankly at the audience in their here and now. Because each staging system I examine operated differently, the stage-audience links established by this look vary. Time and space are most fruitfully examined in terms of specific stage practices and illustrated with concrete examples.[5]

As well as "then," "there," "now," and "here," other verbal markers are important in open address: the verbal positionings of speaker and listeners by deictic words, in particular the stage's "I," "we," "you," "they." Sometimes these words are contained by and restricted to the stage and refer only to the characters in the play. But when open address operates, the words either explicitly or elliptically allude to both characters and audience. In addition to the temporal and spatial markers, I look closely at verbal signals of inclusivity within each staging system.

Open address is a strategy that interrogates, even challenges, playgoers, asks for answers lying outside the stage, in the playgoer/playhouse world. This tradition has little to do with the frequently touted notion of the "fluidity of the renaissance stage." It does not simply mean that a character *can* talk to the audience; it means that in various ways the character *does* reach out to the playgoers and *does* import aspects of the audience world to the stage. These particular exchanges, appearing with great frequency in late medieval drama, continue as crucial stage strategies for Shakespeare, in whose work they grow and change.

CHAPTER ONE

Oure Play

PLAYING CONDITIONS IN THE
GUILD PLAYS

This book opened with lines from *The Killing of Abel* spoken by Cain:

> And hardely, when I am dede,
> Bery me in Gudeboure at the quarell hede;
> For, may I pas this place in quarte,
> Bi all men set I not a fart. (366–9)

Like other plays produced in the cities of Chester, York, and N-Town, *The Killing of Abel* belongs to a cluster of dramatizations of biblical narratives of which Towneley (for Wakefield), Chester, York, and N-Town are the four extant texts.[1] Before focusing on the staging conditions in these plays, I need to deal with two critical issues. First, I have deliberately chosen to use the term "guild plays" to describe these dramas, which are variously called "Corpus Christi dramas," "mystery cycles," "civic plays," and, infrequently, "miracle plays." Each name presents problems. The last – "miracle plays" – is inaccurate; inasmuch as these dramas only occasionally represent miracles; miraculous or marvellous events are more typically the province of the late medieval Saints' plays, such as the East Anglian *Mary Magdelene*, or Croxton's *Play of the Sacrament*. The term "mystery" is semantically equivalent to "guild"; mysteries are guilds. The two designations "Corpus Christi play" and "guild play" both produce controversy in some critical circles. Some scholars suggest that performances of the plays either were, or became, unconnected to the Corpus Christi festival. But

"Corpus Christi" play is what appears most often in contemporary documents, whether or not the performances fell on the liturgical occasion that gave them their name.

In spite of some difficulties about the degree to which trade guilds were involved in dramatic productions, I have elected the term "guild plays" as the most satisfactory. The oldest of these plays clearly arose in a guild milieu, under guild auspices; it was under guilds that this dramatic genre found its characteristic form. Hans-Jürgen Diller comments on the role of the guilds in building these plays: "On our present knowledge we must assume that the guilds and their desire for representation influenced not only the later developments of the Corpus Christi plays but were a decisive factor already at the outset" (74).

For me, the most compelling reason to call them "guild plays" is that they all – including N-Town – represent on stage the workaday world of the crowds watching them (see Davidson, 3). They do not allegorize or romanticize their audiences. Instead, they dramatize the daily, job-ridden lives of the playgoers. It is this, above all, that I want to talk about: the plays' connections with the concrete world of the playgoers. Guild plays represent vast temporal and geographical landscapes – Palestine, Egypt, Heaven and Hell – places, happenings, and people patently outside the here and now of the audience. Yet, as we have seen, Towneley's Cain speaks as if he is in Yorkshire, in the "now" of the spectators, standing among a crowd of English farmers, lords, shepherds, hucksters, merchants, and peasants. Historical, biblical Cain is *also* a farmer in north-east England. Because of England's capricious weather and the Church's heavy tithes, he, like other locals, can only scrape a living. And after being cursed by God, Cain orders his Yorkshire neighbours to be his undertakers.

As noted in the Introduction, Cain implicitly says to these Yorkshire men and women, "I see you; you see and hear me." In doing so, he simultaneously acknowledges the presence of the playworld and of the world of the audience. In every guild play characters move fluidly between talking to one another and talking to the audience. In Towneley, York, Chester, and N-Town, as well as in the two fragments from Norwich and Coventry, figures from a distant history openly notice late medieval people.[2] Whatever the rank or condition of the characters – whether they are divine, or worldly leaders or patriarchs such as Abraham and Noah, or ordinary people such as the shepherds and Joseph – they talk to the crowds standing in the streets. This acknowledgement of the audience – open address – is a constant throughout the guild plays.

The fact that characters in guild plays persistently refer to and talk directly to their audiences has been noted by many critics. There are two major positions on why the plays do so. One point of view is that the actors remind the playgoers of their presence to keep the latter aware that what they are watching is a play and nothing but a play – a dramatization, not reality. The other view suggests that talking openly to the spectators causes them to lose themselves wholly in the play.

The first of these perspectives is best put forward by V. A. Kolve, who argues that the reason guild drama incorporates details of the crowds' lives into the plays and makes direct speeches to the audiences is to keep play and playgoer separate. These dramatic techniques, he says, are employed to remind the crowds that they have no place in the play; in other words, to prevent the playgoers from losing themselves in the performances, from mistaking illusion or "game" for reality: "The aim of the Corpus Christi drama was to celebrate and elucidate, never, not even temporarily to deceive. It played action in 'game' – not in 'earnest' – within a world set apart, established by convention and obeying rules of its own. A lie designed to tell the truth about reality, the drama was understood as significant play" (32).

An opposite view of how this drama relates to its audience comes from Anne Righter. She contends that guild plays involved their audiences utterly, drawing them into the drama so that the crowds became "mankind ... [who] depended for their justification and very existence upon the fact of their involvement in the play" (20). According to Righter, the plays and their strategies tell playgoers how insubstantial and shadowy their lives are, compared with the profound reality expressed by the drama.

My view of audience acknowledgement differs from that of both these critics. I agree with Kolve when he says that guild drama repeatedly urges audiences to be mindful of their everyday reality. However, I think this reminder works in ways quite distinct from what Kolve suggests. I also agree with Righter's view that the plays involve their audiences. But I conceive a kind of close contract between play and audience unlike what she describes. Surely, at the guild play performances there were individuals who stood back and others (both playgoers and actors) who became so completely absorbed that they forgot themselves for a time.

Hans-Jürgen Diller offers a view closer to mine, referring to "audience address" as a vital and significant part of the way guild plays build meaning. He proposes several categories for identifying various kinds of audience address, generating a taxonomy of these speeches in which the Chester and N-Town plays are distinguished from those of York and Towneley. Diller also argues for the importance of looking closely at the nature of character-audience contact: "Only in a very few cases may we hope for some sort of information from the stage directions. More rewarding is the examination of the texts themselves; vocatives and second-person pronouns which cannot refer to characters in the play or information which is familiar to these [characters] can be regarded as sure signs that the audience is being addressed" (113–14).

Where Diller refers to "audience address" I use "open address." He regards the technique as a means by which a playworld ("W^d" in Diller's terminology, as distinct from "W^o," the world of the audience) is constructed, and as a bridge by which audiences cross from W^o to W^d. Although his detailed examinations of types of address are admirable, I am made uneasy by any reading of early drama implying that its dramatists had to struggle with "difficulties" of constructing a valid playworld. Such problems did not arise until the development of an indoor theatre, theatre cut off from daily life in the streets and markets of a town.

Now let us follow the leads of the plays themselves. Much of our thinking about early theatre and its strategies is obstructed by our modern experience of the theatre. In my view, we should reverse much of our thinking about dramatic address in early theatre. Let me start from a different assumption: *Unless* a play indicates that its audience is ignored, we may assume that the actors openly perform to and involve their audiences. And why imagine the crowds as necessarily, in Diller's words, "silent partner[s]" (113)?

Picture plays, then, that mount two playworlds simultaneously: in the case of the guild plays, the biblical and the modern. By persistent references to the contemporary local reality of an audience through face-to-face address, these plays constrained the playgoers to see their own lives on stage as they watched familiar biblical stories. Through this dramaturgical method, the plays showed medieval playgoers where they fitted into the history of the world. It is vital to notice that audiences were never asked, while watching the drama, even for a moment to disregard the facts of their own here and now. They were never instructed to abandon feelings of their communal actuality in order to enter into a deeper existence. They were never asked, even briefly, to pretend to be biblical crowds shouting for Barabbas, or Israelites fleeing from Pharaoh. Audiences did indeed enter the plays: but they entered as *themselves*. These plays about the Bible searched out the contemporary here and now, never letting their audience forget that everything about their everyday world was real and that it all mattered, from its tankards, hammers, and chitter-lings to its silken couches, golden crowns, and costly wines. Every aspect of contemporary identity went onto these stages. This is per-haps what is most extraordinary about this drama – that it staged its audiences as themselves.

"OUR" STAGE

How did it do so? First, by making sure that its stages belonged to the playgoers by spatializing each play as both historical places and the audience's local geography. The plays, of course, talk about distant parts of the world, but the lines and the explicit or implicit stage directions signal strongly to audiences that performances also happen in their home towns, that the watchers own the stage.

Modes of performance varied from town to town. Some plays took place on wagons that moved from station to station, stopping to give performances at various locations in the community, a performance style usually referred to as processional. Internal evidence and the city's compendious civic records indicate that the York play probably used this style. It seems possible that Towneley's play was stationary, perhaps performed on wagons drawn up around a flat space. Inter-nal evidence points to N-Town's play using wooden structures set up around a playing space.[3]

Whether the guilds performed their plays on movable or station-ary wagons or in and around a fixed playing space, they divided the staging into two elements. One, known as the "platea," was an open, flat playing space, either the bed of a pageant wagon or the ground where the crowds stood (city or town streets, marketplaces, or court-yards).[4] The other staging element is variously known as "loca," "seats," "scaffolds," and "towers." It consisted of raised or framed wooden structures marking specific historical locations: Heaven's throne, the hill where Mrs Noah sits spinning, Bethlehem's stable, the cross on Calvary, Hell, and so on.

Reconceiving the operations of platea and locus makes a crucial difference to our understanding of the plays' exchange with the audi-ence. Other scholars have argued that the platea, the playing area lying closest to and often on a level with the assembled crowds, is a neutral stage space, with no specific spatial or temporal signals. Pamela M. King, for instance, considers that the platea "represents non-localized space," and therefore "tends to be thematically neu-tral" except when journeys between loca (framed structures such as Herod's throne) temporarily give it spatial and temporal definition (46). In other words, it is "nowhere," until historical time and geography are signalled. A typical modern critical view of the medieval platea is that of a blank space, a kind of *tabula rasa*, given its meaning by the character and presence of the framed structures, the loca. In Stanley Vincent Longman's description, "The platea is a generalized acting area. The principle behind the platea is the collaboration of the audience in ascribing an imaginary place to the acting area. In its medieval version, the entrance of the actors through one mansion, or scenic piece, and their making their way to the platea invited the audience to transpose the mansion's depicted location to the platea" (157).

In tracking early drama's exploitation of space from liturgical to guild plays, Diller posits that street playing depended on the erasure of the town's spatial features. He argues:

In the liturgical drama place and time – the building of the church and the hour of divine worship – were not a semiotic *tabula rasa*; their signification always shone through and affected that of the representing action. Each represented scene was embedded in the action of the service and received its significance from it. The vernacular plays, performed as they were on the pageant-waggon, the town market or the village green, were not so embedded and had to create their own spatio-temporal foundation. (75)

Again it seems to me that here (as in much criticism of early drama) thinking about medieval staging has been shaped by modern notions of theatre. We put the pageant wagon before the horse. To us, even theatre in the round means entering a designated space, whether indoors or out. But why should the signals of stage space not be those of our immediate surroundings? If this is the case, the theatre can be primarily the buildings of the town. The time-frame of the play can be that of the audience. I think guild plays urge their audiences first to create the "spatio-temporal foundation" of each performance from what they see around them. Historical Jerusalem, Bethlehem, and so on, then mesh with English time and space. This idea builds on the views of Martin Stevens, who stresses how important it was to the York play that the city's architecture was constantly visible (189). I believe it to be not only unlikely but virtually impossible for audiences to have seen the platea as a clean slate onto which the plays wrote an "imaginary place." After all, this acting area had no physical boundary – unless it was the edge of the wagon – between the play's space and where the crowd stood on the cobbles, the flagstones, by the walls of the smithy, the cathedral gate, or the local merchant's house. Even if the platea was the wagon bed, the wagon itself stood against the backdrop of familiar buildings. Further to this, Twycross comments: "The effect of placing these wagons in an ordinary city street is striking. To begin with, they act as frames which mark the play and its actors off from the audience. They localise the actors and give the audience a locus. This is very noticeable when actors who have been on the ground go up into the wagons" (48).

She continues:

In return, the street gives the wagons and actors added emphasis. Plays like the *Creation* or the *Last Judgement* represent events on a cosmic scale. Modern theatre directors tend to interpret this in terms of a sweepingly wide set and scores of actors. But this is unnecessary: it is all a matter of context. When you stand in the street in front of a *Last Judgement* pageant wagon, and your head tilts back to follow the angels climbing up top to take their places on the Heaven deck among the rooftops, you get a real sense of height, and of hier-archy: the three layers – the highest of Heaven, the area 'in the clouds above the earth' where God comes to judge and the ground from which the dead rise and out of which the mouth of Hell opens. Here, as elsewhere, height is used thematically. (48)

Twycross treats the backdrop of the city streets as anonymous. Yet "the Heaven deck among the rooftops" was the upper level of a wagon looming amidst specific, local, recognizable rooftops. It is the local and particular that matters here. If it is taken as the *first* element of guild play staging, our readings change. When the playgoers stretched back their necks to see the angels climbing up to Heaven, they also saw the tops of city buildings; Heaven and all it implies was immanent in York, physically and completely in the spectators' here and now.

The whole playing space, then, was inscribed as the playgoers' here and now and as a stage. Their own town was on show; nothing that happened in the play eradicated it.[5] On the platea, bounded not by wooden framing but by audience and neighbourhood, characters spoke and moved about in the same sphere as the crowds and in proximity to them. Usually, these actors depicted the ordinary people of history, those without rank or power; one such was Christ during the period of his ministry.

Although the large, open platea is sometimes likened to the bare stage in Elizabethan popular theatres, I think it vital to distinguish them. Both Elizabethan platform and medieval platea have in common temporal and spatial flexibility (rather than temporal and spatial definition, as in the framed fixity of a stage shut behind a proscenium arch); nevertheless, each has a distinct kind of fluidity. The two playing spaces are physically very different. In order to see the Elizabethan stage, audiences had to go inside a theatre building. Enclosed by walls, the platform of the early modern public theatre could well have been an "anywhere" or a "nowhere" until defined by the playwright's words. The Globe's stage, for instance, was a separate world from the London world outside. Within playhouse architecture, Elizabethan dramatists exploited something closer to a "neutral stage," an acting area that "lent the playwright freedom" and "cleared the mind of the spectator for conjuring up visions" (Styan, *Stagecraft*, 29–30). Although I hold many reservations about any kind of stage neutrality, playwrights in early modern playhouses could tell their audiences that the stage was "nothing until imagination make it so," and call on them to "eke out our performance with [their] mind" (*Henry V*, 2.Chorus.35). Perhaps we hold on to the notion of neutral space because we tend to read English drama backwards, from popular Elizabethan stages, about which we have ample information, to the stages of early drama, about which we have limited evidence.

Whereas much of the power of the Elizabethan stage lay in a special and qualified version of neutrality, in a potential to be any place and any time that the playwright chose, the staging of guild drama was controlled and owned by its audiences. They gathered in familiar streets, in neighbourhood courtyards, or by their local quarry. As they watched the history of the world, they saw it played on their own territory, in places which, outside performance times, would be the sites of a wide assortment of everyday activities. The real potency of guild play staging lay in the tight relationship of both locus and platea to the concrete actuality in which they were set.

Never neutral, the platea supplied its audiences with numerous locational signals: local landmarks of their home towns. Never a blank space on which to write and erase, the platea was always localized simultaneously by play and audience. The stage was always the biblical world *and* York, Chester, Wakefield, N-Town, Coventry, Norwich. When historical characters crossed this ground, they also crossed the audience's city in the audience's own time.

The complete system is "both/and" staging. Even the fixed staging elements, the loca, signalled both the historical and the contemporary here and now. The loca, which always housed high-ranking figures (for example, God, Lucifer, the angels, Herod, Pharaoh, Pilate, Annas, Caiaphas), marked out specific locations such as God's throne, the stable in Bethlehem, Noah's ark, the lawyers' council house, and Hell's mouth.[6] However, like the platea, loca were first and foremost dramatically defined by the contemporary local world. Historical sites such as Procula's (Pilate's wife's) bed or Bethlehem's stable, or the mound on which Mrs Noah sits stubbornly spinning, were erected in a space that was also York, Chester, Wakefield, N-Town, and so on. Likeness and difference among loca often offered audiences figural readings of separate historical events. For example, loca made apparent the typological connection between the hill on which Abraham goes to sacrifice Isaac and the hill on which Christ is crucified; Mak's cottage locus is similar to yet different from the stable locus of the Nativity. England's farm women, hucksters, citizens, watched these loca come and go as history moved forward. Nevertheless, the really crucial figural link made by loca was between distant events, places, people, and the contemporary world against which the audiences could clearly see them set.

The guild plays' "both/and" staging allows the plays to exploit both likenesses and differences between "there and then" and "here and now." God creates the world outside time and also in medieval York; Abraham sacrifices Isaac on a hillside in the Middle East that is also in N-Town; Mary gives birth in a Bethlehem stable that is at the same time one of Yorkshire's farm buildings; Hell comes right into Chester's streets. In each guild play, the sweep of the whole world's history plays out within – and in purposive tension with – a continually visible contemporary local world. *The Killing of Abel*, as we have seen, uses a familiar landmark, the quarry on the outskirts of town, to make the biblical story of murder simultaneously a local modern story: one about difficult lives in the Yorkshire countryside, about local disputes between farmers and herders, about Wakefield's contemporary potential for meanness, disobedience, and violence. The words of the York episode *The Entry into Jerusalem* stress that Christ enters "oure citée," whose citizens have seen many royal entries (Stevens, 59). As York's people stood in their streets, beneath their towers, they heard Christ refer to "yone castel" and to "this cite" (15). Christ's references to his surroundings do not reconstruct York's buildings as Jerusalem's; rather, they fuse the contemporary northern English city with the historical Middle Eastern one, insisting that both exist fully in the here and now, simultaneous and complete. To take another example, this time from Chester, a biblical shepherd tells a crowd made up of local peasants, shepherds, tapsters, tradespeople, and aristocrats that he has followed his flock for an immense distance. He talks of a weary journey from Wales to Scotland, "from comlye Conwaye unto Clyde," possibly the furthest limits of a known world for many in the local audience (*The Shepherds*). The guild play stage is therefore never in any way neutral; its base-line is always the audience's here and now.

"OUR" EVERYDAY LIVES ON STAGE

Another strategy by which the guild plays kept audiences mindful of their contemporary milieu was showing them that the characters were also members of the city's or town's work force. Although the Church sanctioned the performances, practical production obligations were shouldered by each town's guild members.[7] Wakefield, Chester, and York civic records show that trade guilds paid for the performances, organized rehearsals, built and housed wagons when these were used, collected, bought, and made costumes and props, as well as directed and acted in the plays.[8] Guilds probably took on individual episodes for which they were able to furnish appropriate properties, sufficient actors, and enough money.[9] York's bakers, for example, put on *The Supper of Christ with the Disciples*, presumably because they could provide loaves for the meal, as did Beverley's and Chester's bakers.[10] York's goldsmiths mounted the Herod and the Magi episodes, whose biblical kings needed crowns, caskets for the Magi's gifts, and a glittering star to follow.[11] The same city's vintners supplied the wine for the episode about the marriage at Cana.[12] Its tappeters and couchers supplied a luxurious bed for the ostentatious Procula, its thatchers and tilers put together the stable for the Nativity, and its shipwrights constructed the ark for the Noah episode.[13] Clearly, most of the actors were local: amateurs, people from the neighbourhood, members of the town's guilds (see Higgins, 82–5 and Palliser, 103–6). For instance, the "soldiers" who crucified Christ in York were certainly the city's pinners.[14]

"For the towns themselves the plays were good business. They brought together not only their own citizens but those of villages from miles around, and in a few instances they attracted royalty" (Arnold Williams, 95). There was money to be made from the crowds who attended the plays. In York, for example, sites along the route were rented out by "station holders," individuals who owned and erected scaffolds, or by householders whose windows overlooked the stopping places (REED: York, 829).[15] However, according to John D. Coldewey, although the plays turned a profit for some citizens and for individual guilds, the work involved in putting them on was heavy and not always welcomed by the guilds.[16] Even if reluctantly, many guilds spent lavish amounts on their productions. They also frequently foregrounded their members' participation as players. In some plays, as we have just seen, unmistakeable links were made between biblical characters and local workers. Anne Higgins makes a vital leap when she shows that drawing audience attention to the fact that the players were also local tradespeople was one of the means by which the plays' redactors strove to connect their audiences' local world of work with the world of the play, reminding the crowds of both their likeness to and their difference from people of the past. Higgins contends that the connection sought by the dramatists was primarily figural, a way of looking at history that at once denied and asserted the importance of historical distance and difference from the playgoers' contemporary lives. So as well as giving the cities and the tradespeople of York, Norwich, and Chester useful advertising for local merchandise, putting recognisable neighbours doing their ordinary everyday jobs on stage encouraged audiences to see how the events of history were connected to what was a crucial part of their here and now.

Since guild drama was performed largely in daylight, audiences were able to get a good look at the players.[17] Although in York, for example, some professional players auditioned for parts, spectators certainly knew that most of the biblical characters on stage were played by the same guild members each year, by the town baker, blacksmith, or tanner; by the local goldsmith, carpenter, or cordwainer. According to Kolve, the fact that the players were usually recognizable as local tradespeople prevented audiences from making the dangerous error of confusing "game" and reality. Kolve notes the importance of "the presence of neighbours in contemporary costume" on stage but argues that recognizing the actors as local tradespeople would act as "a major deterrent to illusionism" (55). Nevertheless, everyone in the audience was familiar with the Bible stories: they knew the history of Noah well – who was saved, who was not; they knew that Eden was a fruitful garden; they were aware that soldiers crucified Christ and that at the last supper Christ broke bread and drank wine. So the fact that the actors were recognizable as "neighbours in contemporary costume" (to use Kolve's words) made patent the connection between these historical events and their everyday lives.

Ann Righter asserts that the world of work was something to be abandoned at the play, as it was at church: "From the West Portal of Chartres, the images of the Twelve Months and their labours look out across the cornlands of the Beauce, reminding the worshipper that as he enters the cathedral he turns away from the

world of spring-time and harvest, where birth implies destruction
and the future flows irrevocably into the past" (15). My reading of
the Chartres portal is quite the reverse: the carvings, in fact, welcomed all worshippers into the cathedral as they were, asking the
French artisans to bring their whole selves, including everyday
toil, to their worship. The same completeness was demanded by
the guild players from those who attended their performances. All
playgoers were asked to bring their full identities to the performances; they would then see themselves on stage. York's Noah is
not just a historical patriarch; he employs contemporary medieval
practices of shipbuilding and so is a local artisan as well as a biblical figure. Norwich's Eden has a tree bearing local merchandise,
the fruits and spices imported by the town's grocers: Norwich and
Eden unite.[18] When audiences recognized neighbours or local
tradespeople or artisans on stage, they were guided to consider
what went on in their lives outside the play, to think about yester-
day and tomorrow, when they and the tradespeople-actors were
caught up in daily work, in selling and buying, in making bread,
wine, or rope. Guild play stages signalled their audiences to place
their work and themselves amidst the great events and people of
history.

Meg Twycross claims that in these plays, "Every character can be
his own story-teller." She continues:

Modern theatre, under the influence of Brecht, is partly returning to this
stance: it is not as unfamiliar to us as it was a few decades ago. Medieval
theatre is merely less self-conscious about it. There was no need to create
the "illusion" of naturalistic theatre, the self-contained hermetically sealed
world in which the characters are aware only of each other, and on which we
eavesdrop. If the audience needs to know something, it is told directly. A
character unselfconsciously tells the audience how he feels. He also tells you
"what he is doing at the same time as he is doing it." (54)

I cannot agree with this view. Guild drama did not employ Brechtian
distancing of character and actor; it never sought to promote intellectual rather than emotional response. In fact, in the context of the
guild plays, "player" is not really an issue; "character" and local
inhabitant come together. The purpose is not to unfrock the players
beneath Noah, Joseph, the soldiers executing Christ; rather, it is to
explore the double identity of the biblical man or woman and the
modern worker, the neighbour, the businessman. This purpose is
achieved by foregrounding the characters not as actors, but in their
lives as guildspeople, fellow workers, or just neighbours.

A third strategy used to incorporate audiences into guild drama was to link a myriad aspects of everyday contemporary life with the world of the play. Together with work-related activities, more frivolous happenings of life such as eating and playing appeared on stage, mimicking audience pastimes. For instance, biblical characters would sometimes be seen eating lavish feasts like those of the late medieval rich. They would eat in a way celebrating only themselves. Against the background of the local town, they tried to exclude, shutting out the ordinary people in the play as well as everyone in the audience. York's Pilate and his wife, "dame precious Percula," sip wine before retiring to sleep on their sumptuous couch made by the local tappeters and couchers (*Christ before Pilate 1: The Dream of Pilate's Wife*, 37). When N-Town's Herod thinks the infant Jesus has been killed, he fusses about the quality of the food, wanting an opulent celebration dinner – to be served in elegant late medieval style. He directs his servants to

> sett a tabyll anon here ful sownde,
> Coverid with a corious cloth and with rich wurthy fare –
> Servise for the loveliest lorde that levinge is on grownde.
> Beste metys and wurthiest wines loke that ye non spare,
> Thow that a lityl pint shulde coste a thowsand pownde.
>
> (*Death of Herod*, 144–8)

> (right here set up a sturdy table
> Covered with an elaborate cloth and rich elegant food.
> It will be an experience worthy of the finest lord anywhere
> And don't hold back: don't hold back on providing the very best food
>   and wines,
> Even if just a pint costs as much as a thousand pounds.)

A correct contemporary host, Herod is also tetchy about the seating arrangements.[19]

It is clear that the guild plays spoofed wealthy diners. Sadly, we have no records of how playgoers responded; it is fruitless to speculate who in the audience might have been delighted, who offended, by these parodic meals. As in any audience at any time, such scenes probably summoned up widely differing reactions. The important point is that the staging is explicitly both historical and contemporary. Moreover, it is made to appear at once funny, dangerous, and ultimately foolish. For, say the plays, setting themselves up as exclusive, overwhelmed by their sense of entitlement, believing their luxurious lifestyles will last unchallenged forever, the rich are fools.

The guild players also staged the meals of poor people. Chester and Wakefield shepherds, for example, sit among the crowds to eat what the very hungry might dream of, food in huge amounts: healthy Lancashire and Yorkshire dishes of onions, garlic, leeks, cows' and pigs' feet, chitterlings, oat cakes, a sheep's head soused in ale, and washed down with "ale of Halton and sowre milk" – the peasant fare of the poor, the "liverastes, livers and longes," "sose," "sowse," and "saverraye" (livers, lights and lungs, sausages, sauce, savories) (Chester, *The Shepherds*, 44–5). Dramatizations of common people's dinners were also probably very funny, especially since they were made so excessive. But these feasts were not wholly ridiculed and condemned, as were the dinners of the rich. In west Yorkshire, for example, despite the fact that the shepherds' supper collapses when they have drunk too much and squabble about who has eaten the most, their meal nevertheless ends up being an inclusive act. First, meals like this one were eaten close to the audience; the spectators could clearly see the diners, who themselves probably reflected many in the audience who would have been eating food bought from hucksters and regrators while they watched the performance.[20] Second, the meals of the poor were messy but communal. As such, they were unlike – yet dramatically allied to – the perfect communal meal celebrated each year by the Corpus Christi feast itself, and on each day in the liturgy. Towneley's *Shepherds' Play I*, in particular, openly asserts this connection, reminding the crowds to think about the observances of the Mass. As they raise their bottle, the first shepherd comments: "This is boyte of oure bayll, / Good holsom ayll." (This is the remedy for all our ills: / Good wholesome ale.) (*Shepherds' Play I*, 247–8) The episode reinforces the link to medieval religious observance when, after drinking, the shepherds exchange a kiss of peace: "By my thryft we must kys" (262). Inclusiveness is further stressed when the shepherds propose to collect what is left for the poor (*Shepherds' Play I*, 282–4).

No detail of city or rural life seems to have been too inconsequential to appear in the plays. Mingling with biblical personages were well-known secular figures, traditional characters from folk plays, mummings, and other ritual entertainments.[21] In *Shepherds' Play I*, Mak, Pykharnes, and Titivillus talk with the ribald liberty assumed by folk play fools; in Chester's *The Shepherds*, Trowle is a typically insubordinate folk play servant. In the N-Town play, Den, a court summoner, reads out a list of people bound to sit at an ecclesiastical court hearing. As he shouts out "Malkyn mylkedore," "Stevyn sturdy," "Thom tynkere," "Powle pewtere," and so on (10–30), he is acting like the "caller on" (the announcer) at folk entertainments who draws together audience and characters. As well as making close contact with the crowds, these figures import into the biblical narratives a Bakhtinian "carnivalesque," a nonsensical, subversive, back-to-front version of life.

Folk play opening rituals hailed the entry of biblical villains: kings, officials, or ordinary men such as Cain. Nearly every ruler silenced (or tried to silence) his audience with the conventional calls originating in the processional side of folk drama, phrases long employed by local players to clear a space in which to play. In the guild plays these cries for "room" become threats when bellowed by belligerent rulers, who claim playing space as if audiences should shrink back in terror.[22] For example, Towneley's Pharaoh opens his episode with "Peas! of pain that no man pas! (Silence! On pain of torture no-one is to move or leave.)"(1.1); York's Herod with "Pes, ye brothellis and browlys in this braydenasse inbrased (Keep quiet, you wretches and scoundrels inside this big space.)" (*Christ before Herod*, 1); N-Town's ruler with "Now sees of your talking. And gevyth lordly Audience / Not o word I charge you that ben here present (Now stop your talking, And pay proper attention./ I don't want a word out of anybody present.)" (*Passion Play II*, 1–2).

Popular sports also figured in the plays (see Dobson 159–91). In Chester's Nativity episode, wrestling marked the shepherds' unstable association. Offered a chance to wrestle his superiors, like any folk play hero the underdog Trowle vaunts: "Nowe comes Trowle the Trewe / a torne to take have i fight / with my master (Now comes Faithful Trowle / To take a turn in a fight / With my master)" (*The Shepherds*, 234–6).[23] "Pretend" violence in the medieval pastime of Hot Cockles, pops, or bobbid, a game in which a blindfolded "victim" was punched and slapped, is transformed in Towneley's *The Buffeting* or in York's *Christ before Herod* into actual torture when Christ is tormented.[24] Carnivalesque jests of inversion, such as making a boy a bishop or king for a day, are themselves turned upside down when Christ is designated "boy," seated on a stool, and, with the crown of thorns, turned into a Mock-King (Towneley, *The Scourging*; York, *Christ before Herod*; see Weimann 21–2). Play and real violence merge in a grotesque tournament in a Chester episode. Here, medieval knights massacre Judaean babies, making the children "hop" from spear to spear (*The Slaughter of the Innocents*).[25] A widely-known story, that of the "snow baby," becomes a way to degrade Mary in N-Town's *Trial of Joseph and Mary* by having her judged a lying slut.[26] Fusing past and present yields shocking new perspectives on the Bible stories and on contemporary life.

Perhaps the most ordinary and contemporary things to appear in guild plays were the gifts of the shepherds to the Christ-child, all of them appropriate to poverty, whether biblical or modern. In West Yorkshire the shepherds give the baby a ball, a bottle, "a bob of cherys," a bird, a bell, "a lytyll spruse cofer." In Chester they offer Jesus a bell, a flagon and spoon "for to eat thy pottage with at noone / as I myselfe full oftetymes have donne," a cap, "a payre of my wyves ould hose." York's shepherds present a child's tin brooch, two cob nuts on a band, a bob of cherries, a bird, and a quintessential hungry man's vision of plenty, a horn spoon that will hold forty peas. The educated in the audiences might have picked up symbolic associations in these offerings, but everyone must have attended to the *literal*: each gift is homely and utterly familiar to everyone in the crowd.[27] Everybody, rich or poor, learned or unlettered, saw Mary accept simple things from poor men. In the medieval present as in the biblical past, all offerings proved acceptable, whether they were the Magi's caskets of gold, frankincense, and myrrh, or the shepherds' far less grand equivalents – not a golden orb but a tennis ball, not a phial of precious scent but an empty earthenware bottle.

In their portrayals of work and recreation, as well as the articles belonging to daily life, the guild plays searched out and drew on the reality of their spectators' lives. By presenting on stage the mundane stuff of everyday living, the plays told audiences that what they did each day had deep significance, no matter whether they were rich or poor; worked as vintner, baker, goldsmith, shepherd, tapster, or king. Each moment of daily life mattered, however ordinary or trivial. No-one was told to leave behind his or her home or identity or present time, to forget either work or games. Instead, by linking biblical history to the contemporary world, the plays' redactors urged their audiences to think anew about their own lives.

OPEN ADDRESS FROM LOCA AND PLATEA

I now turn to the main topic of this book: the stage strategy I call "open address." The most powerful dramaturgical strategy for integrating audiences as themselves occurred when figures in guild plays, whether historical or from the contemporary world, looked out at the crowds and addressed them openly. Each character who spoke freely to the audiences can be seen in some sense as a guide, showing the playgoers how to understand the play's action, as well as the way their own world was linked to it. Meg Twycross draws attention to the frequency of use of this form of address:

The use of *ye/you* and *thou/thee* (the singular and thus more direct and intimate form of the pronoun) is frequent; so is the way in which the characters will associate themselves with the audience by using *we/us*. This mode of direct address is again not exclusive to the drama: it is an essential feature of the movement of popular piety that sought to bring the individual into a personal relationship with Christ, suffering for his pain, and loving him for his love shown to us. (55)

Twycross is right in explaining the strategy as an "essential feature ... of popular piety." Nevertheless, it also functions as a fundamental and powerful dramaturgical strategy.

Open address appears in many forms in the guild plays. How each type functioned depended on a combination of factors: where the character stood to speak, how he or she was costumed, what properties were carried by or surrounded the actor, what associations were set up between the character and the crowd's own world. Some characters spoke from loca; some from the platea. Each kind of open address, whether spoken inside framed staging or within a frame consisting only of the audience, operated differently. Nevertheless, all were openly spoken to the audience. Guild plays did not operate by means of oppositional staging: the stage did not set up addresses from loca as wholly distant, historical, and symbolic, or addresses from the platea as wholly local, contemporary, and literal. Characters occasionally did cross from one mode of audience contact to another, that is, from loca address to platea address and vice versa. For example, Abraham speaks both from the platea and from the locus consisting of the hill where he prepares to sacrifice Isaac. In many Herod episodes the king addresses the audience from both the platea and throne loca.

Although they differ in the type of contact they made with the playgoers, addresses from all stage positions worked to guide the audience to an understanding of the play. The most dramatically potent aspect of open address is its capacity to construct and shift relationships between audience and action during the course of the play – from wherever it emanates.

HOW OPEN ADDRESS FUNCTIONS

Address from God

My exploration of the workings of open address starts with the opening words that guide audiences into each guild play, the "*Ego sum alpha et o*" of God, usually spoken on a raised structure decorated to represent Heaven.[28] God, the *"primus et novissimus"* of being, is the first and last voice of the plays. From his high scaffold, in each Doomsday episode he ends the place and time of "this" world. In most plays, the figure of God at the opening overlooked both play-world and audience. Even though N-Town's Threefold God at first walks on the platea, he later climbs up to "Hevyn hille" where he surveys his creation, the playworld, and N-Town's people (*The Fall of Man*, 240). In Chester, God calls down to Noah from "some high place – or in the clowdes, if it may bee" (*Noah's Flood*, Stage Direction, 42). In 1433, York's mercers evidently used a mechanism to lower God from Heaven for their Doomsday episode, since their accounts show orders for a sturdy iron swing on which God ascended to heaven:

iiij Irens to bere vppe heuen iiij finale coterelles & a Iren pynne A brandreth of Iren that god sall sitte vpon when he sall sty vppe to heuen With iiij rapes at iiij corners (REED, York I, 55).[29]

(4 irons to hold up heaven; 4 tapered heavy brackets with hooks and an iron pin; a framework of iron on which God shall rise up to heaven with 4 ropes at 4 corners)

God on his elevated seat was a spectacular sight. Tydeman comments that the materials used for God's locus "were usually as expensive as could be procured or afforded; they were intended to give this area of the stage qualities of radiance and unearthly splendour" (169). Wardrobes for God included furs and skins and expensive imported silks (see Davidson, 61 and Tydeman, 211–12). For instance, Coventry's drapers supplied "iij yards Redde Sendalle for god" (REED: Coventry, 250). In some towns the actor playing God was made mysterious and unknowable by masking him, as in Norwich, whose grocers bought "face & heare for ye Father" (REED: Norwich, 53). In other places, the actor had his face painted: in Chester in 1550 the cordwainers' and shoemakers' guild made a payment "ffor geylding of godes ffase" (REED: Chester, 50). In several towns God was played in costumes made of skins or leather. New Romney, Coventry, and York all record payments for various kinds of skins to dress the actor playing God (Tydeman, 208).

Everywhere, then, God was made magnificent, but his appearance never imitated a human magnifico. This fact is important. All of the God figure's visual signals – that he was raised high, his face made non-human, his clothes made to differ from any worn by anyone in the contemporary world – point to a deliberate effort to engineer a divinity looking and sounding utterly distinct from any human being, whether in history or in the time of the audience. Given that God would not look like anyone in the audience, his appearance could in no way be associated with the ordinary people crowding around the platea, or with the wealthy watching the plays from rented benches set above the heads of the crowd. Consequently, no-one of any class or status was invited to see any resemblance, even any reference, to any human individual in the figure of God. Instead, God was staged as a being outside all human times and places.

The York citizen playing God obviously sat high up as he spoke of creation:

> Here undernethe me nowe a nexile I neuen,
> Whilke ile sall be erthe. Now all be at ones
> Erthe haly, and helle, this hegheste be heuen
> And that wealth shall wield shall won in these wones.
>
> (*The Fall of the Angels*, 25–8)

> (Now here beneath me I name a new place;
> This island is Earth. Now everything exists:
> All of Earth and Hell, and the highest place, Heaven.
> Those in spiritual well-being will live in these places.)

As the God figure directs the townspeople to look at "this" heaven, he is self-contained, non-contingent. He seems neither to demand response nor to look to see whether the people are responding to his words. In fact, his dignified diction appears not to acknowledge any listeners. The theological point here is that neither time nor space exists at the moment God speaks the words of creation. Nothing exists but the deity. Nonetheless, even though God appears to be ignoring York, he is not. In fact, words and staging together told the citizens how to hear the words of creation, and how to imagine themselves connected to them. Because they heard them as they stood in their own city, by Micklegate, or in Coney Street, with York's buildings, the river, the markets, their neighbours, all visible to them, God's words situated their own time and place, their York, within his timelessness.[30] God was treating the playgoers and their city as if they were part of his universal here and now. Thus, in every guild play God's first open address frames not only the play but also the real world, from the play's very beginning, incorporating every town and every person as part of a community made up of all people in all times.

Address from Rulers

Historical rulers such as Herod and Pharaoh and various political officials such as Pilate were also assigned to raised, elaborate locus staging. From these structures, they often said the same kinds of things as God said in his first words: they introduced themselves and told everyone what they planned to do. Like God, human potentates were made to look spectacular, their faces painted or gilded (for example, REED: Coventry, 59, 1040), their costumes and props elaborate, such as Chester's Herod who is "crowned in goulde" (Chester, *Three Kings*, 45–6).[31] However, unlike God, biblical rulers and officials were set firmly in a human world, specifically that of each audience, by their clothing, properties, and words. The plays' kings and lawyers were often costumed in ways playgoers would know mimicked the clothes of local affluence.[32] N-Town's stage directions, for example, ordered historical lawyers to be dressed in accordance with a kind of double representation, as both upholders of the Old Testament law and contemporary clerics:[33]

here shal Annas shewyn himself in his stage, besyn after a busshop of the hoold lawe in a skarlet gowne, and over that a blew tabbard furryd with white, and a mitere on his hed, after the hoold lawe; two doctorys stonding by him in furryd hodys, and on[e] beforn hem with his staff of astat; and eche of hem on here hedys a furryd cappe with a gret knop in the crowne; and on[e] stonding beforn as a Sarazyn, the w[h]ich shal be his masangere. (*Passion Play I*, 230)

(Here shall Annas appear in his place, dressed in a scarlet gown like a bishop of the old law and over that a furred blue tabard with white, and a mitre on his head, as in the old law; two doctors stand with him in furred hoods, and one before them with his staff of office; and each of them on their heads a furred cap with a great knob on the crown, and one standing before like a Saracen, who is his messenger.)

The plays' producers went to considerable trouble and expense to give actors playing the roles of history's tyrants exactly the right props to connect them to the playgoers' world. Coventry gave Herod a modern emblem of political power: in 1490 the town's smiths' guild paid for "a septur for heroud"; it also ordered for him "a creste" and a "fawchon" (curved broadsword) (REED: Coventry, 73). Apparently Coventry's cappers played the role of Pilate so enthusiastically that their medieval weapons – clubs and leather balls – had to be repaired frequently.[34]

Moreover, biblical rulers did not appear to ignore the playgoers' presence as God did. In fact, they grabbed at their audiences, showing off about their English real estate. Lords over "castelle, towre and towne" (Chester, *Three Kings 2*, 171–2), they offered to loyal subjects rewards such as "florens and fryhthis fre / parkys and powndys pleyne" (gold coins, and noble woods, and ponds full of fish) (N-Town, *The Adoration of the Magi*, 181–2). In addition to threatening to injure or promising to reward playgoers in Chester's version of the massacre of the innocents, Herod is the main villain in a medieval horror story, employing henchmen named Sir Waradrake and Sir Grymball Launcherdeepe. As if they have strayed out of medieval romance, these knights grouse about missing out on proper knightly quests, such as killing "Samsoun" or massacring a whole army of warriors like the "kinge of Scottes and his hoste" (*The Slaughter of the Innocents*, 221–2). They are supremely vexed to discover that their mission is to kill mere infants.[35]

Contemporary medieval languages of authority were mimicked on stage. For example, when it seemed timely, rulers swung from English to French, which – whether or not audiences understood it word for word – would be readily recognized as a courtly language, suitable for use in aristocratic or authoritarian contexts. Chester's Herod uses French to toady to the Magi, welcoming those very well-mannered visitors to his court with

Bien soies venues, royes gent.
Me detes tout vetere entent. (*The Three Kings*, 155–6)

(You are very welcome, royal gentlemen.
I would like to know what you intend to do.)

Attempts by biblical figures to use courtly French are always used mockingly. Their French is funny when they manage to speak it because they use it pretentiously, as well as when they cannot because they sound foolish. In the guild plays, address in French serves to comically deflate abusive authority.

The Wakefield Master (inventor of Towneley's many comic characters) has Herod (in *Herod the Great*) become so furious when he can't get his own way that he finds it hard to keep up a high verbal style, even in English. At the opening of the episode, he speaks very down-to-earth English when he curses, brags, and blusters, and when he tries to bribe the audience:

Draw therfor nerehende, both of burgh and of towne:
Markys, ilkon, a thowsande, when I am bowne,
Shall ye have.
I shal be full fain
To gif that I sayn.
Wate when I com again,
And then may ye crave. (462–8)

(Draw around me, close, wherever you're from:
I will certainly hand out a thousand marks to every one of you,
At some time in the future – when I am ready.
I'll be very glad to do what I've promised.
Watch for me
When I come back again
And you can ask me for it.)

Later in the episode the king's paltry supply of courtly phrases runs out altogether. Overwhelmed by doubts about having killed his infant rival, he openly warns the crowds that he brooks no dissent from any subject, including them. He then rushes away, admonishing them that they had better keep quiet even after he leaves them:

For if I here it spokyn when I com again,
Youre branys bese brokyn; therfor, be ye bain.
Nothing bese unlokyn; it shal be so plain.
Begin I to rokyn, I think all disdain
For-daunche.
Sirs, this is my counsell:
Bese not to[o] cruell,
Bot adew! – to the devill!
I can no more Franch! (505–13)

(And if I hear you talking rebellion when I come back again
Consider your brains bashed in; so do as I say.
I've made it so very clear
I won't say it again.
Watch out. I'm starting to feel violent once more.
Don't forget:
I'll take any indication that you're put out by this
To be pure fussiness.
So you can protest as much as you want.
Now, everyone, this is my advice:

Don't be too cruel.
Adieu! To hell with being superior and civilized!)

Address in Latin, the language of the Church and ecclesiastical law, functions in a more complicated manner. It made a different kind of connection with audiences than French.[36] Since Latin was the language of divine and religious authority, it was spoken in God's great formulaic pronouncements. Because playgoers would often have heard it in church, God's Latin did not shut his listeners out. Melissa M. Furrow discusses the levels of familiarity with Latin: "In very practical terms, the Pater and Ave and Creed in Latin were required knowledge for all medieval Christians, even tapsters and fishermen, herdsmen and washerwomen. Next for those who were formally taught came the hymns used in services of the Church and the Psalms, first to be memorized and recited, then to be construed and understood" (36).

Latin address by lawyer-priests such as Annas and Caiaphas, however, is an abusively excluding tongue, intended to shut out the audience. Such characters used their legal Latin to signify personal rank and to generate secrecy, seeming to draw the frames of their loca tightly around them. For example, Towneley's legal clerics, a calculating Annas and an irascible Caiaphas, obscure their plots against Christ with excursions into a Latin that is meant *not* to be understood by others: "*Et hoc nos volumus, / Quod de iure quod possumus. /* Ye wote what I mene:" (*The Buffeting*, 214–16). "We want to do this because we're allowed to within the law," they say, adding with a wink and a nudge: "You know what I mean." Like Chaucer's Summoner, who could fall back on a Latin phrase to impress when he wanted to, ecclesiastical lawyers in the guild plays always use Latin elliptically, meaning to be overheard but also to be obscure.

Mary speaks to the audience in familiar Latin. In Chester's Nativity episode, the stage direction reads: "*Maria gaudiens incipit canticum "Magnificat"*" (Rejoicing, Mary begins the song "The Magnificat") (100). Mary's Latin functions differently from the foreign words of rulers or lawyers. First, hers is unequivocal, not meant to obfuscate meaning. Also, it serves to elevate Mary, reminding spectators that until her marriage Mary devoted herself to a life of study.

Kingly French and legal-clerical Latin serve to signal what was esoteric and closed in contemporary authority. Audiences would all recognize what social or political world these languages came from. Their use in the plays may have elicited mixed responses in the

diverse audiences. Perhaps the educated or wealthy paying to sit up
on their scaffolds laughed knowingly at comic misuses of French;[37]
perhaps the unschooled in the crowd heard the words as pretentious
rubbish, funny even if individual words were incomprehensible. As
with God's and Mary's Latin, word for word understanding did not
much matter. In the case of both the French of rulers and the Latin of
legal clerics, every member of the audience would recognize the
point: that tyrants of every sort turned words to their own selfish and
abusive ends.

As intent as historical rulers were on distinguishing themselves
from everyone, they also constantly claimed audiences as their subjects. Before the entry of Towneley's Herod, a messenger tells the
audience to "downe ding of youre knees / All that him seys" (60–1).
N-Town's Herod charges "you that ben here present," to cease talking (*Passion Play II*, 22). Kings often go beyond merely hurling
words at playgoers. In their lust for power, they burst from their
loca, bulldozing out among the hucksters and townspeople, to
shout at them or bash them about. Consider the famous stage direction from a Coventry episode: "Here Erode ragis in the pagond and
in the strete also" (*The Shearmen and Taylors' Pageant*, 87). I imagine
audiences noisily resisting such assertions of power, for tyrants typically have to quell the crowds before they can get their dramas
under way. Pharaoh, Pilate, and Herod presumably had to subdue
a crowd already shouting back. Towneley's Pilate, for instance,
shouts: "Peas, carles, I commaunde / unconnande I call you" (*The
Conspiracy*, 1). Robert Weimann shrewdly observes that tyrants most
likely provoked mixed responses from the crowds because the figures were "both somber and ridiculous, terrifying and grotesque"
(68). In one of the Towneley plays, for example, Herod threatens
both his servants and the audience with a beating: "With this brand
that I beare ye shal biterly aby" (*The Scourging*, 4). Every king sees
around him in the crowd people – whether playgoers or characters
– whose tongues wag too much. York's Herod promises everyone a
thrashing if his demands for silence are not met:

> Pes, ye brothellis and browlys in this broydenesse inbrased,
> And freykis that are frendely to your freytenesse to frayne,
> Your tounges fro tretyng of triffillis be trased,
> Or this brande that is bright schall breste in youre brayne.
>
> (*Christ before Herod*, 1–4)

> (Keep quiet. You wretches and scoundrels inside this big space,
> And you friendly men, too, learn how to behave properly.

Hold back from talking gossip,
Or this bright sword will bash in your brains.)

In the Towneley play the king's herald tells his master that the present audience is a gossiping crowd who "carp of a king" (78). Herod then warns them to shut up:

Stint brodels, youre din – yei, everychon!
I red that ye harkyn to I be gone,
ffor if I begyn I breke ilka bone
And pull fro the skyn the carcas anone.
yei, perde!
Sesse all this wonder,
ffor I ryfe you in sonder,
Be ye so hardy (*Herod the Great*, 82–90)

(Stop your din, rogues. Yes, all of you here.
I advise you to listen carefully to all that I say.
For, once I start, I'll break every bone in your bodies,
Cut the skin from your carcasses.
Oh yes, don't think of doubting me.
Stop all this interest in rumours of some wonder
And make no more trouble for our royal self
Or I'll tear you apart,
No matter how tough you are.)

Every biblical ruler is, in fact, obsessed by audience presence, fixated on controlling the behaviour and thoughts of "you that ben here present" (N-Town, *Passion Play II*, 1–2). Delighting in their own magnificence, "most royall in richest array" (York, *The Remorse of Judas*, 9–10), they all preen before the spectators. Unlike God, human rulers need admirers. Like Lucifer, they crow about how they look, making sure their audiences notice too. Listen to York's "Pilate of Pounce," as, seated on his scaffold, he expounds on his beauty, at the same time drawing attention to the intrinsic artificiality of his appearance:

For I ame þe luffeliest lappid and laide
With feetour full faire in my face,
My forhed both brente is and brade
And myne eyne thei glittir like þe gleme in þe glasse.

And þe hore þat hillis my heed
Is even like to þe golde wyre,

My chekis are bothe ruddy and reede
And my coloure as cristall is cleere. (*The Remorse of Judas*, 18–25)

(For I am most beautifully wrapped and covered
With extremely handsome features on my face
My forehead is both smooth and broad
And my eyes glitter like the gleam in glass.

And the hair that covers my head
Is exactly like golden wire,
My cheeks are healthy and ruddy
And my complexion is unblemished.)

As the tyrants charged their audiences to gawp at and revere their kingly looks, they diminished themselves and undermined their own authority making both seem cheap and silly. The address they used provoked audiences to position them, then evaluate them, in the actual world. The plays' magnificent God is *self-contained*; he neither needs nor asks for the audience's admiring gaze. But such characters as Herod, Pilate, and Pharaoh are *self-involved*. In demanding that their beauty and the trappings of their power be worshipped, they actually invoke the transience of these attributes.

When biblical rulers claimed medieval audiences as their own people, they talked as if the playgoers consented to the definition. But, in the end, tyrants in the guild plays are shown to be comics or fools, albeit horrific ones. The more forcefully they claimed "You are my subjects," the more they invited shouts of "Oh no, we're not." Two visions of tyranny were being presented. One said that, in the historical there and then, as in the audiences' here and now, tyrants really did appalling things, committing atrocities against people like those in the audiences. The other view simultaneously asserted that, although what human power does to ordinary people can never be ignored or dismissed, when seen as part of the whole sweep of history, the actions of tyrants are limited and circumscribed. In this light, tyrants were and are merely human beings.

It is the latter view that was conveyed by the nature of the exchange between rulers and audiences. The central action and the dialogue showed that, for the historical people living in the same time as the biblical rulers, the horrors perpetrated by the tyrants were appallingly real. But because the audiences never surrendered their contemporary identities, they had an ironic perspective on the actions and words – very much intensified by the provocation to participate and resist – which told them that powerful men from any age were, in the end, no more than empty buffoons, locked into overblown ideas about themselves and their authority. Entwined as it was with the historical world, the contemporary world was staged as one where people knew that reigns of terror would ultimately fall apart. The people, for their part, were able to resist because the tyrants would be shown to be fools. It is not that the horror of human suffering was ever diminished or simplified; indeed, it was so powerfully staged that its impact could not be overlooked. Nevertheless, by the close of the plays, when the Doomsday episodes dramatized the end of time, the tyrants' authority and power had dissipated; all that was left of the bullies were their sins.

Address from Ordinary People

Whereas God always speaks from the locus of Heaven, signalling that the audience's here and now was to be drawn into a timeless world, Christ often addresses audiences from the platea. For the time of his ministry and passion, his words stress that he was joined to the playgoers' here and now, the place and time of ordinary humanity. During the episodes about his ministry, Christ always talks from the platea, moving about near the people in the streets, eye-to-eye with or within touching distance of ordinary people, the members of the audience who could not afford to pay for raised benches or to overlook the performance from rented rooms.[38]

Other important biblical figures were, like Christ, staged without physical structures around them. They were therefore set clearly amidst the places of everyday life: the city walls, stinking gutters, merchants' houses, tradespeople's stalls. Moving epic characters such as Abraham and Noah onto the platea is a vital dramaturgical strategy. These significant historical figures are thereby simultaneously made into ordinary people with problems, sorrows, joys – characters understood as experiencing life as their audiences do. Sharing the playgoers' ground, they lead them into the play, showing the crowds how to link the play with their medieval lives. In every play, the patriarchs talk openly to the audience about their struggles to obey God's orders. Joseph, too, surrounded by the crowd, bewildered, tries in the N-Town and Towneley plays to understand the confusions of his life.

It is also the platea where "barelegged" citizens hailed Christ as he entered Jerusalem in the N-Town play:

Here the four ceteseynys makyn hem redy for to mete with oure Lord, going
barfot and barelegged and in here shirtys, saving they shal have here gownys
cast abouth them; and qwan they seen oure Lorde, they shal sprede ther
clothis beforn him, and he shal lyth and go therupon, and they shal falle
downe upon ther knes all atonys. (*Passion Play I*, Stage Direction, 285)

(Here the four citizens prepare to meet our Lord, going barefoot and barelegged and in their shirts, except that they will have gowns spread over them;
and when they see our Lord they will spread their clothes before him and he
will alight and walk on them, and they will fall on their knees altogether.)

Near the playgoers, mothers screeched their pain, struggled with
Herod's knights, when they watched their babies made to "hopp
uppon [the] speare":

> Owt, owt, and woe is me!
> Theeffe, thou shall hanged be.
> My chyld is dead; now I see
> my sorrow may not cease.
> Thow shall be hanged on a tree
> and all the men in this contree
> Shall not make thy peace.
>
> Have thou this, thou fowle harlott
> and thou knight, to make a knott!
> And on buffett with this bote
> thou shalt have to boote.
> And thow this, and thou this,
> though thou both shyte and pisse!
> And if thou thinke we doe amysse,
> goe baskes you to moote. (Chester, *The Slaughter of the Innocents*, 345–60)

> (Out out, and woe is me!
> Thief, you will be hanged.
> My child is dead; now I see
> My sorrow will never cease.
> You will be hanged on a tree
> And all the men from all around
> Will not help you then.
>
> Take this you foul ruffian
> And you knight, I'll give you a lump;

And a blow from this boot
You can have as well.
And you take this; and you this,
Even if it makes you shit and piss.
And if you think we do amiss
Go and wallow in a ditch of blood.)

The women's curses were shrieked from amidst the audience, seeming to come from the crowds themselves, urging them to join their voices with the mothers'. Countless other unnamed victims stood in the same area, some railing against vicious attacks by cruel leaders, some worrying about ordinary things such as the weather, bossy wives, oversized families, what growing old felt like, or how to get enough to drink and eat. From the platea audiences were reminded that both marriage and work were complicated; that married men, shackled to their wives, would be wise to keep their sighs to themselves. They were told that the local area was dangerous, reminded that they should be on guard where wayfarers could be attacked by "robers and thefeys," "bosters and bragers" with "long dagers" (Towneley, *Shepherds' Play I*, 52, 55–6).

Shepherds often appeared in the guild plays. Though they were biblical shepherds, they also lived medieval English lives. In Wakefield, shepherds stood close to the audience complaining about the problems of contemporary farming: being out on the moors at night in the North's wretched weather; having to put up with oppressive working conditions, in which landowners could make life hard for small tenant farmers. According to the shepherds in Towneley's *Shepherds' Play II*, tenants had to be wary of crossing a liveried official who,"as prowde as po," (37) could demand whatever he wanted from the small farmer – his wagon or his plough – paying next to nothing in exchange. On both sides of the Pennines, close to Yorkshire and Chester, shepherds worried intensely about "the rott," the bane of sheep-keeping: in Yorkshire, Gyb has to beg and borrow because foot rot killed his flock (Towneley, *Shepherds' Play I*, 40). Chester's shepherds stir up herbs and tar for the flock's "taytful tuppes" (lively rams); the third shepherd has been ruining his wife's kitchen pots to boil up "salve for our sheepe" (73), while the first shepherd lists the English herbs, such as henbane, ribwort, radish, and egremont, that made a good remedy for foot rot. By means of such references, biblical shepherds guided their medieval audiences to think about their own local, contemporary setting and so to connect their mundane world with the momentous event of Christ's birth.

In the Chester and Wakefield plays, shepherds were staged with great particularity. Local rustics with typical worries, they were also historical figures who feel a terrifying and universal sense of desolation. As well as grumbling about difficult wives, hard jobs, and sick sheep, Yorkshire's shepherds talk of a loss of hope in life itself. For example, Gyb speaks of despair so great that it makes him envy the dead: "Lord, what thay are weyll / that hens are past! / ffor they noght feyll / theym to downe cast" (Lord, the people who've left this life did the right thing! / They're not on Fortune's wheel anymore. / They don't feel cast down.) (Towneley, *Shepherds' Play I*, 1–2). His is a familiar lament: happiness and prosperity can only be unstable and transitory in this world:

Thus this Warld, as I say
farys on ilk syde,
ffor after oure play
com sorows vnryde;
ffor he that most may
When he syttys in pryde,
When it comys on assay
is kestenn downe wyde,
This is seyn:
When rychest is he,
Then comys pouerté,
Hors-man Iak Copé
Walkys then, I weyn. (10–18)

(In this world we all go up both sides of the road.
After fun and games come sadness and misery.
The mightiest man sitting high up there in pride
Falls down with a crash when put to the test.
I mean, when a man's at his richest
Poverty comes a-calling.
Jack Moneybags on his horse
Then has to go about on foot.)

Such scenes carry a double point of view. From the audience's perspective, the shepherds despair at the brink of the world's greatest moment. Consider this modernized version of the first shepherd's complaints in Towneley's *Shepherds' Play II*:

My God, it's cold. I'm frozen right through!
And my clothes are so thin.
I've been napping so long I can't feel a thing.
My legs fold up under me. My fingers are chapped.
I didn't choose this;
My life was already
Just one aching pain.
Out in all weather: storms, tempests,
Sometimes from the east,
Sometimes from the west.
For men like me it's a wretched life.
And we never get a break
At any time day or night
Or ever.

And another thing: miserable farm-workers
Like us, who spend our days plodding
Through open fields, are well nigh destitute.
And it's hardly surprising if we are poor,
Things being what they are.
You know as well as I do
Our fields are still as unploughed as the floor.

We are hamstrung,
Over-taxed, and ground down
By these gentrified lackeys.
To them we're just little pet dogs.

And they never give us a chance to rest;
May Our Lady curse them for it!
Bound to their lord, they hold up our ploughing.
Some say that's how it should be.
I say that's rubbish.

Here they are oppressing farmers,
To the point of killing us off.
Here they are, keeping us down,
Stopping us working.
It'll be a miracle if we ever prosper.

And nowadays, as soon as his master gives a man
An embroidered sleeve or a badge,
Woe to a working man who annoys him

Or says anything against him,
Even once.

Ignore the force he uses against you?
You'd better or you're in trouble.

On top of that, you can't believe
Anything he says, not a thing.
He can decide what his lord needs from us, ok,
– He boasts and brags about it –
But he can only do it because
His lord protects him.

Then another lord's man, proud as a peacock.
He's come along to borrow my wagon,
And my plough, too.
So I have to be happy to lend them to him.

That's how we spend our lives.
All the time, it's pain, anger and woe.
If he wants it, he's got to have it
Even if I have to go without.
I'd do better to be hanged
Than say "no" to him.

All playgoers were explicitly included in both the despair and its
remedy; "oure play" is linked with "this Warld." The shepherds'
insistently inclusive language joins the contemporary crowds to the
plays' depictions of the birth of Christ.

As well as expressing "popular piety" (in the words of Meg
Twycross), the addresses of such characters as Abraham and Noah
focus on the *particular* ways in which the patriarchs are linked to the
contemporary world. For example, in the Noah episodes individual
words and phrases signal connections between the old world order
and the new (Kolve, 146). The time of the flood is identified as the day
on which God would "fordo all this medillerd [world]", as he would
do again at the Judgment (Towneley, *Noah and the Ark*, 100). The plays
show that cosmic as well as earthly order would be restored when
"the son [Christ] shines in the eest" (Towneley, *Noah and the Ark*, 454).

In addition to making figural and symbolic links, at crucial
moments the characters turn to talk intimately to the playgoers. In
N-Town's *Abraham and Isaac*, after being told by God to kill his child,

Abraham anticipates with horror "this nicht" when he will slay his "awn son" (112–4). No-one is on stage but Abraham and Isaac. It is understood Isaac does not hear his father; only the playgoers hear the patriarch, whose words draw them into his agony:

> Alone right here in this playn,
> Might I speke to myn hart brast,
> I wold that all were well full fayn. (109–11)

> (Alone right here in this plain
> I could speak till my heart bursts.
> I wish that everything were safe and well.)

Every version of the story emphasizes Abraham's suffering and sorrow. Here is the scene as it appears in N-Town:

> Now goddys commaundment must nedys be done
> Att his wyl is wourthy to be wrought
> but yitt þe fadyr to sle þe sone
> grett care it causyth in my thought
> In byttyr bale now am I brought
> My swete childe with knyf to kylle. (*Abraham and Isaac*, 89–94)

> (God's commandment has to be done.
> It is proper to do whatever he wants.
> Yet for a father to kill his son
> Worries me very deeply.
> I am in bitter agony that I have
> To kill my lovely child with a knife.)

Whereas doctrine laid stress on the story as an exemplum of obedience to God's will, the plays also insist that audiences notice the human, emotional cost of complying with God's command, and the dragging temptation to resist.[39] The Bible does not deal at length with the horror Abraham goes through. Indeed, there is some tension between the well-known biblical story and what Abraham says to the audience. The doctrinal reading shows how people, taking Abraham as a model, should relate to God, but Abraham's words on the platea connect him to the audience – in particular, to their emotions – for many playgoers must have known what it was to lose a "swete" child. The plays focus on the love of a man for his son, thrust the human story forward by integrating the patriarch with contemporary

reality. As Erich Auerbach shows, they link the playgoers and Abraham and Isaac, not on the symbolic or the ideal level of meaning, but
on the literal, on the "everyday and real" (*Mimesis*, 138).[40] Living in
an uncertain world like Abraham's, the crowds were asked to feel his
terrible human doubts.[41] But the audiences had an ironic perspective
on the event. They already knew that the story had a happy ending,
and must have anticipated the moment when they would see the
angel move forward to stay Abraham's sword. Nevertheless, they
watched a very human Abraham obey God despite his ignorance of
the outcome.

The addresses of another patriarch, Noah, directed audiences
towards a different aspect of daily life. The flood that destroyed the
world is a very difficult event to make sense of, a most serious matter. Yet this disturbing, sombre Bible story is padded out in the plays
so that it steps sturdily into the world of medieval comedy. Noah's
age is always emphasized:

> And now I wax old,
> Seke, sory and cold
> As muk upon mold
> I widder away. (Towneley, *Noah and the Ark*, 60–3)

> (Now I grow old,
> Sick, sorry and cold.
> Like dung on the earth
> I wither away.)

Throwing off his gown to work in his coat, this Noah mutters to the
audience about his "wery bak" and the stress of having to build a
boat at his age when his "bonys ar so stark." The figure of the
put-upon old man is not confined to Noah episodes: Tired-out
Joseph, with bones as heavy as lead, grumbles to the playgoers
surrounding York's wagon platea that he made a "bad barganne"
the day he married a "yonge wenche" (*Joseph's Trouble about Mary*,
35).

In the Chester, Towneley, and York plays (but not N-Town[42]), the
Noahs lead a chaotic family life drawn straight from contemporary
rough comedy; as well as the foolish old man, there is a harridan,
with plenty of knockabout. They all assume that their situation is
normal, and address audiences as if everyone lived the same way.
Both the weary old husband and his rebellious spouse openly ask for
audience sympathy. Towneley's Noah complains about what he will
face at home (and expects a sympathetic hearing from Yorkshire's

men) when his irascible wife finds out that God has told him to build
an ark:

> For she is full tethee
> For littill oft angre;
> If any thyng wrange be
> Soyne is she wrothe. (*Noah and the Ark*, 186–9)

> (She's always bad-tempered
> And gets angry for almost no reason.
> She goes off the deep end
> Just as soon as any little thing
> Goes wrong.)

Only N-Town presents Mrs Noah as a supportive wife; in Towneley, Chester, and York she is always stubborn, even pig-headed, and
flatly defies her husband. In the Towneley episode she sits on her
hill spinning until the eleventh hour; Chester's Uxor sneers at the
"Ffrenyshe fare" (*Noah's Flood*, 100) her husband has built, refusing
to get onboard unless she can take her ale-drinking "gossepes" with
her; York's Mrs Noah will not travel without her friends and
cousins – she would rather send her immediate family onto the ark
while she goes to town or gathers up her kitchen utensils (*The
Flood*). Every Mrs Noah is as quick as her husband to demand audience sympathy. As elsewhere, Towneley's Uxor speaks directly to
the audience's women who stand around her, when she invites
them to curse all "ill husbandes" who have mastery in that unequal
partnership called marriage. Never doubting their assent, she
grumbles:

> Lord, I were at ese, and hertely full hoylle,
> Might I onys have a measse of wedows coyll.
> For thy saull, without lese, shuld I dele penny doyll.
> So wold mo, no frese, that I se on this sole
> Of wifys that ar here,
> For the life that thay leyd,
> Wold thare husdandys were dede.
> For, as ever ete I brede,
> So wold I oure sire were! (388–96)

> (Well, there's one thing I'm sure of: the day
> They say my pottage is called "widow's food"
> Will be the happiest day of my life.

That day, I'll pay
The pennies for prayers for your soul
With a big smile all over my face.
And so, no doubt, would other wives
Who are here. I see them out there.
They'd like their husbands dead, too,
Because of the life they've had to lead.
Oh, yes, as sure as I've ever eaten bread
I wish our old man was dead.)

In every play except N-Town, Mr and Mrs Noah have a fist-fight on the platea, and, before their quarrel is resolved, beat each other up. In the Chester version, Mrs Noah bashes at her husband with her distaff. In Towneley's episode three fierce skirmishes halt only when Noah's "bak is nere in two," and his wife complains that she is "bet so blo / That I may not thryfe" (*Noah and the Ark*, 503–4). Worn out by it all, Towneley's old man warns the young men among the spectators to avoid his mistakes:

Yee men that has wifes, whyls thay ar yong,
If ye luf youre lifys chastice thare tong.
Me thynk my hert ryfys, both levyr and long,
To se sich stryfis wedmen among (397–400)

(You men out there who have wives,
If you love your lives,
Curb their tongue
While they're young.

I feel my heart, and liver, and lungs,
Split and burst,
When I see the problems of married men.)

The open attempts by the Noahs to elicit partisan responses from their audiences were very indecorous indeed. As in the Abraham and Isaac episodes, audiences must already have been familiar with the official story; they would have been aware that Mrs Noah would eventually enter the ark, and that the whole Noah family would be saved. So, while the episodes stage a well-known biblical story, they also make the audiences take note that the hero and his wife endured patently ordinary human lives in which aging bones hurt and growing old is miserable (particularly if you are told to get on with some strenuous carpentry), where husbands and wives do not always get on, where people often prefer friends to family and would rather go shopping or to the pub than comply with divine commands, and where people sometimes have to be coerced to be saved. Open address in the Noah episodes, then, presents concrete human realities and shows the crowds that, in spite of frailties very like their own, the Noahs were saved.

Some critics raise their brows at the way the guild plays' Noah episodes veer to slapstick, particularly Towneley's account with its three bouts of wife and husband bashing. Rosemary Woolf, for instance, looks askance at the Towneley episode, where she rightly considers that a "fabliau style is most marked" (142). However, she notices the "fabliau style" only to judge that the play's author, the Wakefield Master, has "developed the character pattern of Noah's wife at the cost of obscuring the allegorical significance of Noah" (143).[43] Richard Axton, who examines several Flood episodes, finds that the Towneley play's "knockabout" tends to "get out of hand" ("Modes," 36).

I contest both Woolf's and Axton's evaluations. The episodes are certainly rowdy. They seem to demand active participation from audiences as well as emotional engagement. But their tone in no way distracts from their meaning.[44] By giving them a strongly human comic slant, the dramatists prevent the plays from slipping out of their control. In fact, they purposely make them into something resembling the old participatory folk plays, encouraging ritualistic, "Oh yes, you are! Oh no, you're not!" games among the playgoers. In so doing they engage and position the audiences in a specific way.[45] As in the Abraham and Isaac episodes, open addresses stage the audience in the Noah episodes. On stage, as well as in the Bible story, is the familiar world of contemporary problems, reaffirmed by voices from the audience shouting out for Mr or Mrs Noah. The Noahs thereby guide the plays into modern lives. As they act out stylized yet recognizable everyday conflicts in the guise of familiar characters whose role has always been to elicit response, the Noahs invite the audience to connect the play to their lives. All playgoers know the story, but they have to be told where their lives fit into it.

Address from Non-biblical Characters

Other characters who speak openly to the audience have been added by the dramatists to the biblical narratives. Some engage with the crowds in a straightforward way, others more equivocally. Among the former are characters who steer the audience through the stories.

They appear on the platea between episodes, to announce the next historical event or to interpret for the spectators what they have just seen. In N-Town, for instance, Contemplacio announces several episodes connected to the Nativity: the conception, the presentation in the Temple, the betrothal, the annunciation, and the meeting with Elizabeth. He closes the series with, first, an open address to the audience as "you," then a lyrical cry to God to take pity on the world, involving the playgoers as members, with Jeremiah and Adam, in a historical community:

> A quod Jeremye . who xal gyff wellys to myn eynes
> þat I may wepe bothe day and nyght
> to se oure bretheryn in so longe peynes
> here myschevys Amende . may þi mech myght
> As gret as þe se lord . was Adamys contryssyon ryght
> Ffrom oure hed is falle þe crowne
> Man is comeryd in synne . I crye to þe syght
> Gracyous lord . Gracyous lord . Gracyous lord come downe.
>
> (Epilogue, *The Betrothal of Mary*, 25–32)

> (Ah, said Jeremiah, who will give wells to my eyes
> That I may weep both day and night
> To see our brethren in such lasting agony?
> May your great might amend their torments!
> O Lord, Adam's rightful fall was as great as the sea,
> The crown has fallen from our heads
> Man is held fast in sin. I weep at the sight.
> Gracious Lord, Gracious Lord, Gracious Lord come down.)

In Chester a more prosaic expositor, the Doctor, adds narratives that are not staged and offers Lancashire audiences short sermons on what they should take away from the play. This cleric stresses the importance to the lives of the playgoers of what they have seen on stage. First he sums up the Abraham episode:

> Lordinges, this significatyon
> of this deede of devotyon –
> and yee will, yee wytt mon –
> may torne you to myche good.
> This deede yee seene done here in this place,
> in example of Jesus done yt was,
> that for to wynne mankinde grace
> was sacrifyced one the roode.

By Abraham I may understand
the father of heaven that cann fonde
with his Sonnes blood that bonde
that the dyvell had brought us to. (*Abraham and Isaac*, 460–71)

(Ladies and gentlemen, the significance
Of this act of devotion –
If you wish, you must know–
May cause you to do great good.
The deed that you saw done here in this place
Was an example of Jesus,
Who to gain grace for mankind
Was sacrificed on the cross.
I understand Abraham to signify
Our Father in heaven who undertook
With his son's blood to break that bond
That the devil had brought us to.)

Then he implicates the audience as "we" and "us," kneeling on the platea and saying

Such obedyence grante us, O lord,
ever to thy moste holye word;
that in the same wee may accorde
as this Abraham was beyne.
And then altogether shall wee
that worthye kinge in heaven see,
and dwell with him in great glorye
for ever and ever. Amen. (476–83)

(O Lord, grant us always to be so obedient
To your most holy word,
That we may behave like
The obedient Abraham.
Then we will all of us see
That noble king in heaven,
And live with him in great glory
For ever and ever. Amen.)

In strong contrast to the honest guides are figures taken from old ritual drama: folk drama, sword or plough plays, and mummings (see Tydeman, 1–22). These characters tend to have peripheral roles in the guild plays, occupying a curiously disengaged or unembroiled stage position, moving casually in and out of the narrative. For instance, the Wakefield Master adds the servants Pykharnes and Froward to his dramatizations of the killing of Abel and the buffeting of Christ respectively; and the word-mongering Titivillus to the last judgement episode. N-Town has Den, a vicious court summoner; Chester has the canny yet foolish Trowle. None of these characters ever fails to notice his audience.

Then there are the plays' stage demons, who poke at the crowds, both verbally and physically. In Towneley's last judgement episode, frantic minor demons rush about trying to save Hell. One needs to call a council meeting like "a pere [peer] in a parlemente" (120). Another reminds him that to get to the devil's court they must travel "up Watlyn Strete."[46]

All the extrabiblical figures whose origins lie in folk drama have a word-mongering reductiveness allied to a slippery amorality that veers to the diabolic. Titivillus, on a platea that is also Hell, reads out a list of sins from his bag of documents, mocking the people of York-shire for their transgressions. He then takes aim at the women in the audience:

> When she is thus paynt,
> She makys it so quaynte
> She lookys like a saynt –
> And wars then the deyle. (*The Last Judgement*, 264–8)

> (When she's painted herself up
> And acts so elegantly
> She looks like a saint
> And is worse than the devil.)

Next, he taunts well-dressed fools who spend so much money on clothes that their children starve:

> Here be, I gesse, of many nice hoket,
> Of care and of curstnes, hething and hoket,
> Gay gere and witles, his hode set on koket,
> As prowde as pennyles. His slefe has no poket –
> Ful redles.
> With thare hemmyd shoyn,
> All this must be done,
> Bot sire is out at hye noyn
> And his barnes bredeles. (*The Last Judgement*, 233–41)

(I have here, I would say, people
Who excel in foolishness,
Who cause trouble and wickedness, who scoff and play tricks.
One here wears bright clothes but is totally witless.
Cocks his head jauntily;
He's as proud as he's penniless.
Money slips through his fingers –
Must have holes in his pockets.
He rejects good advice.
He wears fancily stitched shoes –
Must always be fashionable –
And at mid-day this father goes out strutting
While his children go without food.)

The master trickster, the devil, uses guile rather than force to invade the playgoers' world, usually treating the watchers as confidants. In York's *The Temptation*, the devil professes faith in the playgoers' collusion with his plans. Before each temptation, and after Christ answers him, he confers with the audience. For example, when Christ rejects food, before turning back to Christ the devil says to the spectators as if they obviously agree: "Ah slike carping nevere I kende / Him hungres nogt, as I wende" (I've never heard such words before. / It's just as I thought, he isn't hungry.) (*The Temptation*, 85–6).

The devil in N-Town's *Passion Play I* is the most strikingly polished of these diabolic figures. Unlike other devils who may leap "in to the place in the most orryble wyse" (N-Town, *Passion Play II*, stage direction after 465), this devil (decked out in exaggerated late medieval fashion), is an engaging smoothie. This episode may have been performed not on wagons but with loca set up in and around a platea, with one locus representing Hell. The devil would enter the platea from this locus and, although he would ignore its presence, the Hell locus would remain visible to N-Town's crowd. As he speaks, the devil disengages from any verbal or physical link with his locus, positioning himself squarely on the platea, in contemporary N-Town. He preens himself; as if lording it over envious friends, he flaunts his garments to the N-Town crowds. Here is the devil crowing over the balanced harmony of his clothes:

Eche thyng sett . of dewe naterall dysposycion
and eche parte Acordynge . to his resemblauns
Ffro the sool of the ffoot, to the hyest Asencion. (*Passion Play I*, 66–8)

(Each thing is placed in its natural order
Each part set out according to its appearance
From the sole of the foot,
All the way up to the very top.)

The plays' other richly costumed characters, the tyrants, also drew
attention to their appearance, unwittingly making themselves fools
in the spectators' eyes in the process. The devil, on the other hand,
consciously plays the fool as he parades about in his gaudy clothes.
With the "thy" and "thee" of intimate address, as if speaking to one
individual only, he urges each member of the audience to covet and
to imitate the latest fashions. He locates his open address in a parody
of N-Town's sartorial excesses:

> Cadace, wolle, or flokkys, where it may be sowth,
> To stuffe withal thy dobbelet, and make thee of Proporcion
> Two smale legges and a gret body (thow it ryme nowth)
> Yet loke that thou desire to an the newe facion. (77–80)

> (Packing, wool or flock, where it can be found,
> To stuff your doublet, and make you well-proportioned –
> Two small legs and a great body,
> Though they don't go together very well
> Show that you want to be in the latest fashion.)

The devil exhorts the crowds to admire his flea-ridden hair-do, a
coiffure that may also make reference to medieval Jewish style:

> With side lokkys, I schewe, thine here to thy colere hanging down
> To herborwe quweke bestys that tekele men onyth. (85–6)

> (With side-locks, just look, and hair hanging down to your shoulders
> Provide a small home for the crawly things that tickle at night.)

Look at every article in my up-to-date outfit, right down to the decorations on my shoelaces, he urges his putative friends, piling detail
upon detail:

> Of ffyne cordewan, A goodly peyre of long pekyd schon
> hosyn enclosyd . of þe most costyous cloth . of Crenseyn
> þus a bey to a jentylman . to make comparycion
> With two doseyn poyntys of cheverelle . þe
> Aglottys of syluer feyn. (69–72)

(Of fine Spanish leather, a handsome pair of long pointed shoes
Enclosing stockings of the most expensive crimson material:
This is the boy for a gentleman to compare himself with – me –
With two dozen laces of kid leather
And eyelets of good silver.)

N-Town's devil, the very epitome of contemporary – and illegal –
artificiality, exhorts the citizens to embrace profligacy, pride,
violence, and envy, and to disregard their sumptuary laws: "thou
sette hem at nowth" (76).[47]

As he peacocks around N-Town's platea, the devil draws laughter
at himself; he must surely have leaned close to individuals in the
audience to let them finger his garments. At the same time, he makes
his audience laugh at anyone resembling the parody he presents.[48]
This is the nub of the devil's dramatic contract with the playgoers: it
is purposely divisive. "Byholde þe dyvercyte of my dysgysyd
varyauns," he says, showing off his costume (65). The words could
equally well apply to what he wants from his audience. The tapster
in the Chester *Harrowing of Hell* who, as she enters, identifies her sins
and warns her fellow tradespeople not to follow her example, invites
rather than denies the possibility of a fair and equal community. The
devil, by contrast, works to split the N-Town audience into contest-
ing individuals. Even his "thou," a spurious caress for each separate
"friend," is meant to fracture the crowd, to foment comparison and
competition. He urges each member of the audience to slide his or
her eyes over others: "A gowne of thre yerdys loke thou make comparison / Vn-to all degrees dayly . that passe thin astat" (Make sure
you compare this gown made of three yards of material / With the
garments of those, of no matter what social rank, who pass you
daily.) (*Passion Play I*, 81–2). Pretending camaraderie with everyone,
however clothed, he subtly urges disunity. As his preening fashion
display and his address make fun of some people – those who could
afford and were legally entitled to be richly fashionable, they are also
reminding others of what they lack. When he begs the spectators to
"giff me your love. grawnt me my Affecion / And I wyll unclose . þe
tresour of lovys Alyawns" (Give me your love, give me the affection
due to me / And I will make clear the treasure of love's allegiance.)
(61–2), the devil is staging N-Town not as diverse but as divided.

FUSING PLAY AND PLAYGOERS:
FOUR EPISODES

I will now consider how open addresses in four plays made the connection between the world of each audience and the world of the play. The different episodes guide playgoers into the drama in distinct ways. In this section, I will first look at how audiences are claimed openly by more than one speaker. In the case of Towneley's *The Killing of Abel*, three characters address the audience; I examine the contradictions among their open addresses. From the brawling world of Towneley I move to York's pinners' episode, then to Chester's cooks' episode. Both explicitly address their audiences as members of the local contemporary world of work. Finally I speak of the silence of Christ in N-Town's *The Woman Taken in Adultery*, examining Christ's unspoken words as an open address that is the very centre of the episode.

Towneley: The Killing of Abel

As we have seen, the Wakefield Master invented a servant for the biblical Cain. In his version of Abel's murder, three stage characters speak openly to rural Yorkshire: Cain, his servant Pykharnes, and God. Each asks the audience to be a different kind of listener, and each urges playgoers to reject the addresses of the other two.

Both Cain and his brother Abel play on the platea, surrounded by Yorkshire people. Cain makes his entry to the platea trying to control a team hauling a plough. There he counts sheaves he has set aside for sacrifice, pretending his meanness is thrift. Abel is saddened and worried by his brother's trivialization of the pious transaction. In this episode, the God who awaits the sacrifice is plainly visible, present throughout, set up on a high seat or scaffold. Abel repeatedly urges Cain to bear in mind that this sacrifice is meant for God. He reminds his brother: "Cam, I rede thou tend right, / For drede of him that sittys on hight" (245–6). Nevertheless, Cain carries on being a resentful Yorkshire farmer who treats God as if they were engaged in human bargaining.

Throughout the episode, Cain is locked in an angry reductive particularity. He sees nothing beyond local farming troubles: bad weather, failed crops, no money, high taxes. He complains that the priest has taken his last farthing. Cain has a very narrow moral vision; he sees getting money as the only end in life, and demands that his listeners share his view. His idea of sacrifice is tit for tat: God gave him poor crops, so God gets a paltry sacrifice. Speaking on the platea, he says of God:

For he has ever yit beyn my fo.
For, had he my freynd beyn,

Othergatys it had beyn seyn.
When all mens corn was faire in feld,
Then was mine not worth a neld.
When I shuld saw, and wantyd seyde,
And of corn had full grete neyde,
Than gaf he me none of his;
No more will I gif him of this.
Hardely hold me to blame
Bot if I serve him of the same. (119–29)

(He's always been my enemy.
If he'd been my friend
I'd certainly have known.
When everybody else's wheat was growing well
Mine wasn't worth a needle.
When it was the time for me to sow
And I was short on seed
And had a real need
For wheat,
He never let me have any of his.
He'll get the same amount from me.
You can scarcely blame me
For treating him the same way he treated me.)

Cain's servant Pykharnes also speaks from the platea. He takes his master's viewpoint even further, telling the audience that it is possible to have no moral vision whatsoever. His opening words in this dramatization of brother killing brother are a cheerful greeting: "All hail, all hail bothe blithe and glad, / For here come I, a mery lad" (1–2). One of Pykharnes's roles is to parallel, emphasize, and at times surpass Cain's coarseness – for example, when he says that Cain offers God a sheaf no bigger than one "as he might wype his arse withal" (237). However, from the very beginning, his most important function is to prod the audience towards a kind of depravity different from Cain's.

Pykharnes abuses his audience. He invites the crowd to watch the play, with obscene warnings:

Bot who that janglis any more,
He must blaw my blak hoill bore
Both behind and before
Till his tethe blede. (6–9)

(Anyone who wants to carry on chattering
Can blow my arse hole
From the front and the back
Till their teeth bleed.)

Pykharnes summons the audience into the play by suggesting that
rural Yorkshire already knows Cain well: "A good yoman my master
hat – / Full well ye all him kan" (15–6). He has a subversive affilia-
tion with both his master and the audience that parallels Cain's relationship to God. Striking his master back when he is hit, he flattens a
hierarchical association into a disturbing kind of equality: "Yai, with
the same mesure and weght / That I boro will I quwite [repay]"
(51–2).

Similarly, Cain wants to force God into his own mould, to pull God
into the human realm and to guide the audience to do the same. After
the murder, God calls out from his high seat: "Cam, why art thou so
rebell / Agans thy brother Abell?" (291). Cain wilfully misunderstands; his reply is intended to shrink the raised-up, magnificent
deity to a rural hobgoblin: "Why, who is that hob over the wall? /
We! who was that piped so small?" (297–8). This must surely have
been a tremendously funny and, at the same time, disturbing joke.
One imagines a huge voice resonating from an elaborate, mysterious
figure located above the platea and audience. God speaks to Cain
again, asking him this time: "Caym, where is thy brother Abel?"
(344). Cain answers the question with an evasive question of his own:
"What askys thou me?" (345). The Yorkshire artisans, farmers, and
merchants in the audience surely knew that God, speaking as he does
from the high, omniscient seat of Heaven, does not need to ask for
information. His words announce, to the audience as well as Cain,
Cain's spiritual and moral condition. Cain tries to browbeat God, and
God resists.

At this point God in his locus speaks familiar biblical words that
address both the people of the bible and contemporary Yorkshire
men and women, resounding high over both playworld and audience:

I will that no man other slo
ffor he that sloys yong or old
It shall be punyshid sevenfold. (371–3)

(My will is that no-one ever kills another.
And he that kills you, whoever he is,
Will be punished for the deed seven times over.)

The words link the biblical and the contemporary worlds. God's ban forbids everyone in Wakefield – its millers, farmers, butchers, shearers, bailiffs, and priests – from touching the murderer standing close by them.

Even though God has commanded that no-one may kill him, Cain is nervous of those nearby. Not wanting to risk getting too close to potential killers, Cain places Pykharnes between himself and the audience. He orders Pykharnes to cry the king's peace to them. However, Pykharnes's version of Cain's proclamation sends out messages meaning the opposite of what Cain says. For instance, Cain wants the audience to believe that the highest human authority will protect him: "The kyng will that thay be safe" (428). Pykharnes turns this into an elemental wish irrelevant to Cain: "Yey, a draght of drynke fayne wold I hayfe" (429). By counterpointing each of his master's announcements with one of his own, Pykharnes reduces to further nonsense Cain's already futile attempts to control the rural Yorkshire community.

What the playgoers have heard so far are three conflicting orders. God has spoken to them in their identity as dwellers in a universal, eternal world, as members of a community in which each person bears responsibility for the others. Everyone understands that this is a command that can never be repealed, ignored, or modified by any human person. God's announcement carries a meaning that is unequivocal, stable, and universal, and therefore irresistible. But Cain wants to lead the spectators into the action as either those who will slay him or those who will clear his name. Both are impossible roles for them to play, since both would cause the onlookers to join in his efforts to challenge God. Finally, Pykharnes, in giving the audience his fool's upside-down version of Cain's words, invites them to join in his aberrant, uncaring attitude to God, murder, and life.

The three voices present the audience with three incompatible visions. Cain's is immoral and narrow, insisting on the paramount importance of a selfish individual. Pykharnes's is amoral, casually valuing everything and everyone at nothing. God's moral vision values all actions and all people, including those watching.

At the end of the episode, with a final gesture at the people standing around him, Cain slinks off through the Yorkshire platea to the locus of Hell, where he will forever sell his grain in a stall in the infernal marketplace. Hell, like Wakefield, is a town with streets and markets. Unreformed and unrepentant, Cain will go on counting crookedly.

Now faire well, felows all, for I must nedys weynd,
And to the dwill be thrall, warld withoutten end.
Ordand ther is my stall, with Sathanas the feynd.
Ever ill might him befall that theder me commend
This tide.
Farewell les, and farewell more!
For now and evermore
I will go me to hide. (443–50)

(Well, goodbye everyone
I have to move on. I've got no choice.
It's been solemnly decreed
That I'll be living with that fiend Satan.
I'm to be his servant in hell, for ever and ever.
Even so, I wish ill-luck on anyone
Who wants me to go there now.
So, goodbye, those of you who aren't very important
And fare well those of you with all the power,
I'm off to hide myself forever.)

York: The Crucifixion

The members of York's pinners' guild were responsible for staging their city's dramatization of the Crucifixion.[49] The daily work of these artisans bore a clear resemblance to the activities they performed on stage as Christ was attached to the cross. The episode makes no attempt to mute this disturbing connection; on the contrary, the pinners guide York's other citizens to take a hard look at the link between themselves and the people involved in the Crucifixion, to consider the connection between daily work in York and the work of the soldiers attempting to place Christ's cross in a mortice the pinners made.

All the action of the episode takes place on the platea where, close to the audience, four soldiers stretch Christ out to fit the cross. The pinners who play the soldiers simultaneously represent history's ordinary underlings, ordered by "lordis and leders of owre lawe" to carry out an execution, and workers in York's here and now. Like any workmen, they are a familiar mix of efficiency and fumbling, ready to get on with the job, showing themselves anxious to do "this werke" well as they prepare to "crosse him." Haste seems to be of the essence as they get everything ready for "this dede." They have their tools to hand, "both hammeres and nayles large and longe." The cross, with holes bored into it, is laid out on the platea. The soldiers order "þe ladde" to lie down on "þis tree." They remain standing, watching as he does so, staring down at him. So, presumably, are the citizens of York. Stretched out on the ground at their feet, Christ speaks:

> Almyghty God, my fadir free,
> Late þis materes be made in mynde:
> þou badde þat I schulde buxsome be
> For Adam plyght for to be pyned.
> Here to dede I obblisshe me
> From þat synne for to saue mankynde,
> And soueraynely beseke I þe
> That þai for me may fauoure fynde.
> And fro þe fende þame fende,
> So þat þer saules be saffe
> In welthe withouten ende –
> I kepe nought ellis to craue. (*The Crucifixion*, 49–60)

> (Almighty God, my noble father
> I ask you to recall our business:
> You asked me to be willing
> To be tortured for what Adam caused.
> For the sake of mankind I pledge myself
> To be killed here for the sin he did.
> I ask especially, because of me, that
> Mankind find favour with you.
> Defend them from attacks of the devil,
> So that their souls are safe
> In endless joy.
> There is nothing else I desire.)

The action continues, showing with horrific detail how the soldier-pinners botch their work. They argue about who is responsible for each task. To "fetter" Christ to the cross, it takes all four of them to wrench his limbs. Every violent move they make is intensified by their detailed account of their actions; they bring Christ's hand to the "bore," using a short thick nail, a "stubbe," which will go through bone and sinew. They have miscalculated the condition of Christ's body when they bored the holes, and his sinews are so shrunken that his hands reach far short of the holes. They resort to hauling his arms along the cross with rope. That done, all four attend to his feet, lugging again on a rope to stretch the body to fit the cross. When they heave Christ up, the cross teeters. They have made a mess of the mortice and have to insert wedges to make the cross stand firm.

Though the spectators hear nothing from Christ, they hear a great deal of grousing from the soldiers to the effect that their shoulders hurt, that body and cross make a "wikked" weight. The soldiers also talk about how Christ is being shaken asunder, how the "cordis have evill encressed his paynes," (145) and how the pain "þis ladde" feels as the cross drops into the hole is "more felle / þan all the harmes he hadde" (247–8). Every grumble is spoken near the audience, on the platea. The cross, with Christ stretched on it, rises close to playgoers too. The people of York are being drawn into this horror.[50] Standing back to admire his work, one soldier asks, "Saie sir howe do we thore?" (105), implying that he wants the crowd's approval. Several times the soldiers seem to notice that standing around them are people who might lend a hand with their hideous task. Uncertain they can manage with just the four of them, one soldier says: "Now sertis I hope it schall noght nede / To call us more companye" (169–70). When the soldier later complains that he cannot find his hammer, his query, "Where are oure hameres layde / The we schulde wirke withal!" (239–40), seems to invite the people in the streets to yell out the answer, for surely they can see where the tools lie. Throughout, the spectators are guided into being on the edge of complicity in the killing of Christ.

An extraordinary tension between comedy and horror mounts as York's citizens watch their neighbours perform, certainly recoiling from the work being imitated, perhaps answering calls for involvement, possibly leaning close to hear the joking exchanges, pulling back from the brutality of the action. The tension builds further as the soldiers shout at the figure on the raised cross: "Say sir, howe likis you nowe / þes werke þat we haue wrought?" (249–50). Christ replies:

Al men that walkis, by waye or strete
Takes tente ye schalle no travaile tine!
Biholdes min[e] heede, min[e] handis, and my feete,
And fully feele nowe, or ye fine,
If any mourning may be meete
Or mischieve mesured unto mine. (253–8)

Everyone who walks by road or street,
Take care that none of the work is wasted.
Look at my head, my hands, my feet,

And think carefully, now, before you finish
If any mourning or misfortune is equal to mine.

His words ignore the individual men and the specificity of their question. Facing them and York he speaks to everyone, collapsing time and space, soldiers and pinners, biblical people and the medieval crowd. The tension is resolved; everyone in the streets – burghers, maids, butchers, chandlers, as well as pinners – is included by Christ's words among those who must be and are forgiven.

What is particularly gripping about this episode is that the playwright does not leave it there. The audience is not allowed to rest, anguished by the sight of the cross but ultimately comforted by forgiveness. Instead, while the tortured body hangs in front of them, they hear the soldiers mocking Christ's words as jangling and prattling, praising themselves for a job well done, drawing lots for Christ's coat, and agreeing not to squabble about their gambling. The playgoers are led back by the soldiers into a very ordinary world. Even though they are still standing on the platea, the soldiers no longer acknowledge York's presence. The two identities on stage, historical and contemporary, converge. Christ addressed and forgave all people, including biblical soldiers and contemporary citizens. But the full meaning of the play now resides in York, with the city's people, who understand the significance of Christ's words.

Chester: The Harrowing of Hell

Chester's *The Harrowing of Hell* begins with the release from Hell of Adam, Esau, Isaiah, Simeon, John the Baptist, and the repentant thief who was crucified with Christ. A dejected Satan sits alone in his framed space, *"in cathedra."* A local tapster then steps from among the Chester crowd and walks towards Satan bearing the "cuppes and kannes" of her brewing trade. She will be a damned soul:

Woe be the tyme that I came here,
I saye to thee nowe, Lucifere,
with all thy felowshipp in fere
that present be in place. (277–80)

(Lucifer, I say to you now
Woe to the time that I came here
With all this company of people
Who are present in this place.)

She must exchange being a "taverner / a gentle gossippe and a tapster / of wyne and ale a trustie bruer" (285–7) for whatever companionship the inferno offers. The tapster has earned damnation because she cheated her Chester customers. The audience finds out that she served them short measure and adulterated her products with "esshes and hearbes" (295). She turns to speak to the citizens directly, warning any tradespeople among them that if they do not clean up their business they will come to an end like hers:

Tavernes, tapsters of this cittye
shalbe promoted here with mee
for breakinge statutes of this contrye. (301–3)

Pub owners and tapsters of this city
Will be informed on here with me
For breaking the laws of this land.

Her first words are addressed to Satan; she then turns unmistakably to face her fellow citizens. Her "this cittye," "here," and "this contrye" locate Hell firmly in Chester along with its ale-houses, taverns, and inns. Her next address to the audience links Hell and Chester together, making sure the playgoers know unequivocally that the two places co-exist. In her first open address the tapster uses "this" to indicate Chester, her hometown and the audience's; now she uses "this" to point to the nearby Hell: "therefore this place nowe ordayned ys / for such ylldoers so mych amysse" (309–10).

Having made it perfectly clear where Hell fits into the spectators' lives, she lists what goes on among her city's crooked tapsters, telling of sharp practices such as "castinge malt besydes the combes, / myche water takinge for to compound / and little of the secke" (314–5). She describes wine-makers who make drinkers sick by selling them adulterated or improperly fermented drink:

With all mashers, mengers of wyne, in the night
bruynge so, blendinge agaynst daylight,
sych newe-made claret ys cause full right
of sycknes and disease. (317–20)

(This applies to all mixers and stirrers of wine
Who add mixtures at night, before it is light,
There no doubt about it; such newly-made claret
Causes sickness and disease.)

Standing on the platea, the tapster invites the inhabitants of "this cittye" to go with her to "this place":

Thus I betake you, more and lesse,
to my sweete mayster, syr Sathanas,
to dwell with him in his place
when hyt shall you please. (321–4)

(And so, no matter whether you're big or small,
When you're ready, I'm taking you all
To Sir Satan, my sweet lord,
To live in his realm with him.)

With her inside information on the tricks of the brewing trade, the tapster is a familiar figure, one of Chester's sinners made comical. But neither the realism nor the comedy of her character and words is an end in itself; both are part of a larger dramaturgical strategy. They combine with the simple English words – "this," "here," and "now" – she so insistently uses and with an open address that explicitly fingers everyone in Chester to make her, unmistakably, one of Chester's citizens. Her roll-call of local corruptions does not include great historical crimes; she and her fellow tapsters are not Cain or Herod. Her sins are the trivial crookednesses of any of medieval Chester's workers, whether brewers, fletchers, cordwainers, drapers, or ironmongers. Hell is a promise for anyone who hurts "this commonwealth."

Chester's crowds watch the devils welcome their neighbour. Satan is glad to see his "dere daughter." The second demon promises to marry her:

Welcome, sweete ladye! I will thee wedd,
for manye a heavye and dronken head
cause of thy ale were brougt to bedd
farre worse then anye beaste. (329–32)

(Welcome sweet lady! I will marry you,
For those your ale made sick, laid low,
Those many heavy drunken heads
In a state far worse than any beast's.)

The third demon, meanwhile, invites this "deare darlinge," who in Chester has used "cardes, dyces, and cuppes smale," to a party in Hell.

At the beginning of the episode, the patriarchs and the repentant thief address Chester directly, telling the audience of their joy at their release from torment. The tenor of their words differs considerably from that of the tapster's speeches, however. Although these great men are connected to the audience by their position on the platea, they retain historical dignity in their speaking. While their diction is not high-flown – they speak with simplicity – the tone of their addresses is lyrical. Using familiar images from the Bible, they remind contemporary Chester of their historical lives. For instance, Isaiah guides the playgoers to remember his visions:

> Yea, secerlye, this ilke light
> comys from Goddes Sonne almight,
> for so I prophecyed aright
> whyle that I was livinge.
> Then I to all men beheight,
> as I goostlye sawe in sight,
> these wordes that I shall to myght
> rehearse withowt tarienge. (25–32)[51]

> (Yes, surely, this very light
> Comes from God's almighty Son,
> For that's the prophecy I made
> When I was living.
> Then I promised everyone
> According to the spiritual vision that I had
> The words that I'm about to recite to you
> Right now.)

Chester's version of the harrowing of Hell does not stop with the biblical account. By incorporating a local tapster, it does what Auerbach observes medieval Christian drama doing in general, "it opens its arms invitingly to receive the simple and the untutored" (*Mimesis*, 135). The tapster insists on the place of the concrete here and now in the episode – what the people of Chester might otherwise fail to see if they heard only prophets speak, the things that sum up their part in the drama. When their neighbour eyes them from Hell, the Chester crowds cannot miss seeing where they fit in.[52] Even those among Chester's citizens who have not committed the tapster's specific crimes cannot except her point: that every action, however petty, matters in the here and now as well as in the eternity represented in front of them.

N-Town: The Woman Taken in Adultery

One of the most compelling medieval dramatizations of the Christ figure appears in N-Town's *The Woman Taken in Adultery*. This episode is unlike others in the N-Town play cycle in its simple staging.[53] There is only one locus, possibly a simple wooden frame, representing the door of the prostitute's house. The dramatic power throughout depends very much on audience presence close to the action.

As the episode opens, Christ enters alone onto the platea. He addresses N-Town's people as the communal "Man" in an urgent present tense, linking the citizens to Adam and to all people for all time:

> Man for þi synne take repentaunce
> If þou amende þat is amys
> Than hevyn xal be þin herytaunce
> Thow þou haue don Agens god greauns
> Yett mercy to haske loke þou be bolde
> his mercy doth passe in trewe balauns
> All cruel jugement be many folde.
>
> thow þat Your synnys be nevyr so grett
> Ffor hem be sad and aske mercy
> sone of my ffadyr grace Ye may gett
> with þe leste teer wepynge owte of Your ey
> My ffadyr me sent the man to bye
> All þi Raunsoun my-sylfe wyl dye
> Iff þou aske mercy I sey nevyr nay. (1–16)

(Mankind, repent of your sins.
As long as you repair what is amiss
Then you will inherit heaven.
Even if you have done dreadful harm to God
Make sure you ask for mercy.
When truly measured, his mercy surpasses
Many times all cruel judgment.

No matter how great your sins
Regret them and ask for mercy.
And soon, when the smallest tear weeps from your eye,
You may receive grace from my Father.
Mankind, my Father sent me to redeem you;

I must pay the whole of your ransom.
I myself shall die out of love for you.
I shall never refuse you if you ask for mercy.)

The call to repent and seek mercy implicates all onlookers. Christ also
warns against failure to show mercy to others and against vengeance
on neighbours:

Vppon þi neybore be not vengabyl
Agaeyn þe lawe if he offende
lyke as he is þou art vnstabyl
thyn owyn frelte evyr þou attende. (25–8)

(Do not be vengeful against your neighbour
If he offends against the law.
You are weak like him.
Pay attention to your own weakness.)

When Christ ends his speech, a scribe, an accusator, and a Pharisee who are huddled together on the platea confer about the trouble Christ causes them. Like all lawyers on guild play stages, rather
than explicitly acknowledging the playgoers as listeners, as Christ
does, they turn them into eavesdroppers. N-Town's people, to
whom Christ has just given the new laws about justice and mercy,
watch these men planning to trick him. They hear him defamed as
"þat ippocrite" and "þat stinking beggere," words spoken by figures who seem to glare at Christ over their shoulders. The Pharisee
hopes to embroil Christ in a fake dispute: "A fals quarrel if we
cowde feyne" (57). Throughout their plotting, the silent figure of
the Messiah stays on the platea, clearly visible to everyone in the
audience.

Among other issues, the episode explores ideas about communal
responsibility and public shame, and persistently draws on audience
nearness to the action in so doing. For instance, Christ himself talks
openly to the crowds about community. The conspirators, on the
other hand, very much aware that N-Town's citizens surround them,
anxiously refer to the danger of the "pepyl."

Near the plotters is the house of a social outsider, the harlot:

A fayre Yonge qwene here-by doth dwelle
both ffresch and gay upon to loke
And a tall man with here doth melle
the wey in to hyre chawmere ryght evyn he toke. (69–72)

(A beautiful young whore lives close by
Who is always bright and cheerful
A handsome man often goes with her
And he's just gone into her room.)

They aim to use her to catch Christ in "ryghte good sporte" (66). Advancing to the house, they roar for the "quene" to come out in a tone very different from their deliberate, careful plotting. If necessary they are ready to shoulder the door down. A young man, his shoes untied, his pants off, rushes out. The stage direction reads *"hic juuenis quidam extra currit indeploydo calligis non ligatis et braccas in manu tenens"* (Here a young man runs out in his jacket, his shoes untied, and holding his trousers in his hand) (204). The scribe and the Pharisee hurl vile alliterative epithets at the woman, chanting with the brutality and bravado that come from safety in numbers:

> Come forth þou stotte com forth þou scowte
> com forth þou bysmare and brothel bolde
> com forth þou hore and stynkynge bych clowte
> how longe hast þou such harlotry holde.
>
> Come forth þou quene come forth þou scolde
> com forth þou sloveyn come forth þou slutte
> we xal the tecche with carys colde
> A lytyl bettyr to kepe þi kutte. (145–52)
>
> (Come out you slut, come out you trollop
> Come out you shameless woman, you bold wench!
> Come out you strumpet and stinking bitch-rag
> How long have you been a whore?
>
> Come out you slattern, come forth you nagger
> Come out slovenly cat, come out slut
> We'll teach you with our deadly torment
> To keep your body to yourself.)

The woman begs for mercy in simple terms: "ffor goddys loue," "for charyte." The audience hears someone shout: "Stow that harlot, sum erthely wight" (125). It seems as if the N-Town crowds, rather than the plotters who lurk on the platea, perhaps nervously staring at the young man's dagger, are called on to arrest the young man racing out with his breeches in his hand. He, meanwhile, trying to get away from the three bullying cowards, also sees the citizens and twice shouts out at them. First he hails them as fellow sinners who surely sympathize with his narrow escape:

> In feyth, I was so sore affraid
> Of yone thre shrewys, the sothe to say
> My breche be nott yett well up-teyd
> I had such hast to renne away. (137–40)

> (In faith, I was very afraid of those three
> Louts. To tell you the truth,
> I was in such a rush to get away
> I still haven't tied my trousers up properly.)

Then he shifts their identity, turning the people of N-Town into allies of the three officials: "Adewe, adewe, a twenty devil way! / And Goddys curse have ye everychon" (143). This parting shot echoes and parodies Christ's final warning, that each man should "evyr ask mercy whil he hath space" (40). The young man is comic, vulgar, trivial.

The action is nasty; on the platea there is shouting and hustle. The woman's door is broken down, the young man curses, the plotters spit obscenities at the woman. The prostitute first begs for mercy, then asks "privily" to be put to death "in þis place," rather than be shamed publicly. She petitions, "lete not the pepyl upon me crye / If I be sclaundryd opynly / To all my frendys it shul be shame" (Don't let the people publicly taunt me. / I shall be shamed before my friends / If I am slandered openly.) (172–5). But the Pharisee screams for her to be put on show instead, for everyone to vilify:

> Fie on thee, scowte, the devil thee qwelle!
> Ageyn the lowe shul we kill?
> First hange thee the devil of helle
> Or we such folyes shulde fulfill! (177–80)

> (Shame on you, whore, may the devil kill you.
> You want us to kill you secretly,
> When the law requires you to be stoned publicly?
> The devil of hell can hang you
> Before we'd commit such a foolish act.)

It is disturbing that these upholders of the law can so heartily relish their part in the melee. Not only do they abuse the woman verbally; they also look forward to beating her up. The accusator: "I xal geve þe such a clowte / þat þou xalt fall down evyn in þe way" (I'll give you such a smack / That you'll fall down on the spot.) (187–8). The scribe: "Such a buffett I xal þe take þat all þe teth I dare wel say / with-inne þin heed ffor who xul share" (I'll give you such a smack that will I'm sure / Make your teeth shake in your head.) (189-91).

Although Christ remains on the platea, nothing in the text indicates that he attends to the brawl in any way. He has no lines; during the brutal insults and desperate pleas, Christ is abstracted and silent: "*Hic ihesus dum isti accusant mulierem continue debet digito suo scribere in terra* (Here, while they are accusing the woman, Jesus must keep writing on the ground with his finger)" (206). The stage directions suggest that Christ is ignoring all that goes on around him, writing in the earth on the platea. The three accusers call out to "sere prophet" that they have a woman to be judged. They try to attract his attention, to badger him about how he would apply justice to this matter, but he remains silent, continuing to scratch the ground: "*Jhesus nichil respondit sed semper scrybyt in terra* (Jesus doesn't answer but keeps writing on the ground)" (207). He remains silent so long that the scribe is disconcerted. He calls out to Christ: "in a cold stodye me thinkyth ye sitt" (225). The stage directions here are explicit, showing for a third time that the silent Christ goes on writing: "*Hic ihesus iterum se inclinans scribet in terre* (Here Jesus, stooping down again, will write on the ground)." Then the directions read: "*Et omnes accusatores quasi confusi separatim in tribus locis se disiugent* (And all the accusers, looking confused, will move apart to three separate places)." Utterly unnerved, the accusers leave the woman behind with Christ and go their separate ways.

Christ's silent writing must have made a potent dramatic moment. His stooping figure writes continually in the earth ("*semper scribit in terra*") on the audience's own ground, very close to them, ignoring the frantic activity around him. The biblical account has Christ write only twice. In the play, the prolongation of Christ's act of writing heightens both the drama and the focus on N-Town's ground.[54] Contributing to the mystery of his action is his very position. Perhaps some in the crowd had their view blocked; with Christ crouched so low, they couldn't see without shifting to find new sight-lines, making them rather like the accusers trying to see what he's up to. Though he never does answer them, Christ's act of writing turns out to seem significant to the scribe, the accusator, and the Pharisee. In fact, they are panicked by it. Each interprets

Christ's writing as broadcasting his personal sins. They all shift
about to see; they try to read. Once separated from each other, they
murmur their fears. The Pharisee, certain that his sins are written
on N-Town's earth, is terrified of his fellows: "Iff that my felawys
that dude aspye / They will telle it bothe fer and wide" (If my colleagues saw that, / They'd tell everyone, far and wide) (237–8).
The accusator is also afraid of what his peers would do if they
knew all about him: "If that my felawys to them toke hed / I kan
not me from deth aquite" (If my colleagues noticed them / I could-
n't save myself from death) (243–4). So the conspirators skulk off
the platea to find somewhere to hide, not only from each other, but
also from N-Town's citizens, who they assume have also read their
no-longer-hidden sins.

The playgoers see them slink away, but Christ does not acknowledge their leaving. He asks the woman: "Where be thy fomen that
dude thee accuse / Why have they lefte us two alone?" (265–6). Safe
now, the woman answers that they fled in shame. She repents her
"lewde lyff," Christ forgives her, then turns his address outwards to
N-Town:

> Whan man is contrite and hath wonne grace
> God wele not kepe olde wreth in mynde
> but bettyr loue to hem he has
> Very contryte whan he them fynde
> Now god þat dyed ffor all mankende
> saue all þese pepyl both nyght and day
> and of oure synnys he us vnbynde
> hyge lorde of hevyn þat best may. (289–96)

> (When people are contrite and have won grace
> God will not keep in mind his former anger.
> When he finds them very contrite
> He will love them with a better love.
> Now may God who died for all mankind
> Save all these people, night and day.
> And may the high Lord of Heaven,
> He who may best do so,
> Deliver us from our sins.)

"Þese pepyl" are N-Town's citizens; "oure synnys" are their own. It
is the artisans, clerics, lawyers, and harlots of N-Town who are forgiven. They are also vital witnesses to Christ's writing; ranged
around him, they must surely have craned like the three plotters to

see what he was scratching in the dust, as if their sins too might be inscribed in the earth of their own city.

On the platea there have been two kinds of address. One is that of the plotters, holding tight to their law books, much as they clutch their repressive version of the old law and talk secrets, first furtively in a group, then as isolated individuals. They use words to connive and entangle, to abuse, to shut out, to attack. Their world is literate but enclosed, upheld by secrecy, trickery and bullying. N-Town is not allowed into their world; its people are over-hearers, not members.

Then there is the address of Christ, the woman, and her customer, all of whom openly include the audience in their addresses. The woman is allied to N-Town by her position on the platea; in other words, no staging distinguishes her from the audience. The young man is made an N-Town inhabitant when he directly confronts the townspeople. The markers of their words are inclusive language ("we," "our") and silence. Christ's silent act of writing also implicitly draws in the spectators. Whether literate or not, every member of the audience doubtless strained to make out what was on the ground. Perhaps Christ's finger did no more than make scratches in the earth. To the unlettered, the marks meant as much or as little as writing; to the literate, they may have been equally puzzling. The point is that Christ's silence, accompanied by his writing is not exclusive and private, like the plotters' words; rather, it is inclusive and public.

The crux of the play is what the audience brings to the action. It is the people of N-Town who can shame or be shamed, who must wish for mercy and also show mercy.

Every year audiences were staged in "oure play." When each guild play ended, its audiences were still on stage. They continued to live on that stage for the rest of their lives. They went about their ordinary business in their own streets and markets, where once a year characters from history mingled with them and spoke to them openly.

CHAPTER TWO

Nonce Plays

THE STRAINS OF TUDOR PLAYING

At the end of the sixteenth century, Shakespeare's London players impersonated an Athenian company of actors in *A Midsummer Night's Dream*. When not acting, the "Athenians" Quince, Bottom, Flute, Snout, Snug, and Starveling work as carpenter, joiner, weaver, bellows-maker, tinker, and tailor. Primarily, they are artisans of trades other than acting, like England's civic tradespeople who year after year turned actor and took part in their town's guild productions. The guildsmen of Shakespeare's Athens, however, struggle with theatrical problems that were never faced by English guildsmen players. One difficulty is that they are not putting on a play telling their own and their audience's history, but rather a distant fiction, the classical tale of Pyramus and Thisbe. Another problem is that, unlike many of the English guild players, they expect to earn a fee for their performance.[1] Lastly, they are plagued with worries over methods of staging, concerns of a kind quite unknown to English guild players.

The "Athenian" troupe's theatre is not that of English guild drama: the players' and audiences' home towns. Instead, they are booked to perform in someone else's home, the house of Theseus, their ruler. They need, therefore, to build a production suited to the physical conditions of their employer's hall. At a secret rehearsal in the forest, this proves one of their biggest puzzles: how do they produce something fit for playing in a space where they do not usually belong, a temporary stage in the dining hall of the most powerful man in Athens?

Furthermore, all actors, including those involved in the seventeenth-century London *A Midsummer Night's Dream* production, must worry about pleasing their audiences. Terrors about audience response grip Bottom and company to fever point; they fret about how to convince, yet at the same time not to offend these playgoers who largely control their lives. Bewildered by the possibilities of getting no money for an unconvincing performance or of being executed if they perform too well, they assign an over-sized chunk of rehearsal time, as well as much of the actual performance, to sorting out how to accommodate their audience, people who inhabit a world very different from their own. The players' fears, although comic, are also based in fact; they have a tough assignment. They have to perform for those in immediate authority over them, people who control their lives outside the play, including one who has been seen willing to condemn a young woman to celibacy or execution for loving the wrong man.[2] They must entertain not their everyday neighbours but very important people, an audience of quite different social identity from their own, leading lives very unlike their own. And they have to do it in unfamiliar territory – the palace of Theseus.

Shakespeare's fraught "mechanicals" must juggle concerns about drama, staging, and audience far removed from any encountered by the actors and organizers of medieval guild plays. Bottom and crew have to balance getting paid against the appalling thought that a lion's roar that might "fright the Duchess and the ladies" could "hang [them], every mother's son" (*Dream*, 1.2.76–8). They have to please a social group distinct from (and more powerful than) their own; they must do so with a story unconnected to anything in their lives; they have to make good theatrical use of an unfamiliar space, a room usually serving as a dining hall in a palace. All these concerns plaguing the "Athenians" were also often encountered by Tudor players, actors of drama running concurrently with the late years of the guild plays and continuing beyond the latter's demise into the late sixteenth century.

These Tudor plays are what I have chosen to call "nonce drama." First, they expressly address certain stories. Second, they are usually short plays, not omnibus vehicles or enormous productions like the guild plays. Third, these plays make it clear that they are to entertain for a brief time only: for the nonce.

This chapter will examine some of the significant theatrical characteristics of a selection of plays of the mid- to late sixteenth century. The discussion should not be read as either a comprehensive description or the final word on the theatre of the period. As noted in the Introduction, there was no straight chronological path in English theatre as a whole or in its dramatic strategies. There was, rather, considerable overlap in all aspects of the drama. The guild plays continued to be produced in the streets and open spaces of many cities until the mid-sixteenth century. Morality plays such as *Mankind* and *Everyman*, secular, folk, academic, and scriptural plays, small and large, amateur and professional, itinerant and parochial, were also performed throughout English cities, towns, and villages. With this in mind I now explore how talking openly to the audience operates in some plays I consider representative of a new staging system. The chapter centres on the exigencies of practical playing conditions. I will show how, under these new conditions, the function of open address changes from that in the guild plays. The new functions of open address reveal much of interest about the native dramatic tradition in England.

SOME CHANGES AFFECTING PLAYING CONDITIONS

Shifts in economic distribution taking place throughout England and Europe meant that provincial guilds faced increasing financial difficulties during the late fifteenth and early sixteenth centuries.[3] By the middle of the sixteenth century, the power of the guilds outside London had significantly eroded; many provincial craft organizations found the massive production costs of the cycle plays beyond their now-diminished resources. C.V. Phythian-Adams observes that "by the mid-sixteenth century, late medieval urban society and culture in the well-established towns had become too elaborate, too costly to be sustained by contracting economies and populations" (*Urban Decay*, 178).[4]

The great amateur productions also fell victim to religious pressure. After the Reformation, the plays were subjected to performance restrictions, and their producers were ordered to cut what was now perceived as offensive or unorthodox material.[5] Above all, in the turbulent first seventy years of the century, with an uncertain regnal settlement and strong fears of political insurgency, large gatherings of people were perceived as constituting a threat to the Protestant authorities.[6] Those in power became very edgy about allowing huge crowds to watch guild performances:

The celebration of Corpus Christi could raise difficult problems for public order for those towns in which they took place. And plays could undoubtedly be unsettling, even when they contained no potentially subversive content, simply because of their tendency to loosen social constraints and inner controls. A case in point is that of the York Fergus play: a straightforward cycle play on the theme of the funeral of the Virgin Mary, but which included some particularly hilarious slapstick comedy effects. According to its sponsors, the Mason's gild, however, it not only caused irreverent noise and laughter, but also quarrels and fights and lawsuits among the onlookers. There is no doubt that assemblies for play and game, whether these were of the dramatic sort, or had the character of folk festival, could lead to sedition. A Lent carnival at Norwich in 1443 precipitated a revolt. Sometime in the 1550s the staging of one of the cycle plays at York – the play of Thomas the Apostle – provided the occasion for a papist disturbance. The Kett revolt was sparked off by a play at Wymondham. All this is a large part of the explanation why folk festivals, like the Hox play at Coventry or the Yule Riding at York, aroused the same sort of disapproval in Puritan circles as did the cycle plays, and were done away with more or less at the same time. The sixteenth century privatization of the drama by the development of the play, the theatre and the professional actor parallels the privatization of religious and civic ritual, and arose from much the same causes. In the setting, then, the public ritual and public drama of the Corpus Christi feast no longer had any place. (James, 28–9)

Government grew increasingly uncomfortable with people attending plays that talked to them about a now-rejected communal identity, that dramatized a public self with religious and political affiliations regarded as inimical to the state. Protestantism and English history replaced Catholicism and universal history. In 1563, the feast of Corpus Christi was excised from the church calendar in the Elizabethan Book of Common Prayer (James, 21, note 66). One of the last holdouts, Towneley's Corpus Christi performances, continued until 1576, when an injunction was issued against them by the Diocesan Court of High Commission. Nine years earlier, the first London playhouse had opened (Gardiner, 78).[7]

Nevertheless, in various parts of England, amateur and semi-professional playing, outside the auspices of civic guilds and unconnected to the major morality plays, remained part of the sixteenth-century drama. John Wasson has found evidence of amateur playing in Kent, where parish church accounts show that plays, heavily advertised in surrounding districts, raised money for local projects such as mending church roofs. He describes a very active drama scene; in the 1520s at Lidd, "players from 11 different neighbouring villages came to town to perform. The Kent records reveal that in the

1520s 24 different parishes sent their plays or bann criers to neighbouring villages" (73). However, records of small local amateur productions such as these vanish completely by the 1590s, perhaps coin-
ciding, as Wasson speculates, with religious changes and the opening
of the professional theatres in London.

Provincial producers seem occasionally to have supplemented
amateur production teams with professional personnel. John Coldewey identifies the "professional property player" in the records of
counties around London. He describes how local communities paid
professional theatre men, usually from London, to come in to organize and direct their often very elaborate plays.

The mid-sixteenth century was predominately the era of professional players, however precarious a living these actors made.
Thanks to the fine work on that century's players and playing
by Richard Southern, Ian Lancashire, Robert Weimann, William
Tydeman, and in particular David Bevington, we know that there
were many kinds of players among the wage-earning actors.[8] At the
top end of the theatre's social scale were players who acted in the
productions at the royal court. Henry VII and his son, for instance,
favoured performances by their own resident acting companies
(Bevington, *From "Mankind"*, 13). Adult companies such as these
were permanently attached to the court and worked nowhere else,
performing only for their royal employers and their guests. These
resident actors were, in effect, servants of the royal household, a job
offering a certain security, putting the players' feet firmly under
someone else's table. The court also housed boys' companies, such as
those who acted before Mary (a monarch who was particularly fond
of children's performances) in Heywood's *Play of the Weather*
(ca 1525–33).[9] Like their adult counterparts, the boys' troupes never
toured outside the court.

Other companies entertained in the houses of the aristocratic or
well-to-do. Sir John Paston, for instance, employed his own actors.[10]
Occasionally, some of these players, like a few of the court players,
were not permanent resident companies. They were employed to
perform only on special occasions, the rest of the time earning a living by playing around the country.[11] W. R. Streitberger, examining
the Revels accounts for the court at the beginning of the sixteenth
century, finds that companies like these were much in demand,
especially at Christmas. The Revels accounts show evidence of
"well over 50 performances by acting troupes at court between 1491
and 1509, most concentrated during the Christmas season" (33).
Many troupes of various types appeared at sixteenth-century
courts: "the King's Men, the Prince's Men, and Essex's Men, the

Players of St Albans, Lord Burgavenny's Men and as well anonymous troupes including players from France" (Bevington, *From
"Mankind"*, 35).

Among the itinerant players, the more fortunate wore the livery
of royalty or landed gentry and could thus be quickly identified by
local authorities as being in regular employment. Peter Thomson
points out the importance of the uniform; following the "Acte for
the punishment of Vagabonds and for the Relief of the Poor and
Impotent" of 1572, which brought the acting profession under the
terms of the Poor Law legislation, "the nomadic life of the Tudor
actor made it unwise for players to set up unless they were
licensed by and wore the livery of a nobleman" (*Theatre*, 171).[12]
Other itinerant players – the unlicensed, unliveried groups such as
the anonymous companies who performed *Mankind* or the Croxton
Play of the Sacrament – were in a much less secure legal position as
they travelled from town to town. They were always in danger of
falling foul of laws enacted to police the countryside and to control
the vagabond problem (Gurr, *Stage*, 36).

Both liveried companies such as the King's Men and anonymous
troupes of actors might include tradesmen fallen on hard times and
dislodged from their home towns together with those who had
deliberately chosen acting. For example, Bevington notes that the
King's Men included "a merchant tailor, a tailor, and a glazier"
(*From "Mankind"*, 12). Early in the sixteenth century, all travelling
troupes of players were small, made up of four or five men only,
meeting the demands of their plays by innovative doubling of roles
and great versatility in playing styles.[13] Like American summer
stock companies or the small repertory groups on provincial English circuits in the early and mid-twentieth century, these companies probably carved out an uncertain living, playing all over the
country, in inns or wherever there was a suitable venue and a
potential audience. By the end of the period, when numbers in the
companies had increased to about eight (often now including a
boy),[14] many itinerant troupes had gravitated to the lucrative new
theatre market in London (Bentley, 3–11).

In contrast with the scope and unity of the guild plays' narrative
of world history, the topics of nonce drama are narrow and diverse.
Moreover, compared with the guild plays' two-hundred-year run,
the latter came and went very quickly.[15] The medieval morality
plays had followed a structure and subject matter that were
to prove less intransigent politically and religiously for later
playwrights than those of the guild plays.[16] Their innocence-fall-
repentance-redemption plot was more easily adapted to mid-

sixteenth century concerns than the guild plays' plot involving the whole of world history. The morality plays' mix of generalized human and allegorical, rather than historical and local, characterization was also better suited to the new theatrical conditions, especially the reduced numbers of players, the smaller amounts of money for props and costumes, and the necessity for moving from place to place.[17] Many dramatists therefore remoulded the old morality subjects and structures to fit the needs of professional playing companies.

Plays from the mid-Tudor period usually confine themselves to a single theme, though taken together they cover a diversity of subjects from many points of view, reflecting and responding to the tremendous religious, political, and social upheavals that characterize the five reigns from Henry VII to Elizabeth I. From the beginning of the sixteenth century on, many then-current political anxieties appear on stage, including the terms of the succession in *Horestes* (1567) and the nature of political authority in *Magnificence* (ca 1515–23) and *King Darius* (ca 1556–65). Nonce drama also concerns itself with the period's intellectual changes, such as the growth of humanism. Some plays, such as the early *Four Elements* (ca 1517–18) by John Rastell,[18] dramatized humanist ideas about the importance of education in transforming English society, or about Calvinist approaches to education, as in the representation of ignorance as a source of moral degeneration and damnation in Ulpian Fulwell's *Like Will to Like* (ca 1558–68).[19]

Throughout the period, too, plays shift allegiance in their portrayals of religious beliefs. Within a span of twenty-five years, there appeared on stage virulent denunciations of Roman Catholic policies and practices (in Bale's *King John* of the 1530s, for instance), portrayals of Protestants as treacherous fools (as in *Respublica* of ca 1553), then the re-identification of Roman Catholic practices and oaths with folly and moral degeneracy in such plays as *Enough is as Good as a Feast* (ca 1558–69).

Secular topics such as economic bad management and financial extortion appear in *All for Money* (ca 1558–78) and *The Trial of Treasure* (ca 1567), plays adapting the old morality structure of innocence-fall-redemption while inventing new topical allegorical figures to warn about contemporary political and social abuses and their consequences.[20] This allegorical-morality form lingered on in late hybrid history-romance plays such as *Cambises* (ca 1561) and *King Darius* (ca 1558–65). Like many of their predecessors, Tudor dramatists – at least those who wrote for the intellectual elite – drew on classical learning to deliver political advice, as in *Gorboduc* (ca 1562), or to entertain, as in *Gammer Gurton's Needle* (ca 1550).

While medieval guild players staged their productions on home ground, the Tudor professional players had to perform on someone else's territory. The resident players at court or manor, for example, always performed for their employers in the latters' homes. The stages used by resident companies or by troupes under contract for occasional performances were built from whatever the royal court or the aristocratic houses could offer. In the case of the court, this invariably meant that the troupes played in a sumptuous theatrical setting (Bevington, *From "Mankind"*, 26–48). Plays written for court performance offer internal evidence of expensive production techniques and properties (Bevington, op. cit., 54). Court records, too, show that players at court had plenty to work with: expensive settings, lavish costumes, large companies, trained singers and musicians.[21] In the homes of the gentry, players customarily used the dining hall, a space normally reserved for eating. Richard Southern speculates about a typical hall performance in which the players would act before an audience gathered for supper, "setting up their play amidst the bustle of the servants, and [playing] to spectators seated at long tables" (128). He imagines a "long room with a space cleared for playing at the end of the hall nearest the kitchen. The players make use for exits and entrances of the two doors which led to the kitchens, with a screen set across the door to cut off draughts and the sight of the kitchen" (128). Plays such as *Fulgens and Lucrece* (1497) and *Hickescorner* (ca 1500–20) were evidently staged much as Southern describes.[22]

Players who toured the countryside had to adapt themselves to constantly changing stage conditions. Understandably, they played in indoor venues whenever these were available, such as "parish houses with large assembly rooms upstairs and churches" (Goodman, 155). More frequently, the travelling companies rustled up audiences in marketplaces or inn-yards, usually using the inns' galleries as audience seating or as part of the play's staging and its gateways to control admission (Gurr, *Stage*, 36). There is evidence of this kind of performance at various London inn-yards, including the Bel Savage, the Bell, and the Boar's Head (Goodman, 155). Sometimes itinerant players set up a trestle or stage, the sort of wooden structure that seems to have been erected for *The Marriage of Wit and Wisdom* (before 1570).

The changes in playing conditions we have considered led to three main features of playing that distinguish Tudor nonce drama from medieval guild drama. First, the early plays spoke to their heterogeneous audiences about everyone's reality, staging both characters and audience in their familiar dramatizations. The later nonce plays, on the other hand, although they might represent or talk about some aspects of their spectators' lives, never attempted to stage the entire history or universe of both characters and spectators. Indeed, the stories told by nonce drama were not always familiar to the audience.

Second, whether they performed for the elite or before a social mix, actors in nonce drama were not *primarily* artisans: carpenters, tilers, or bakers. Rather, many were professionals whose craft and trade was acting; their job was the entertainment of their public. Whether paid by fee, by collection, or by direct subsidy, their wages came from the people they entertained. Unlike in guild drama, players and playgoers were separated by money. Whatever the status of their audience, players were distinguished from them by their status as paid actors. Nor were they likely to be their audience's immediate neighbours.

Third, players in nonce drama did not perform in a space belonging equally to audience and actor. Rather, the places where they performed belonged to their audiences, whether to the social superiors who owned the court or dining hall or to the communities in whose local inns the transient companies set up.

As a result of these developments, by the mid-sixteenth century plays were no longer "oure" plays. Audiences gathered together to be united as a community just for the time of performance; players set up, then moved on; subjects and plots came and went; space was shared for performance time only. Plays, then, were performed for the nonce. Wrestling with problems of playing, story, and stage, Shakespeare's "Athenians" are clearly mounting a nonce play.

OPEN ADDRESS IN NONCE PLAYS

Despite changes in playing conditions, open address survived; nonce plays continued to acknowledge audience presence, to talk explicitly to the playgoers. Many of the old recognition styles and signals lived on: self-introductions, admonitory speeches, and calls for room, for admiration, for adulation.

Nonce play characters often notice what the crowds are doing at the moment of performance, or pick on individuals or groups among the playgoers. In the early *Hickescorner*, for example, characters notice that the audience is eating dinner while watching the play. Several times, characters in the playworld comment on the presence of "sovereigns" and "lords" in the dining hall theatre (2, 546, 767);[23] at one point they go so far as to order a fresh round of drinks for their audience (158). They also pick out the young men from among the diners (297, 568), implicating the youthful spectators in the play's narrative of grasping ambition by having the rascally Hickescorner enter from among the young men's "bosoms"(297). Young playgoers at performances of *Youth* (ca 1513–29) come under the scrutiny of a reprobate character when Riot, hunting for the protagonist, Youth, has to spot him among the young men in the crowd. Both these plays draw parallels between the young men on stage and in the audience, proclaiming that to be young is also to be at risk morally. In *Lusty Juventus* (ca 1547–53), youth is presented as heedless. The protagonist, a young gamester called Juventus, wants friends to sport with, so he turns to the crowd and asks, "What shall I do now to passe away the day? / Is there any man here that will go to game?" (*Lusty Juventus*, 58–9)

Later in the century, Elizabethan playwrights preserved early strategies of noticing the presence of the audience. In *The Marriage of Wit and Wisdom*, a play performed in inn-yards in London and nearby communities, Idleness is disguised as a local rat catcher, a perfectly appropriate job in a pub courtyard. Idleness treats the playgoers to sexual innuendo:

> Have you any rats or mice, pole-cats or weasels?
> Or is there any old sows sick of the measles?
> I can destroy fulmers [polecats] and catch moles;
> I have ratsbane, maidens!
> To spoil all the vermin that run in your holes. (2.1.1–5)

This salacious address to the audience is followed by a stage direction making it quite clear that Idleness stays physically intimate with his listeners: "Here he espieth Search coming in, and goeth up and down, saying, 'Have you any rats and mice?' as in the first five lines." In another Elizabethan play, William Wager's *The Longer Thou Livest the More Fool Thou Art* (ca 1558–69), the character Ignorance (represented as blind) highlights the playgoers' presence by his inability to tell whether they are there at all. Peering around blindly, he asks "Is there anybody here in this place?" (234). Many of the plays, even those presented to an elite audience, keep up a close, confiding relationship with the spectators, leading everyone into the play by treating lords and servants alike as familiar companions. John Heywood's *A Mery Play Betwene Johan Johan the Husbande, Tib His Wife, and Sir Johan the Preest* (ca 1520–3), for instance, relies heavily on audience proximity in the dining hall for its effect. Like Noah, Joseph, and the shepherds in the guild plays, Johan Johan regards the audience as sympathetic listeners to his complaints. At one point he hands over his coat for a playgoer to hold, then, becoming suspicious of the person, snatches it back again. Throughout, the humour of the play depends very much on Johan's firm belief that the playgoers are his understanding friends – and his only; for example, he confides in them his intention to beat his wife. However, what Johan's confidants actually see is that his spouse always gets the upper hand; for instance, Johan fiddles with wax to mend a punctured bucket as he chats to his "friends" while, behind his back, his wife fiddles with the local priest (Bevington, *Medieval Drama*, 987).

Nonce plays often begin with an earnest address spoken openly to the audience. During the first part of the sixteenth century, in plays that often closely follow the morality structure, virtuous figures directly instruct playgoers about life. *Youth* opens with the figure Charity, who blesses the crowd as "you" and urges its members to see the need for charity in the world:

> Jesu, that his arms did spread
> And on a tree was done to dead,
> From all perils he you defend.
> I desire audience till I have made an end,
> For I am come fro God above
> To occupy his laws to your behove
> And am named Charity. (1–7)

In *Hickescorner*, Pity is the first to speak to the spectators, also addressing them as "you":

> Now Jesu the gentle, that brought Adam fro hell,
> Save you all, sovereigns, and solace you send!
> And of this matter that I begin to tell
> I pray you of audience till I have made an end. (1–4)

Pity goes on to warn them about the heedlessness of wealthy people who forget that they live in an inconstant world.

Mundus et Infans (ca 1500–22) also begins with an acknowledgement of audience presence. In this play, though, the opening speech is a vaunt delivered by the worldly Mundus, in a manner typical of the boastful rulers of medieval plays. After demanding silence with "Syrs, cease of your sawes, what-so befall,/ And loke ye bow bonely

to my byddynges" (1–2), he explains to his listeners that he is everyone's king, including theirs:

> Lo! here I sette semely in se!
> I commaunde you all abedyent be,
> And with fre wyll ye folowe me. (21–3)

In the two speeches just quoted (Pity's in *Hickescorner* and Mundus's
in *Mundus et Infans*), note the use of "this" and "here." In guild plays,
these deictic words indicated sharing between the playworld and the
world of the audience. In the nonce plays, however, "this" and "here"
signal what belongs solely to the playworld; they mark a separation
or a drawing back from the playgoers.

As in the guild plays, fools (as well as wise characters) make close
contact with audiences, coquetting about the nonce stages as they did
in the medieval streets or marketplaces, showing off to their
supposed admirers. In *Magnificence*, John Skelton parodies the idio-
cies and abusive extravagance of court life – the life of many watching the play. Foolish characters chat comfortably to the assembly,
assuming everyone agrees with what they say. First, Fancy speaks to
the spectators:

> Now let me see about
> In all this rout
> If I can find out
> So seemly a snout
>
> Among this press,
> Even a whole mess!
> Peace, man, peace.
> I rede we cease. (990–7)

Then the stage directions indicate that Folly enters: "*Hic ingrediatur
Foly quesiendo crema et faciendo multum feriendo tabulas et similia*" (Here
enters Folly shaking a bauble and making a commotion beating on
tables and such like) (117). All of the play's various fools, boasters,
and gulls treat the hall as their own space where they notice friends
among the dinner guests. Magnificence, bedazzled by Fancy's cun-
ning, thinks he is above the rule of fortune and shares his delight
with the playgoers: "For Now, sirs, I am like as a prince should be:/
I have wealth at will, largesse and liberty" (1458–9). In this play, too,
figures of retribution mete out warnings meant to include the immediate contemporary world. Adversity, on striking down stupid and

proud Magnificence, explains to the people in the dining hall that his role is like that of death:

> For I strike lords of realms and lands
> That rule not by measure that they have in their heds
> That sadly rule not their household men. (1939–41)

All the speakers discussed above – announcers, salacious intimates, virtues, and fools – make addresses that carve out a physical space in which to play for the nonce. For example, in inn-yards or dining halls, getting through the crowds to the playing area could be a problem. In Rastell's *Four Elements*, the taverner called in by Sensuall Appetyte complains that he has had difficulty reaching the stage through the audience:

> *Sensuall Appetyte:*
> Than I beshrew the[e], page, of thyne age!
> Come hyther, knave, for thyne avauntage.
> Why makyst thou hit so tow?
> *Taverner:*
> For myne avauntage, mary, than I come.
> Beware, syrs! how! let me have rome!
> Lo, here I am! What seyst thou? (551–6)

> (*Sensual Appetite:*
> Then I curse you, wretch, for your age!
> Come here, knave. It will be to your advantage.
> Why do you do it so awkwardly?
> *Taverner:*
> To my advantage, then I'm coming.
> Watch out, sirs! Yes! Make room for me!
> Lo, here I am! What are you going to tell me?)

Under Tudor playing conditions, a playing area had to be established by open address at the start of each play. Then it had to be freshly defined by open address as *other* than the audience's space. Spectators out-of-doors in inn-yards, or indoors in a dining room were likely to have been elbowed out of the way by the nonce plays' villains. Although the style is hardly distinguishable from the way medieval bullies and ruffians pushed and shoved playgoers about, the purpose and effect are different in nonce drama. Playing space must be *wrested* from the Tudor audience. So must time; the spectators are asked to suspend their everyday selves for new identities as playgoers. Outdoors or in, characters pretend that the people who watch them are obstacles to be pushed aside or weaklings to be cowed by ranting words; the old folk formula of demanding room remains of practical use until the advent of the public theatre, with its containing walls and separate stage space.

Occasionally the characters establish the play as a play by bullying the crowds. In the early plays of the period, such as *Hickescorner*, *Mundus et Infans*, and *Youth*, the vicious characters are aggressive to stage characters and audience alike. In *Hickescorner*, Free Will – depicted as immoral, both a political gangster and a social snob – openly demands that the diners in the audience recognize him as their social superior:

> Aware, fellows, and stand a-room!
> How say you, am not I a goodly person?
> I trow you know not such a gest! (156–8)

Pushing through, he then mocks them as his social inferiors, using words reminiscent of the guild plays' Herods:

> Make you room for a gentleman, sirs and peace!
> Dieu garde, seigneurs, tout le presse!
> And of your jangling if ye will cease,
> I will tell you where I have been.
> Sirs, I was at the tavern and drank wine.
> Methought I saw a pece that was like mine,
> And sir, all my fingers were arrayed with lime,
> So I conveyed a cup mannerly. (646–53)[24]

Later, in the Elizabethan period, too, audiences are pushed around by sinister characters. In Wager's *The Longer Thou Livest the More Fool Thou Art*, Cuthbert Cutpurse bashes his way through the crowd:

> Make room! stand back in the devil's name!
> Stand back, or I will lay thee on the face. (636–7)[25]

In the guild plays, audiences were jostled by ruffians, devils, and tyrants in order to stage abusive power as involving contemporary people. In the nonce plays, audience space and playing space coincide – but only briefly. The purpose of talking openly to audiences has changed. Space is now separated into stage and playgoer areas to allow the play to go on.

THE AUDIENCES OF NONCE PLAYS

Anne Righter regards as problematic the strategies used by Tudor dramatists to maintain audience contact: the introductions, the bullying, the confiding. She laments that, after the demise of medieval dramatic forms, playwrights continued to build audiences into plays. According to Righter, early Tudor drama is spoiled by "meaningless audience address" inserted by playwrights hampered because they have not yet learned to ignore the presence of spectators (34). The main thrust of her argument is that playwrights work towards an illusionistic theatre, one that does not explicitly allude to playgoer presence – a goal both inevitable and desirable. But Righter misses the point that nonce playwrights made open audience acknowledgement function in changed ways. They purposefully adapted the old tradition of open address to bear the strains of new playing conditions, and invented a new kind of audience for a new staging system.

Unlike Righter, T. W. Craik values Tudor drama's open audience recognition. He regards the intimate alliance between the two worlds, expressed largely in the strategies of various kinds of open address, as one of the drama's defining characteristics as well as one of its greatest pleasures: "The special dramatic virtues of the best Tudor interludes ... are intimacy and spontaneity. The characters from their first entrance, put themselves on familiar terms with the spectators, and will turn aside to address them during the action; the action itself seems unpremeditated, developing from casual encounter between disputants holding opposed principles" (39).

Open acknowledgement of audiences – disliked by Righter, admired by Craik – serves the practical necessities of Tudor drama well. As in guild drama, talking directly to playgoers does not serve simply to characterize or to supply information about a play figure. It also functions as a powerful dramaturgical device for connecting audience to play. Even under changed playing conditions, the strategy still serves to tell audiences what to attend to and how to attend to it. In nonce plays, characters talk openly to playgoers to make the play happen; their words delimit time and space for the play. Direct references to playgoer presence recognize the crowds as people watching a performance – that is, they identify them as an audience.

Fulgens and Lucrece offers an early example – theatrically remarkable at any time – of the new distinction between player/character and audience. In his play, Henry Medwall exploits the intimacy and the diversity of the watchers, servants as well as diners, in the dining hall. He does so in a double-layered fashion, by having some speeches notice the audience and others ignore them. The play presents two interlocked stories: a tale of Romans, cast partly as an ideological debate about the nature of true nobility, alongside a tale of two adamantly English servants. These two comic English characters act as guides leading the audience into both parts of the play, framing and punctuating the political Roman story and weaving together contrasting dramatic modes.[26]

Medwall, like Bottom and crew, had a difficult audience to cope with. He was Chaplain to Cardinal Morton, at whose dinner the play was performed. Thus he was directly employed by a powerful member of the audience – none of whom Medwall could risk boring, or worse, offending, by potentially unpalatable material, especially in the debate section of the play. In the Roman section, which leads to the debate, Lucrece, a noblewoman, is wooed by two suitors. She chooses for her husband a man who has made his own way in the world, someone who has proved his nobility by his actions rather than by being born rich and aristocratic. While Lucrece's reasoning is in some measure, as Weimann points out, a "subject of genuinely current interest in early Tudor England" (107), it might also have been perceived as a slight to those among the diners who had inherited wealth or power.[27]

One method Medwall uses to defuse potential offence or touchiness in his audience is to have Lucrece speak directly to them, to explain that her choice represents an individual case and need not be taken as a precedent or model for their contemporary world. She concludes by asking them to take her decision in the right spirit: "I pray you all sirs as many as be here take not my words by sinister way" (II, 767–8). Whatever the diners may have thought of Lucrece's choice, Medwall clinches its inapplicability to present company by having the two comic figures, the English servants, make it very clear that she has demonstrated poor judgment in opting for "a churl's son" rather than "a gentleman born" (I, 836). These two staunch supporters of the English hereditary class system close the play by asking the diners to tell them what they think, apparently assuming (as Mr and Mrs Noah did in the guild plays) that they will readily split into separate interest groups. Servant A wants to hear the women's opinion: "Is it to your guise to choose all your husbands that wyse? By my truth then I marvel!" (II, 849–51) B warns "wedded men everyone" that, if this case is anything to go by, they had better watch out for themselves. So while Lucrece denies that there can be any general or immediate application of her decision, the servants try to thrust it back into the audience's world.

From the very opening of his play, Medwall lets the diners know that they have to think of their contemporary reality as separate from the world of the play. Servant A talks about B's stepping out of the frame and into the play's central action, certain that the move will ruin an evening's entertainment. In answer to A's fear that he will "destroy all the play" (I, 363), B assures his friend that everyone watching will remain in an actual, not a dramatic, world: "The play began never till now," (I, 365) and urges A to get himself hired by Lucrece's suitor Flaminius. Throughout the play, A and B take note of the facts of the immediate occasion, remarking on the progress of the dinner, calling for a break to allow hungry guests to resume their banquet, playing mock hosts and shouting for another round of drinks for everyone: "Usher! get them good wine there to fill them of the best" (I, 1419–20).

Servant A opens the performance by entering the dining hall, where he introduces himself to both guests and servants as someone outside the present posh society where people are eating Christmas dinner with a cardinal. Looking about in awe, he urges his social superiors to go on with their feast, astonished that anyone eating a free dinner can seem as dull as this group:

> For goddes will
> What mean ye, sirs, to stand so still?
> Have ye not eaten and your fill,
> And paid nothing therefor?
> Ywis, sirs, thus dare I say,
> He that for the shott pay
> Vouchsafeth that ye largely assay
> Such meat as he hath in store. (I, 1–8)

Servant B puts to rest A's worries about whether the diners are enjoying their evening by telling him they are about to be entertained by a play. B is insulted by A's suggestion that he might be a player, explaining that both he and A are simply audience members allowed to enter the hall "By the leave of the marshall" (I, 149) as the other guests have. Shortly after this, Cornelius, the rich, high-born suitor, looks for a servant from among the audience: "So many good fellows as [B] in this hall" (I, 354). B seizes his chance to make a bit of money and to cross over the dramatic threshold by joining in the play as Cornelius's servant.

After the break between parts, A and B resume their close contact with the audience. A hurries into the dining hall, complaining to the diners of having to scramble back in time for the second part of the play. Acting as theatrical compere, he recalls for them the story so far, reminds them that they will be able to make up their own minds about the argument, and assures them that he and the rest of the actors want to "content / the least that standeth here" (II, 42–3). There is a banging on one of the dining room doors; A sends one of the audience (perhaps a servant) to check it out: "One of you go look who it is" (II, 175). B enters grumbling that the household has been too slow letting him in. Throughout the second part of the play's central action, A and B play the well-known traditional role of cheeky servants who get messages wrong, invert the meanings of whatever their masters say, and discover sex everywhere.[28]

After Lucrece chooses the poor but noble Flaminius, A and B figure out that her decision means the play is over. They wind up the performance by drawing attention to the play's author, apologizing on Medwall's behalf:

> The auctor thereof desyreth
> That for this season
> At the lest you will take it in pacience
> And yf therbe ony offence –
> Show us where in or we go hence –
> Done in the same,
> It is onely for lacke of connynge
> Is there of to blame. (II, 906–14)

B tells the audience the author has done his best and will accept amendments:

> And so he wyllyd me for to say
> And that done, of all this play
> Shortly here we make an end. (II, 919–21)[29]

Robert Weimann's discussion of *Fulgens and Lucrece* includes a brilliant assessment of the dynamics of the play:

The significance of the subplot is primarily a theatrical one. All through the play "A" and "B" rub shoulders with the humble folk in the hall; in fact, their social identity is dramatically stylized in a brilliant induction. Before the play begins they stand idly about the hall, but since they are "maysterles" (I, 398), and so in search of work, they hire themselves out to the gentlemen suitors in the interlude. The performance begins before they cross the borderline between the real world and the play world, for such a crossing assumes, at the outset, the function of a dramatic effect and indicates the first phase of a significant movement: "spectators" become actors, the masterless servants in the hall become servants acting on the "place." This extradramatic counterpoint is ironically underlined when "B" energetically denies that he is an actor (I, 46 et seq.), so that "A" then fears he will "disturb the play" (I, 363). (107–8)

In *Fulgens and Lucrece* then, there are events that never happened in medieval drama: A and B "cross the borderline between the real world and the play world" (Weimann, 108; my italics). What is astonishing about Medwall's play is its innovation; for the first time, there *is* a dramatic threshold to cross. Moreover, it is a threshold built through address in response to practical necessities: the social realities of Medwall's stage and audience, and his need as a playwright not to irritate those governing his life. Medwall makes much of the gap between acting and not-acting, between those who play and those who watch, in his repeated references to the facts of performance. In other words, he invents a dramatic boundary: on one side of the imagined fence is the world of acting, playing space and players; on the other (for this particular play) is the world of diners, servants, and feasting.

Medwall sets up this barrier from the very opening, when Servant A enters. A and B purport to belong to neither world. They lounge about, but they are very obviously pretending to be servants, an impersonation underscored by A's mistake about actors and costume. When they do enter what they call the world of the play, they are never fully of that world either. Their stagey Englishness, recalling folk performance, jars against the Roman world of debate and verse.[30] Their comic concern with contemporary realities continues in the classical world. And although their speech style and approach to life might align them with the audience, they subvert even this potential alliance by inappropriately playing up the unlikelihood of being hosts at the banquet, and claiming to have been let in by the marshall, like the dinner guests. Robert Jones describes A and B as creating "a realistic frame" for a fictive story (42). But A and B are eminently theatrical creations as stagey as the rest of the play – except that, very importantly, they pretend that unlike the audience they know when a play is a play, and repeatedly tell the playgoers so. This is their central function: to announce the theatricality of the whole event, and by doing so, to define everyone present, both diners (those presumed quick to take offence) and servants, as audience.

SPACE, TIME, AND OPEN ADDRESS
IN NONCE DRAMA

Wherever they staged their productions, before whatever class of spectator, all professional players of the Tudor period were obliged to carve out a physical space for each performance, then to define it as a playing area, distinct from the ground occupied by the bystanders. Early in the period, *Hickescorner*'s Virtuous Living establishes his own place and time alongside the playgoers in the dining hall:

> And now here will I rest me a little space
> Till it please Jesu of his grace
> Some virtuous fellowship for to send. (30–3).

In *Mundus et Infans*, the mixed crowd at the performance in an inn-yard draws notice. First, after fighting Manhood, Folye notices those standing around and offers to beat them up:

> On all this meyne [people] I wyll me wouche [offer],
> That stondeth here aboute. (560–2)

Then Perseverance speaks to those who presumably are sitting quietly:

> Now good God, that is moost wysest and welde of wyttes [most
>   knowledgeable],
> This company counsell, comforte and glad,
> And sue [draw together] all this multytude that semely here syttes. (749–51)

Increasingly, open addresses identified the crowds specifically as audiences. In *Impatient Poverty* (ca 1547–53), Abundance acknowledges the hall where the play is being performed, as well as the people in it: "Joy and solace be in this hall! / Is there no man here that knoweth me at all?" (200–2). He continues by asking the audience further questions. Playgoers were being told that they were a different brand of people from whoever was on stage, and that the place where they stood or sat and the time in which they watched were distinct from the place and time on stage. By Elizabethan times, people who attended plays were often explicitly spoken of and to as "audiences," a designation not previously used.[31] The crowd at

Enough is as Good as a Feast, for example, is claimed by the actors to be
"our audience"(236), a category of people different from the play's
performers and characters.

In almost every nonce play, an announcer or guide first greets the
spectators with some kind of request or explanation, and later bids
them goodbye with thanks and apologies. Sometimes characters with
a role in the play itself speak the beginning and finishing addresses;
in other plays, expositor characters with no part in the central action
speak them.

The prologues often make practical requests, such as asking the
crowd to be a patient audience:

> Now Jesu the gentle, that brought Adam fro hell,
> Save you all, sovereigns, and solace you send!
> And of this matter that I begin to tell
> I pray you of audience till I have made an end. (*Hickescorner*, 1–4)

Occasionally, prologues offer apologies for what playgoers are about
to receive. *Grim the Collier of Croydon* (revived 1598) opens with a
comic prologue (one that might have been spoken by *A Midsummer
Night's Dream*'s "rude mechanicals"): "You're welcome; but our plot I
dare not tell ye, / For your fear I fright a lady with great belly" (5–6).
The Marriage of Wit and Wisdom begins with reference to players
readied to put on the show: "The proof, the sequel shows, for I
have done my charge,/ And to the actors must give place to set it
forth at large" (Prologue, 29–33). It then moves straight into charac-
terizing the listeners as people gathered specifically to see a
performance:

> Ah! sirrah! my masters! how fare you this blessed day?
> What, I wean [think] all this company are come to see play!
> What lackest thee, good fellow? didst thee ne'er see men before?
> Here is a gazing! I am the best man in the company when there is no
>   more (1.2.1–4)

A play performed at court, *Apius and Virginia* (ca 1559–67), has a
guide to announce that its players will *"come in* to play" (my italics):

> But my goodwill I promised them to do,
> Which was to come before to pray of you,
> To make them room, and silence as you may,
> Which being done, they shall come in to play. (11–14)

The announcements also highlight the fact that performers become characters. In *The Interlude of Health and Wealth* (before 1570), the audience is reminded that actors are waiting to assume roles: "Al these partes ye shal se briefly played in their fashion" (1). These speeches emphasize that a play is a fictional construct, not part of the playgoers' world. In *Respublica*, a noble audience is told that the play is "the thing we shall recite" (10). These examples and many others of the period demonstrate that prologues were used to draw the playgoers' attention to three major aspects of playing: performance as event; play as artefact; and themselves as audience – all identities set up for the nonce.

Epilogues, such as those in Skelton's *Magnificence*, were used to the same effect as prologues. After Magnificence has been brought to acknowledge his sinful foolishness and has promised to make amends, three Virtues salute the audience and sum up the play's moral import. The play closes with their speeches, made directly to the audience. Redress's speech contains a theatrical as well as a moral message, as he reminds the listeners that the play has been a temporally limited event:

> Unto this process briefly compiled,
> Comprehending the world casual and transitory
> Who list [chooses] to consider shall never be beguiled,
> If it be regist'red well in memory. (2506–9)

Circumspection reiterates the point that the play speaks to everyone about right conduct. He then explains to the playgoers how best to understand what they have seen and heard: "A mirror encleared is this interlude, / This life inconstant for to behold and see" (2520–1). The playwright introduces a double metaphor for the play, one that will appear often on the later Tudor stage and again combines a theatrical and a moral assertion: the play is a mere reflection of life, an unreality which, at the same time, clarifies life's moral values, distinguishing sin and virtue.[32] The third Virtue, Perseverance, then directs the spectators' attention to the play's status as a piece of writing constructed for an immediate occasion, that is, for their present edification and entertainment as audience: "This treatise devised to make your disport / Showeth nowadays how the world cumbered is" (2534–5).

The nonce play is an uncertain thing, capable of yielding truth (particularly to attentive listeners), but with an ambiguous relationship to everyday reality. Circumspection explains:

This matter we have moved, you mirths to make,
Pressly purposed under pretence play,
Shoulth wisdom to them that wisdom can take. (2548–50)

Redress closes the play by pointing out the gulf between the people on stage and those at the banquet. Just as the play is a limited, special kind of event, the people watching it are a particular kind of community, grouped temporarily for a specific purpose and a single occasion, people who, once the play is over, will disperse, all going their separate ways.

OFF STAGE IN NONCE DRAMA

In nonce drama, when players and dramatists carve out a distinct stage space, they gain the further potential to build around and behind it an additional world, one wholly aligned neither with the stage nor with the audience's world. In nonce plays, characters pop on and off stage with remarkable rapidity, moving in and out of both the playworld and an unseen world. For example, in *Hickescorner* and *Youth*, good and bad characters apparently come on stage from, and go out to, the sleazy parts of London, an invisible city of debauchery and violence whose off stage existence is powerful in shaping the play's dynamics. Bevington notes, for example, that *Youth*'s protagonist and the characters Free Will and Imagination all talk a great deal to the playgoers about their off stage experiences (*Tudor Drama*, 41). In *The Longer Thou Livest the More Fool Thou Art*, the wilfully ignorant protagonist, Moros, is relegated to a disciplinary off stage area where he is supposedly taught doctrinal lessons, while on stage his religious instructors, Discipline, Piety, and Exercitation, discuss how to reclaim their stupid and wilful pupil. Behind them, the audience can see the recreant poking his head out from the off stage schoolroom. (The stage directions read "between whiles let Moros put in his head" (38).) Moros is beaten by his teachers, out of sight but well within the audience's hearing.

Exigencies of staging drove the invention of various off stages. Because of their limited resources, it was a theatrical necessity for many playwrights to double up roles, to have characters go on and off stage to change costume and become someone else. John Bale showed himself a master of this technique when he wrote for the small company that performed *King John*. The play is a vehement denunciation of Roman Catholic dogma and practices. A convert to Protestantism, Bale was a vigorous propagandist for his new beliefs and wanted to reach as many people as possible with his warnings about the ever-present dangers of Catholic tyranny. Under the patronage of Thomas Cromwell, Bale wrote *King John* for a small professional troupe to be performed before mixed audiences (Bevington, *From "Mankind"*, 51–2). The play dramatizes the story of a king persecuted and finally murdered by members of the insidious network of the papal empire. *King John* owes a debt to the two major forms of medieval religious drama: to the morality play for its allegorical figures, and to the guild play for its figural approach to history. It is essentially a history of England in which the reign of Henry VIII is figurally connected to a series of historical moments from the Old and New Testaments, from England's distant past, and from recent English history.

Bale's skilful use of a small company was a vital theatrical contribution. Bevington describes Bale as "a pioneer" in the techniques of stage doubling (70): the players who appear as weak-minded and spiritually vulnerable courtiers (Civil Order, Nobylyte, Clergy) also take the roles of allegorical figures such as Usurped Power and Private Wealth, as well as of historical figures such as Stephen Langton, Pope Innocent III, Pandulphus, and Simon of Swinsett. These shape-changers, particularly the play's arch-villain Sedycyon, all dash on and off stage (much of the exiting and entering would have to be done very quickly), building the impression of a sinister off stage world. That world is constructed and maintained by on stage open address. For instance, while Nobylyte, Clergy, and Dyssymulacyon are changing costumes – and roles – Sedycyon holds the stage alone, inviting the audience to share his interests and at the same time suggesting the existence of a nearby place of depravity:

> Haue in onys a-geyne, in spyght of all my enymyes!
> For they cannot dryve me from all mennys companyes;
> And, thowgh yt were so that all men wold forsake me,
> Yet dowght I yt not but sume good women wold take me.
> I loke for felowys that here shuld make sum sporte:
> I mervell yt is so longe ere they hether resorte.
> By the messe, I wene the knaves are in the bryers,
> Or ells they are fallen into sum order of fryers!
> Naye, shall I gesse ryght? they are gon into the stues;
> I holde ye my necke, anon we shall here newes. (626–35)

> (Here I am, back again, in spite of all my enemies!
> They can't drive me from the company of every human being;

And even if it happened that everyone abandoned me,
I don't doubt but that some good woman would take me in.
I'm looking for men now who would like some fun.
I am amazed it's been so long since they last gathered here.
By the mass, I swear the rascals are hiding in the hedges
Or else they have fallen in with a bunch of friars!
No, let me guess the real truth. They're visiting brothels;
I'd stake my life on it. We'll soon find out.)

This kind of suggestion of an off stage existence is found only once before: in the travelling play *Mankind*, where attention is drawn to the immanent hidden presence of Titivillus, a diabolic figure, who will materialize only if the spectators shout for him and pay over their money.[33] Bale creates a much more fully developed and sustained off stage world than that of *Mankind*. It suggests a place like those in the audience's actual lives, but over which, at the time of the playing, they have no control and in which they do not participate. The characters, not the playgoers, inhabit this place. It is useful to compare Bale's off stage world to the stage world of the guild plays. In the earlier drama, there was no off stage; not only was the physical world as a whole implicated in the play, but there was no mystification attached to any part of the staging. All was embedded in the familiar, the contemporary; the stage space and audience space were wholly aligned. Bale, by contrast, manages to build around and into his playworld an ominous other world, a "somewhere" very close, just off stage. It is a world of sinister monastic practices, political duplicity, and foreign treachery, not precisely and fully identified with the playgoers' own lives, but rather paralleling the events they see and experience.

While some characters disappear to this mysterious "somewhere," others, often left alone on stage, hold the audience in conversation. Speaking directly to the playgoers, these characters engage their attention while behind the scenes other players change costume. What happens is that, as the audience listens, the characters' words are charged with the general knowledge that comic or dreadful transformations are happening somewhere out of sight. In the guild plays, *everywhere* was the stage; off stage as well as on stage belonged to the audience's world. Now, part of the theatrical world has been eroded. In later Tudor drama, there would be nothing outside the stage during performance; the players would claim it all. Whereas audiences used to designate where the play was by their simple presence, by the end of the Tudor period plays would start to define all playing space.

NONCE PLAY IMPRESARIOS
AND THEIR TALK

Earlier in this chapter the word "guide" was used for a character who openly addresses playgoers and leads them into the play. In this part, another term for a specific type of character is introduced – this one for the figure in the native English tradition usually known as a "Vice." For several reasons, I have chosen the term "impresario" for this stage figure. The impresario has a complex heredity; his dramatic existence harks back to more than the morality plays' allegorical Vices. He is also descended from guild drama's riddling, cheeky servants, such as Pykeharnes, Garcio, and Froward; from its extrabiblical rascals, such as Mak; and, most significantly, from its devils, including Titivillus, the word-tangler.

In nonce plays the impresario's features and functions show his mixed heredity. Often he is named allegorically, like characters in morality plays, as a direct parody of sins or foibles. He turns upside down and rejects authority, like the rebellious servants in folk plays. He is an inveterate liar, like Mak. Above all, the impresario is a wordsmith, as arrogant, persuasive, and divisive as the guild plays' devil. He enjoys having audiences, to listen to him and to stare at him. My chosen term, "impresario," embodies all these things, and also implies the particular, smooth and sleazy entrepreneur type who runs the show, insinuating himself between the central action and the audience.

The impresario performs functions made necessary by the new playing conditions of nonce drama. As noted above, this figure has an insatiable appetite for audience attention. From early morality plays such as *Mundus et Infans* to the Elizabethan hybrid plays, the "gallimaufreys"[34] of history-romance-tragedy such as *Cambises* and *King Darius*, impresario schemers talk intimately and volubly with their audiences. As Weimann notes, Inclination, the impresario of *The Trial of Treasure*, for example, "occupies the stage for three-quarters the acting time"(155).

Why does the impresario hog the nonce stage? First, of course, the character is funny, outrageous, great theatre material, popular with audiences. Another reason for the pervasiveness of the impresario has to do with practical need. This figure has often been written of as the most self-consciously theatrical of all Tudor stage figures.[35] Many early plays depicted Vices and poseurs; Weimann shows that equivocator figures are deeply entrenched in native English dramatic tradition and locates the impresario's early origins in the word play and choric role of folk-drama fools (120). Even in guild drama

and morality plays, sinful characters carry a strong aura of theatricality into their addresses to the audience. Guild drama's cheeky servants, its bullies, its devils such as Towneley's Titivillus, cavort
about, preening flamboyantly for the crowds. In the morality plays,
Vices are often deceivers costumed as Virtues, playing roles in order
to gull Mankind. In the nonce plays, latent theatricality becomes
very much manifest and, by early Elizabethan times, the impresario's "showmanship" (Spivack, 153) and his part in performance
as "producer, manager, and commentator" (Spivack, 156) define his
relationship with the audience.

Ambidexter, the duplicitous impresario of *Cambises*, illustrates the
new exchange well. He is an arch-schemer who drives the central
action relentlessly forward; at the same time, he filters events in the
play for the audience by commenting on them. Here he is talking to
the playgoers after Cambises' marriage, describing the king's wedding and the "royall and superexcellent" entertainments it afforded:

> Running at tilt, iusting, with running at the ring,
> Masking and mumming, with eche kind of thing, –
> Such daunsing, such singing, with musical harmony,
> Beleeve me, I was loth to absent their company. (942–5)

Next, Ambidexter turns description into disquisition, first on his own
ideas about marriage, then on marriage in general. He lectures the
audience directly:

> I muse of nothing but how they can be maried so soone;
> I care not if I be maried before to-morrow at noone,
> If mariage be a thing that so may be had.
> How say you, maid? to marry me wil ye be glad?
> Out of doubt, I beleeve it is some excellent treasure, –
> Els to the same belongs abundant pleasure.
> Yet with mine eares I have heard some say:
> "That ever I was maried, now cursed be the day!" (950–7)

Later he enters weeping, crying crocodile tears for the cruel treatment of the queen by her husband. This time he prods the contemporary world and the people in it:

> A, a, a, a! I cannot chuse but weepe for the queene!
> Nothing but mourning now at the court there is seene.
> Oh, oh, my hart, my hart! O, my bum will break!
> Very greefe so torments me that scarce I can speake.

Who could but weep for the losse of such a lady?
That cannot I doo, I sweare by mine honestie.
But, Lord! so the ladies mourne, crying "Alack!"
Nothing is worne now but onely black:
I beleeve all [the] cloth in Watling Street to make gowns would not serve, –
If I make a lye, the devill let ye starve!
All ladyes mourne, both yong and olde;
There is not one that weareth a points woorth of golde.
There is a sorte for feare for the king doo pray
That would have him dead, by the masse, I dare say.
What a king was he that hath used such tiranny!
He was akin to Bishop Bonner, I think verily!
For both their delights was to shed blood,
But never intended to doo any good. (1133–50)

Ambidexter is the audience's constant mediator with the play; at the same time, he makes the spectators, too, the butts of his jokes and commentaries.

Like the guild plays' devils, tyrants, and extra-biblical figures, then, impresarios do not share audience space – they invade it. Their incursions are often verbal: insistent demands or outright abuse. For example, the audience is badgered by an apparently offended impresario in the pre-Elizabethan *The Interlude of Wealth and Health*:

Why is there no curtesy, now I am come
I trowe that all the people be dume
Or els so god helpe me and halydum
They were almost a sleepe.
No wordes I harde, nor yet no talking
No instrument went nor ballattes synging
What ayles you all thus to sit dreaming
Of whom ye take care?
Of my coming ye may be glad. (1–9)

Impresarios may also demand physical action from the people in the inn-yard or dining hall. In *The Longer Thou Livest the More Fool Thou Art*, Wrath expects his appearance to reduce the crowd to acts of homage:

No God's mercy? no reverence? no honour?
No cap off? No knee bowed? No homage?
Who am I? Is there no more good manner?
I-trow, you know not me nor my lineage. (1038–41)

The devil of guild drama acts as a guide who would, if playgoers believed him, disunite them into contending individuals, fracturing any sense of community that they might ordinarily have or that is fostered by the rest of the play. Likewise, the nonce impresario often singles out individual members of the audience. In the Elizabethan *Like Will to Like* (whose cautionary message is that villains and fools attract their own kind), Nichol Newfangle picks on the women among the crowd: "How say you, woman? you that stand in the angle? / Were you never acquainted with Nichol Newfangle?" (5). This clothes-horse is also a gamester, and invites the audience to gamble with him. At one point in the play, he enters with a "knave of clubs in hand" which "as soon as he speaketh he offereth up to one of the men or boys standing by" (4). He makes sure the individual gets the message, ordering, "Stoop, gentle knave and take up your brother." At the end of the play, when Cuthbert Cutpurse and Pierce Pickpurs – who, Newfangle reminds the spectators, have plied their trade amongst them while they've been watching the play – get their just deserts, Newfangle is in at the kill, making sure that the audience also feels implicated: "he bringeth in with him a bag, a staff, a bottle, and two halters, going about the place, showing it unto the audience" (67).

Nichol Newfangle turns out to be as careless of his own spiritual fate as of that of his companions, riding off cheerfully to Hell on Lucifer's back. All impresarios demonstrate a similar lack of commitment to any moral or ideological values, whether those of the play or of the actual world. They also seem to have no belief whatsoever in the reality of either world.[36] They build a space of their own from which they talk to both, noticing that they can see both audience and playworld but never admitting that either is substantial. Like that of the extrabiblical figures of guild drama, their ontological position with regard to play and audience is ambiguous. Although famous impresarios such as Ambidexter, Nicholas Newfangle, and Haphazard (in *Apius and Virginia* [ca 1559–67]) are part of the narrative of the play's main action, their contract with the play and with the public is eminently unplaceable.

Yet nonce play impresarios display a particular propensity for talking about, as well as to, this insubstantial public. They riddle with and unsettle meaning in both the playworld and the world of the audience, thus guiding their listeners into a confused and confusing world. From early plays onward, impresario figures make it clear that they will not be tied down to any clear statements about either the playworld or the real world:

Lo sirs, here is a fair company, God us save!
For if any of us three be mayor of London,
Iwis, iwis, I will ride to Rome on my thumb.
Alas, a, see! Is not this a great farce?
I would they were in a mill pool above the arse,
And then, I durst warrant, they would depart anon.

(*Hickescorner*, 443–8)

In their self-definitions, which they offer with frequency and gusto, impresarios are just as equivocal; in fact, they make it virtually impossible to read any certain identity in what they say about themselves. Haphazard gives his listeners a voluble, alliterative, but thoroughly indecipherable self-description:

Yea, but what am I? a scholar, or a schoolmaster, or else some youth.
A lawyer, a student, or else a country clown:
A broom-man, a basket-maker, or a baker of pies,
A flesh or a fishmonger, or a sower of lies?
A louse or a louser, a leek or a lark,
A dreamer, a drumble, a fire or a spark?
A caitiff, a cutthroat, a creeper in corners,
A hairbrain, a hangman, or a grafter of horners?
By the gods, I know not how best to devise,
My name or my property well to disguise.
A merchant, a May-pole, a man or a mackerel,
A crab or a crevis [crayfish], a crane or a cockerel?
Most of all these my nature doth enjoy;
Sometime I advance them, sometime I destroy
As big as a beggar, as fat as a fool,
As true as a tinker, as rich as an owl:
With hey-trick, how troll, trey-trip and trey-trace,
Troll-hazard with a vengeance, I beshrew his knave's face;
For tro and troll-hazard keep such a range,
That poor Haphazard was never so strange:
But yet, Haphazard, be of good cheer,
Go play and repast thee, man, be merry to yere.

(*Apius and Virginia*, 181–206)

The open address of impresarios is not the disconnected, ritualistic riddling of the folk-play fool; nevertheless, their words do not make complete sense, either in the world depicted on stage or in ordinary experience. In *The Trial of Treasure*, for example, Inclination moves onto the stage to describe to the crowds where he has appeared from.

He tells them his story in such a way that, while it makes reference to
known locations and events in the audience's world, it so scrambles
up geography, history, myth, sense and nonsense that, in the end, he
seems to have stepped out of nowhere:

> I can remember since Noe's ship
> Was made, and builded on Salisbury Plain;
> The same year the weathercok of Paul's caught the pip,
> So that Bow-bell was like much woe to sustain.
> I can remember, I am so old,
> Since Paradise gates were watched by night;
> And when Vulcanus was made a cuckold,
> Among the great gods I appeared in sight.
> Nay, for all you smiling, I tell you true.
> No, no, ye will not know me now;
> The mighty on the earth I do subdue.
> Tush, if you will give me leave, I'll tell ye how;
> Now, in good faith, I care not greatly,
> Although I declare my daily increase;
> But then these gentlemen will be angry
> Therefore I think it best to hold my peace:
> Nay, I beseach you, let the matter stay,
> For I would not for twenty pounds come in their hands;
> For if there should chance to be but one Dalila
> By the mass, they would bind me in Samson's bonds! (211–12)

Impresarios refer their comments directly to the audience; their
pact with the playgoers is immediate. Yet Inclination's words simultaneously deny both what the playgoers hear elsewhere in the play
and what they know to be reality. Typically, impresarios import recognizable fragments of everyday life into the fictional discourse of
the play, then re-sort them and fuse real facts with nonsense, creating
a new, unrecognizable, unstable world. This is the world into which
they guide their audiences,[37] for nonce play impresarios take charge
of both play and audience.

In other words, the impresario controls a *theatre*. In his hands, characters in the play and people in the audience are no longer "us": playgoers have become "you," people who are separate from the play and
do not belong to it except as observers. This entrepreneur, barker, and
master of ceremonies tells all present who they are and what they
must do. He is the primary organizer of crowds, the one who tells
them that this event, into which they move for the nonce, will ignore
the familiar rules of life. The impresario's loudest message to play-

goers is to leave their daily reality behind them for the performance. They do not need it – and it will not help them.

I end as I began with Shakespeare's "Athenian" actors. Although these players try to round off their nonce play with an epilogue, neither Theseus nor Shakespeare allows them a final address to their audience. Instead, Puck makes excuses directly to the London crowd, and when he does so he speaks as impresario of the play as a whole:

> If we shadows have offended,
> Think but this and all is mended,
> That you have but slumbr'd here
> While these visions did appear.
> And this weak and idle theme,
> No more yielding but a dream,
> Gentles do not reprehend.
> If you pardon we will mend
> And as I am an honest Puck,
> If we have unearned luck
> Now to 'scape the serpent's tongue
> We will make amends ere long;
> Else the Puck a liar call
> So, good night unto you all.
> Give me your hands if we be friends,
> And Robin shall restore amends. (*Dream*, 5.1.423–38)

Although Puck's closing speech is full of open references to the London audience, they are addressed as a community distinct from those on stage. The people in the playhouse yard and galleries are "you," while the players on stage are "we." Puck invites this "you," the audience, to favour and to applaud "us," the players. The two separate communities become a tentative "we" and temporary "friends" only under specific conditions: when they are brought together by the playhouse, in which each pursues a distinct role. In Puck's words, we hear references to some features that Shakespeare inherited from the nonce plays: players who are professional actors, playing on a stage separated from the auditorium, to people identified as "audience" watching a story that is not about their lives. Shakespeare also inherited Puck himself – an impresario, a stage figure whose function it is to mediate between the disjunctive worlds of "us" and "you."

This heritage, the native tradition of open address to the audience, shifts again when London's permanent playhouses set up business, as we shall see in the next chapter.

CHAPTER THREE

I Know You All

THE PUBLIC PLAYHOUSES

Although troupes of players continued to tour provincial towns and villages, setting up temporary stages in inns, markets, guild halls, or the dining halls of aristocratic homes (Coldewey, "Enterprising," 5–12) by the last quarter of the sixteenth century the story of English professional theatre was primarily one of London.[1] Encouraged by the presence of the royal court, with its promises of patronage and frequent performance opportunities,[2] by the growing prosperity of the capital – in contrast with the economic slump in the provinces, especially in the formerly well-to-do northern towns (Phythian-Adams, "Urban Decay") – and by London's burgeoning population – the city grew from 150,000 people to about 200,000 during the time of greatest theatrical activity, 1574–1642 (Gurr, *Stage*, 196) – professional players headed for what promised to be a lucrative theatre market. They were further encouraged to get off the roads by the "Acte for the punishment of vagabonds" (1576–1600). This law, intended to control and limit the wandering and gathering of transients and masterless men through the countryside and in the towns, required each troupe of travelling actors to be legitimized as players by being licensed by either one member of the nobility or two judicial dignitaries (Gurr, *Stage*, 28).

At first, as they had often done, players set up their trestles in inns. The Bel Savage Inn and the Boar's Head, both within London proper, were winter venues for itinerant players.[3] Then, in 1567, John Brayne built the Red Lion in Stepney, east of London, an open air structure about which little is known, but which seems to have been based on a mix of the old inn playing space and the public arenas where people were entertained by bull- and bear-baiting.[4]

London's civic authorities, however, frowned on inn performances, or on any playing in the city. The city fathers saw plays as
threatening civic order by promoting unruly gatherings and by taking people from work and worship. In 1559, the London council tried
to oust professional players from the city by issuing a prohibition on
playing. When this injunction proved ineffectual, in 1574 they for-
bade all inn playing unless tavern owners obtained licences from the
civic authorities (Foakes, 2; Chambers, 324). Civic antagonism made
the city proper a difficult place in which to perform, yet it is clear –
partly from how hard the authorities fought against it – that late
sixteenth-century Londoners had a growing appetite for professional
drama.

To satisfy this enthusiasm and take advantage of an opportunity to
make money, in 1576 John Brayne, in partnership with his brother-in-
law the carpenter James Burbage, moved the Red Lion enterprise
outside London's limits to the north-east of the city. Here, in the liberty of Shoreditch, they built a new playhouse, the Theatre; the next
year they erected a second one, the Curtain, in the same neighbourhood. For the following forty years, entrepreneurs continued to build
playhouses outside London's city limits, drawing enough people
to make Philip Stubbes complain in 1583 that Londoners went to
"Theatres and curtains" while "the church of God shall be bare and
empty" (Chambers II, 223). In 1587, Philip Henslowe erected his playhouse, the Rose, in the liberty of the Clink, on the south bank of the
Thames. Within this area, a red-light district of brothels, bear-baiting
pits, and inns of dubious character lying beyond London's gates and
jurisdiction, two more theatres were built: the Swan in 1595, in the
Manor of Paris garden, and the Hope in 1614.[5] At the end of 1598,
James Burbage's son Richard moved the Theatre playhouse, pulling
apart the wooden structure and transporting the boards and beams
across the frozen Thames by night, using local carpenters to reconstruct it on the Bankside as the Globe.[6] In 1600, to the north of London, just beyond Cripplegate, Philip Henslowe (as co-owner with the
actor Edward Alleyn) put up the Fortune theatre, a wooden building that burned in 1621 and was rebuilt two years later in brick. Near
the Fortune, also north of the city, the Red Bull Inn was rebuilt as a
playhouse in 1605.[7] Steven Mullaney summarizes the particular distribution of London's public playhouses: "By the turn of the century
the city was ringed with playhouses to the north and south, posted
strategically outside its jurisdiction and beyond the powers of civic
containment or control" (18).

London's civic authorities continued to oppose public playing
houses even after they had moved outside the precincts of the city,

although private playhouses operated around 1576–1590 within the city proper. In 1597, after Nashe and Jonson's *The Isle of Dogs* (a lost play) attacked national and civic government, the Privy Council issued an order that, according to Thomson, "ought to have spelled the end of the still-youthful professional theatre of England":[8]

Her Majestie being informed that there are verie great disorders committed in the common playhouses both by lewd matters that are handled on the stages and by resorte and confluence of bad people, hathe given direction that not onlie no plaies shalbe used within London or about the citty or in any publique place during this tyme of sommer, but that also those play-houses that are erected and built only for suche purposes shalbe plucked downe. (*Theatre*, 4–5)

But playing companies had the royal court's liking for plays on their side, so public playhouses continued in business.[9] Despite consider-able difficulties – disputes with city authorities, bans on playing in Lent, troubles with censorship, repeated closures because of the plague – playhouse business flourished.[10]

The commercial playhouses, all of them open air and most of them wooden structures, seem to have attracted and held large audi-ences.[11] Using the rediscovered sites of the Globe and the Rose in Bankside, Andrew Gurr and John Orrell estimate that the Globe was a polygonal building, measuring approximately 100 feet in diameter from each outside wall and with the inside of the walls stretching about 70 feet (114). Its yard may have accommodated about 800 peo-ple, while another 2000 could be seated in its various galleries. In the public playhouses, the entrance fees began at 1d., which entitled the theatre-goer to stand in the yard; for 2d., he or she could sit in the first gallery; an extra penny rented a cushion to sit on (Gurr, *Stage*, 63). Inside, the audience saw a raised flat platform – in the case of the Red Lion, some forty by thirty feet (Gurr, *Stage*, 112). At the Fortune, a playhouse built as an eighty-foot square, the yard measured fifty-five feet along each side and the stage was forty-three by fifty-five feet (Gurr, *Playgoing*, 18–19). The platform was set up a little lower than head height for most of those in the yard, possibly with a low railing around it (Hattaway, *Popular*, 23).[12] In some cases the sight may have been quite grand. Foakes writes, "The stage façade was highly deco-rated, and the Elizabethan playhouses offered their public colour, spectacle, and richness" (21). In most playhouses (certainly at the Globe and Fortune), a canopy was spread over the platform stage, its underside painted with stars, moons, signs of the zodiac, resting on elaborately carved pillars (Gurr and Orrell, 119). Two doors in the

back wall of the stage led to the tiring house, the off stage space serving as dressing and storage areas (Dessen, *Conventions*, 8).

The Tudor period had seen the proliferation of professional players. With the building of public playhouses, these actors became
members of a wider commercial enterprise. Although the playhouses were owned and controlled by the entrepreneurs who built them,
plays were mounted by collectives of "sharers," who rented the playhouses from their owners, paying them a percentage of the take for
the use of their buildings (Bentley, 42).[13] Often the sharers were a
company's principal players, men who made enough money from
their trade to buy into the venture and to share the costs of whatever
was needed for putting on performances.[14] Player-investors had
various duties:

the purchase of new costumes and costume materials; paying for new plays
by freelance dramatists; getting scripts approved by the Master of the Revels,
paying him for licenses for the theater and for occasional privileges, like
playing during parts of Lent; paying the company's regular contributions to
the poor of the parish, assessing fines against sharers or hired men for
infringement of company regulations; calling rehearsals; collecting fees for
court and private performances; supervising the preparation and distribution of playbills; and perhaps for paying the hired men. (Bentley, 147–8)

The sharers also hired the rest of the company: the acting members –
both adults and boy apprentices – and the technical crew – the stage
keepers, wardrobe keepers, prompters (or book-holders) – in short,
everyone who was needed to keep the performances running
(Bentley, 148).

Named for royal or aristocratic individuals and under their patronage, playing companies on the whole made a good living, though the
need to tour in times of theatre closures because of outbreaks of
plague made life somewhat unstable (Foakes, 41).[15] The popularity of
individual companies with their London public waxed and waned.
At various times different companies were favourites. In 1577, Leicester's Men, who played at James Burbage's Theatre, was the chief
London company. By 1583, the Queen's Company had the edge; by
1588, Worcester's Men had overtaken them; by 1590, Admiral's and
Strange's companies had amalgamated to produce the city's most
popular group of players. The Chamberlain's Men was formed in
1594. This company, later renamed the King's Men under James I,
was originally run by James Burbage and his son Richard. It offered
its chief members, including William Shakespeare, shares in the playhouse buildings where the company acted: the Theatre, the Globe,

and Blackfriars. As Peter Thomson points out, to stay in business the entrepreneurs and the companies had to please their customers – all of them: "A theatre company that misjudges its appeal rarely lasts long or lives well ... An Elizabethan artisan could have afforded the penny admission, but he would have paid it only if his interest was genuine" (*Theatre*, 24–5).

Because the acting companies were businesses taking financial risks – their outlay was considerable –[16] they structured their internal organization tightly. Michael Hattaway describes how rigidly hierarchical they could be:

Each company had about five or ten 'sharers' who, in return for investing capital in the company, took their profits by dividing among themselves the receipts from one part of the house, first the yard, later the galleries. Shares in companies could be bought, sold, bequeathed, or divided among several individuals. The rest of the takings went to the owner of the playhouse and to support the rest of the organization: the tailors and tire-men who had care of the costumes, the book-holder and stage-keepers, and the gatherers – as well as the hiremen and the boys. For before he could acquire the status (or the capital) of a sharer, a player often progressed through two stages analogous to the degrees found in most Elizabethan trades, that of apprentice and that of hireman and journeyman. (Hattaway, *Popular*, 70)

By the last quarter of the sixteenth century, the formally structured and financially successful collectives of actors were somewhat like other civic guilds (Hattaway, *Popular*, 71). A mark of their efficiency and business acumen (and of their theatrical talent) is that they attracted Londoners regularly and in considerable numbers to their playhouses, as well as being called on to perform regularly at court.[17] Gurr notes that for "nearly 40 years London had at least six playhouses and four regular companies performing daily except on Sundays, Lent or plague"(*Stage*, 76).[18] He estimates that during this time playhouses regularly attracted nearly 15 to 20 per cent of Londoners (Gurr, *Stage*, 196), as well as tourists from Europe.[19]

Anne Jennalie Cook suggests that these audiences were composed of men and women from a largely educated and wealthy class, whose "own ranks were tremendously varied, reaching from bright but impoverished students, younger sons of gentry families set to a trade, and minor retainers of noble households all the way up to lords, ambassadors, merchant princes, and royalty itself" (272). Gurr rejects Cook's view of audience composition. He argues, first, that she uses a misleadingly "generous definition of the privileged" and, second, that her estimate of the proportion of the crowd they formed is an "oversimplification." According to Gurr, Cook's description of playgoers during the period 1576–1642 (from the opening to the closing of the playhouses, both public and private) ignores changing patterns in playgoing, particularly the shift after 1599 when playgoers had a variety of playhouses to choose from (*Playgoing*, 64). Using evidence from the play texts, eyewitness accounts, and other writings, including attacks on the theatre, Gurr arrives at a description of audiences at public playhouses before "the revival of the boy companies and the hall [private theatres] in 1599" that is much broader than Cook's: "The artisan and servant classes joined with the citizens and gentry at playhouses. Those few descriptions which suggest that the full range of society was present at plays come from around the 1590s, when only the amphitheatres [open air public playhouses] were open" (*Playgoing*, 65–6).[20]

A.R. Braunmuller suggests that, once the playhouses were in business, London customers were always hungry for new plays: "When Elizabethan entrepreneurs risked the capital to erect permanent theatres in the 1560s and 1570s and actors joined into formally organized companies, they created a staggering, and continuing, demand for new material" (53). An entry from Henslowe's diary shows "15 different plays performed over twenty-five playing days" (Hattaway, *Popular*, 51). Since all the companies worked a gruelling repertory system in which types of plays changed rapidly, London audiences could potentially see as many as five different plays in a week.[21] All were subject to censorship by the Master of the Revels, having to be approved by his office before they were staged; at times, certain plays were refused a license altogether, or required alterations to the text.[22] Nevertheless, the overall range of plays available to London audiences was remarkable: citizen comedies, romances, dramas concerning topical events (such as the then-recent murder in *A Yorkshire Tragedy*),[23] tragedies, histories – Polonius in *Hamlet* lists the repertoire.[24] Margot Heinemann comments that "anyone who could put a penny in the box" had the opportunity to see in the commercial playhouses dramatizations of a welter of topics, including current politics (167). Gurr observes that this fecundity of subject matter was largely due to the release that came with the new kind of theatrical business transaction occasioned by playhouses and audience-customers:

Only when the plays were offered to a crowd which had gathered and paid exclusively to enjoy a play were the poets made free to create offerings like *The Spanish Tragedy* and *Tamburlaine*. In the 1560s use of an open market place or a banqueting hall meant that authority's frown was a recurrent danger. Moreover audiences in halls and even at markets usually gathered for reasons more weighty than seeing a play. Plays in banqueting halls were a garnish to the feast supplied by a generous host. Brayne's and Burbage's commercial playhouses thus created the first regular means for every playgoer to buy just the garnish of his or her own entertainment. The plays designed to feed such a well-focussed hunger came afterwards. (*Playgoing*, 116)

Gurr regards the opening of the Red Lion in 1567 as marking the start of a shift in the history of English drama, whereby professional players were emancipated from having to rely on collections from audiences during or after performances, from having to seek accommodation by innkeepers, and from placing their hopes in widespread communities' wanting to see and pay for their playing (Gurr, *Playgoing*, 6). The date 1567 is therefore important for this book.

PERMANENT STAGES AND THEIR AUDIENCES

When nonce players packed up at the end of their performances, they dismantled a complete theatre; after they had removed themselves and their equipment, innyards or halls resumed their original and primary character. But London's commercial public playhouses (Gurr calls them "amphitheatres"), owned, controlled, and operated by entrepreneurs, for the first time in the history of English theatre offered players permanent acting sites: theatres that were always theatres. Players no longer had to build and dismantle a stage for every performance.

Moreover, the public playhouses had fittings and stage decorations that were permanent fixtures. Instead of having to exit behind a makeshift curtain or through dining hall doors, as early Tudor players had been obliged to do, actors in London's play houses could make their entrances and exits through stage doors. Behind these lay an off stage which was only that, not also a kitchen, an inn, or a market. Just as important, the doors led London's commercial players to a tiring house where there was permanent storage for all the materials of playing: costumes, props, playbooks (the scripts), musical instruments.[25] A secure storage space, of course, offered the potential for more and more elaborate stuff to be stored. Henslowe's diary, for instance, lists the costumes and the wide range of properties packed in his theatre's tiring house. The inventory includes lavish costumes made of expensive materials (satins, velvets, cloth of gold) often bought from rich men's and women's wardrobes.

Whether London citizens and visitors went to the north or northeast suburbs, or crossed the Thames to Bankside, as they handed over their entrance fee they paid to enter a space belonging primarily to the owners of the playhouse and to the sharers who were principal players in the acting companies. It is important to note that the space entered by the playgoers was specifically used for playing; it was never also used as a school, kitchen, refectory, or innyard.[26] Thus, London's playgoers, already invented as a new type of community – an audience – by Tudor playwrights, also walked into a freshly minted type of space. After 1567, then, however varied or numerous, whether "understanders" (those standing in the yard) or gallery sitters (those paying more to sit in the tiered walls of the playhouse), London audiences watched commercial players on stage, seeing their neighbours only as fellow members of the audience.[27]

With the opening of the Red Lion and other playhouses, drama became a fully professional commercial enterprise.[28] Both stage and auditorium were permanent and distinct physical areas. The platform stage, the playing space, belonged to and was organized by each theatre's owners, its resident acting company, and its playwright – not the audience. In London's commercial theatre, an actor was a member of a separate, recognized profession, a guild unlike others in the working world. In other words, the working identities of audiences and players no longer overlapped, nor did audiences lend players their space to work in, for the nonce. The bare stage was solely the place of the play, a space that – even when it stood empty before the play began and was neutral as far as the play's fiction was concerned – signalled to playgoers a "there and then" separate from their "here and now." Those entering the playhouse were customers, permitted to enter because they put their pennies in the box. When they did so, they abandoned at the door their city, their usual identity with its workaday preoccupations. Inside the playhouse there were playgoers watching drama played out in its own self-contained world, not in the audience's city, not even in an aristocrat's hall or in a neighbourhood innyard. It is true that the gulf between stage and audience was always mitigated: actors and spectators were close to one another and could see, hear, and smell each other's near presence. But no matter how the London crowds cheered, "mewed," jostled, or booed in their contemporary space, they did not have the same kind of temporal and spatial connections with the play on the platform as their ancestors did. Commercial playhouse drama was not "our" play, as guild drama had been; nor was it set up for the nonce. The English stage had become more independent of its audiences than it had ever been. Tydeman expresses regret over the loss of intimacy between play and audience that accompanied the growth of commercial theatre:[29]

As commercial considerations came to dominate, no longer did hard labour and varied skills, time, talent, and monetary levy, weld together people and presentation; no longer was a public dramatic performance the result of widespread communal activity but something to be purchased like any other commodity; no longer could spectators identify with local performers whose personal habits and usual daily pursuits they recognised and acknowledged. The new theatres might inherit some conventions and customs from an earlier age but now an invisible wall had sprung up between the paid actor on his apron stage and the paying audience in pit and galleries. It has still to be demolished. (245–6)

But here excitement lies: Shakespeare uses open address, the close exchange between play and audience, on the new stage. The numerous strategies used by Shakespeare to erect and to demolish that "invisible wall" form the subject of the rest of this book.

SHAKESPEARE'S CLOSED STAGE

At the start of Shakespeare's career, the "invisible wall" closing off the commercial platform offered a young dramatist great freedom. When Shakespeare wrote the three-part chronicle of *Henry VI* (1590),[30] then *Titus Andronicus* (1591), he made use of the material assets of the playhouse: access to machinery, to the tiring house and its props and lavish costumes (Hattaway, *Popular*, 30–3, 36). He had permanent staging: the platform, the trap, the "aloft," a playing area that at every performance could be anything and anywhere the playwright chose. Most of all, he had a stage that was always and only a stage. Shakespeare wrote these plays for a permanent company of professional actors – master players, hired men, and apprentices – who performed regularly to audiences avid for new plays. He had spectators, inherited from the nonce plays as audience, who paid to see his plays, who were sometimes noisy, who interrupted performances (Hattaway, *Popular*, 46), but whose world did not need to be imported to the stage for a play to make complete sense.

Shakespeare's early histories, the three parts of *Henry VI*, first performed at the Rose playhouse by the Admiral's Men, as well as the revenge play *Titus Andronicus*, show a heady awareness of the power made available to a playwright by a permanent playhouse and a closed stage. Young Shakespeare employs every asset of the Rose's scaffold stage: the doors, the platform, the tiring house wall, the upper level. In the first history play, for instance, the action moves vertically between the platform from where a French gunner prepares to shoot and the "aloft," the upper level where the English have built a tower "to overpeer the city" of Orleans (*1 Henry VI*, 1.4.11).

The action is sketched bold and fast in these early plays, spectacle enhanced by sound effects and by the musical instruments available in the playhouse,[31] as in the sensational comedy called for by the stage directions where Simpcox fakes a miracle: "Here do the ceremonies belonging, and make the circle; Bolingbroke or Southwell reads, 'Conjuro te, etc.' It thunders and lightens terribly; then the Spirit riseth" (*2 Henry VI*, 1.4.S.D. 24). The action is powerful, loud, amazing. But it remains wholly on a stage that ignores the immediate tangible presence of playgoers.

Early in his career, Shakespeare rarely left his stage empty. Nor did he allow his characters to speak to the people in the Rose's yard and galleries. Very occasionally characters are left on stage alone (Cade, Talbot, and Richard, for example). But when they speak, their speeches do not operate to notice the playgoers or connect them to the play; they serve rather as narrative or expository links (usually set at the beginning or end of scenes) in these long, episodic dramas. Talbot, for instance, appears on stage alone after La Pucelle drives the English army away before her, saying:

> Where is my strength, my valor, and my force?
> Our English troops retire, I cannot stay them
> A woman clad in armour chaseth them. (*1 Henry VI*, 1.5.1–3)

Even though Talbot calls the disappearing army "our" troops, they are not the playgoers' army. He does not invite the audience into this "our." On stage is English history, Talbot's history – but not the audience's history. When Talbot describes the action to the crowds, he talks about *his* experience, offering them elucidations and recapitulations of his on stage world. What the audience hears, even when characters are alone, are speeches that largely ignore their presence: declamatory public assertions on a closed stage rather than intimate talk from an open stage.[32]

Drawing on Elizabethan anti-theatrical discourse such as the writings of Stubbes and Gosson to track the story of England's disintegration into social chaos, Jean Howard argues that the *Henry VI* plays make reference to issues touching on the contemporary world of the Rose's customers (*Struggle*, 130–9). Annabel Patterson also points to connections between the trilogy's subject matter and then-current English events, in particular to similarities between the plays' dramatization of Cade's rebellion and "the Southwark happening," a confrontation between Southwark felt-makers and guards at Marshalsea Prison in 1592 (36, 51).

While the early Henry plays may allude to recent Elizabethan events, they glance at them from inside the "invisible wall"; they do not reach out across it to talk directly to the playgoers about contemporary concerns. The stage remains closed; the crowd's physical presence in the yard and galleries is largely ignored by the characters on stage. No-one on the scaffold challenges, questions, or appeals to the spectators; no character mediates between them and the play's action, not the angry Cade, malevolent Richard, or honest Talbot.

In *Titus Andronicus*, the young playwright again uses everything his stage can offer. As in the Henry trilogy, although his audiences share the daylight with the play, their presence again goes unremarked.[33] In this play, Aaron the Moor, lover of Tamora, Queen of the Goths, is given time alone on stage. Aaron is a full-blown villain who characterizes himself to Lucius with the vaunt: "I curse the day ... wherein I did not some notorious ill" (5.1.125–7), and who boasts of evil actions, from murder and rape to impoverishing small farmers: "I make poor men's cattle break their necks" (2.1.1). Presumably motivated by lust and ambition (like others in this playworld) or by grotesque excess, his appetite for and relish in evil is like physical greed. Aaron, devil-like, stands slightly to the side of this story of Romans and Goths. But though he echoes devils and villains of native English tradition, unlike them he does not taunt the playgoers, demand their response, or invite them in any way to participate in the play.

In these early plays, few characters – including Aaron, though he comes the closest – say "we" inclusively, meaning both themselves and the people surrounding the platform or peering down from the galleries. Few even say "you" while pointing to the playhouse's customers. At the opening of his career, Shakespeare uses little open address in which characters assume that their audiences share in their conflicts or delights. The dramatic energies of these plays, however carefully choreographed, are designed to be largely confined by the verges of the platform. The audiences at *Henry VI* and *Titus Andronicus* remain outside the "invisible wall" as people who have paid to be awed, amazed, and thrilled, but not to be consulted.

THE PERMANENT STAGE AND OPEN ADDRESS IN SHAKESPEARE

Meanwhile, it seems that a huge bare platform on which anything can happen was too stark, chilly, and fixed a place for Shakespeare. A closed stage is potent; it has the capacity to thrill – but Shakespeare soon made his stage appeal openly to the playgoers. Another early play, *The Taming of the Shrew* (1591), puts on stage the audience's sleeping shadow in the staunchly English figure of Christopher Sly. The Italians Petruchio and Katherine both speak addresses that spill off the stage into the yard and galleries (Petruchio at 2.1.169–181 and 4.1.188-211; Katherine at 4.3.1–16.). In *Two Gentlemen of Verona* (1590), Proteus, Julia, and Launce all speak at length to the playgoers about their lives and loves. Standing alone on the stage in *Love's Labours Lost* (1594), Don Adriano de Armado avows that he loves, Berowne regrets that he loves, and Costard swears by money. So Shakespeare plays his playhouse as well as his stage, introducing audience presence as an essential element in the play's meaning. No longer content to use only the platform, the trap, the aloft, he adds another dimension to the physical stage: the *playhouse* with all its contents, including the playgoers.

From the nonce plays Shakespeare inherited an off stage with a presence capable of putting pressure on the scaffold action.[34] From both guild drama and the nonce plays he received a rich tradition of creating meaning through visual effects[35] or by the grouping of characters on the platform.[36] Shakespeare used all these strategies, and added to them the new stage's potential to be a closed place bounded by the scaffold edge and ignoring the proximity of the playgoers. The result is an amalgam of closed and open playing space, where characters have the option to ignore or to notice the presence of the audience. As his career continued, then, Shakespeare not only had characters speaking alone on stage, but increasingly built on the potential of open address to incorporate into the play the presence of people standing, drinking beer, or sitting on rented cushions. His plays consistently register the fact that audiences as well as actors were inside the playhouse walls, and that those spectators stood or sat very close to the scaffold. As in the guild plays, the type and degree of contact with the playgoers varies; however, it always imports to the play, as it did in medieval drama, markers of the concrete, the real, and the literal. Shakespeare's audiences increasingly heard from his stage addresses not simply expository or declamatory, but more like the inclusive address of characters on the platea of medieval plays, the kind of "we," "you," "here," and "now" that served to connect the medieval playworld with the world of the audience.[37] Once more, without asking the playgoers to shift their ordinary identities, these words position them as contributors to the play. And because the playgoers are located in real lives, Shakespeare, despite a playing space identified primarily as a stage, can use them to locate the play.

Richard III: "Now" and "We" in Open Address

The protagonist of *Richard III* serves as an excellent example of a character who plays not just the stage but the whole playhouse. Like a medieval devil who wants to draw everyone onto his side, or like the devil's progeny the nonce play impresario, Richard intends to run the show. With his audience standing around the stage or gazing down at him from the galleries, Richard begins his play:

Now is the winter of our discontent
Made glorious summer by this son of York;
And all the clouds that low'r'd upon our house
In the deep bosom of the ocean buried. (1.1.1–4)

This is quite unlike the earlier Richard's expository speeches in *3 Henry VI*. His "now" and "our," his deictic address, is seductive; he treats his listeners as if they must surely sympathize with his obsessive delight in this "now."[38]

Richard's insistent friendliness towards the playgoers and his relentless demands on them are important. Richard is modelled, I think, on the guild plays' devil figure. Like the medieval devil and the nonce play impresario, this character filters the action before the spectators have a chance to see it for themselves. He puts them in a particularly troubling position when he favours them with unpalatable confidences, forcing them to contrast his evil but energetic presence with the lacklustre personalities of many around him. It is to these confederates in the yard and the galleries that Richard exults after winning the widow Anne: "Was ever woman in this humour woo'd? / Was ever woman in this humour won?" (1.2.227–8). The first word of the play signals the contract Richard demands from his audience: he wants them sympathetically embroiled in his idiosyncratic personal sense of time. He means the playgoers to partake in his urgency to grab the moment, to know the surging in his "now." The prosody of Richard's speech is compelling. He opens with a trochee, in which "now" is so heavily stressed that the word must matter. Richard's "now" – made vital because it opens the action, made both accessible and memorable because it is short, simple, and spoken only to the audience – resonates throughout the play. As the members of the audience stand or sit close to Richard, he, like a guild drama devil, proposes to them that they should think only of the present moment, a time pulled from *their* now, then re-made and supposedly controlled by him alone.

Because Richard initiates the play (perhaps to the extent of locking eyes with his listeners in the playhouse), his notion of time is
always more substantial than the present inhabited by other characters on stage.[39] Almost immediately after establishing the temporal frame, however, his use of "us" and "our" pushes the audience – heirs of the civil wars – away. With a gesture over his
hunched shoulders, he sends towards the tiring house doors
through which the other characters will appear a sneering "our"
("our brows," "our bruised arms," "our stern alarums"). Clearly
ironic, these words of community signal the royal "we" to which
he is not entitled at the same time that they signal Richard's contradictions: his simultaneous alliance with and alienation from the
rest of the playworld, his confederacy with and dissociation from
the playgoers.

Richard III builds sharp alternations between Richard's open
address and his return to the closed world of English politics. Within
the latter, the playgoers see for themselves the rest of the English
court appearing as absorbed by thoughts of time as Richard. Their
temporal obsession, however, enervates rather than energizes them.
The dying king is gripped by guilt about his past. Clarence foresees
his own death and fears the past and the future. Old Queen Margaret,
caught up in ritualized past and future terrors, denounces everyone
around her. All these characters inhabit paralysed time, a temporal
frame that stays cut off from the playhouse. Only Richard lives in a
present that invites the audience in.

As the play progresses, Richard's position relative to the playgoers
shifts; his communion with them shrivels. But real time has been signalled by his direct contact with them and the time of an actual world
marked by their acknowledged presence. This time continues to run
and cannot be wished away. Harried, Richard tries to regain control
by ignoring the audience to make his stage closed. He steadily
retreats to relocate himself within the frame of a "now" that excludes
everyone but himself.

Like a medieval Herod or Pharoah, Richard has believed himself
invulnerable, atemporal; he has asserted that his "now" would run
forever. Yet in the scene before the Battle of Bosworth Field, as he lies
awake in his tent, his "now" disintegrates. Richard is harried by the
past, by the people he has murdered. Isolated and hopeless, he struggles in the present, alone. Where he once flung his words at the playgoers, he no longer sees them, although they are there listening,
aware of what his fate will be. Richard is imprisoned in a spiralling
solipsism:[40]

Cold fearful drops stand on my trembling flesh.
What do I fear? Myself? There's none else by.
Richard loves Richard, that is, I [am] I.
Is there a murtherer here? No. Yes, I am.
Then fly. What, from myself? Great reason why –
Lest I revenge. What, myself upon myself?
Alack, I love myself. Wherefore? For any good
That I myself have done unto myself?
O no! Alas I rather hate myself
For hateful deeds committed by myself.
I am a villain; yet I lie, I am not.
Fool, of thyself speak well; fool, do not flatter:
My conscience hath a thousand several tongues,
And every tongue brings in a several tale,
And every tale condemns me for a villain.
Perjury, perjury, in the highest degree;
Murther, stern murther, in the direst degree;
All several sins, all us'd in each degree,
Throng to the bar, crying all, "Guilty! guilty!"
I shall despair; there is no creature loves me,
And if I die no soul will pity me. (5.3.181–201)

The playgoers surround him still as he repeats "I," "I," "I." But the stage signals isolation; it is fatally closed. Richard is unable to reach out to anyone, framed by his tent in a psychological and spiritual isolation. He cannot seek or hear any response from the audience. There's no-one there, no-one here. The permanent stage thrusts its invisible threshold between him and the audience; it clamps its edge around him. Thus barriered, Richard discovers that neither "now" nor "I" is or ever was subject to his individual will. Richard's singular self is no longer a source of energy; and the present moment, the "now" he so revelled in, has become terror. Much of the power of this speech derives from the isolation of Richard on a closed stage shutting him off from the playgoers, in a lonely "now" of political defeat.

THE UNHEROIC STAGE

We have seen that the "invisible wall" of Shakespeare's stage is sometimes impenetrable, sometimes permeable. Shakespeare derived tension and drama not from the technical capabilities of the stage but from his management through open address of the whole playhouse. I will now propose an approach to reading the plays that argues the centrality and continued influence of the old dramatic strategy of open address in Shakespeare's work. This perspective considers open address as a deflationary, diversifying, and complicating stage strategy. Shakespeare used what I call "the unheroic stage" to construct playworlds that refuse to let the singular, the romanticized, the heroic, take over. Through close contact with the audience, open address from this stage creates a complex, diversified on stage world.

To take an example: *Henry V* (1599) is managed throughout by a patriotic Chorus, an enthusiastic upholder of Henry as hero who intervenes repeatedly to persuade the playgoers that they are watching a glorious past. This loyal supporter appears by the end to see quite a different play from what actually occurs on stage. He promises, for instance, that the audience will see a Christ-like king who with a "largess universal like the sun" (4. Chorus. 45) and "liberal eye" (4. Chorus. 46) will comfort the dejected English army. This is not what happens. Instead, the ordinary soldiers challenge several notions of heroism and of kingship. Later, Henry, alone with the audience, does not talk about the care of these soldiers, or of all the English; instead, he gripes about the burdens of being a king rather than a commoner. By the close, the play seems to have escaped the control of the Chorus; he can end it only by apologizing to the audience for the playwright's deficiencies, his "rough and all-unable pen" (Epilogue 1).

In the rest of this section, I will look more closely at two other plays that, like *Henry V*, use open address to show the audience an unheroic stage: *1 Henry IV* and *Troilus and Cressida*.

1 Henry IV

In *1 Henry IV* several worlds are dramatized: the "official" disillusioned hauteur of the royal court, the emotionally charged military world of Hotspur and Glendower, and the "unofficial" world of a London tavern. On the whole, these worlds are closed; that is, the stage largely ignores audience presence. But the stage also makes open contact with the audience; in fact, two kinds of contact, both ambiguous.

Falstaff, a self-styled "Vice," organizes himself a place between the closed world on stage and the world of the audience.[41] At times, he seems almost to be standing among the playgoers, although he never directly says "you" or "we" as platea characters did.[42] Since Falstaff never explicitly refers to the audience, his connection with them is robust yet shady. With a knowing wink, the fat old reprobate sometimes teases the playgoers about their familiarity with old stage conventions: he threatens, for example, to "beat Hal out of [his] kingdom with a dagger of lath" (2.4.136–7). Given the opportunity, Falstaff talks as if all his listeners (and often these are only the audience) share his way of seeing life. Indeed, he goes further: he assumes that they must believe his life fuller, more substantial, than the lives of other characters in the play – as he does. Falstaff acts as if he has established a rapport with people who just want to get by, with friends who prefer lives that are not heroic, with those who dislike anything that fails to recognize the supreme importance of living inside a comfortable body.[43]

There are many voices from the closed stage. Henry's voice is one of weary kingship: "So shaken as we are so wan with care" (1.1.1). Hotspur's speaks of pugnacious valour: "Not speak of Mortimer? Zounds I will speak of him, and let my soul / Want mercy if I do not join with him!" (1.3.128–30). Hal's voice is that of rapid manipulative wit: "Thou art so fat-witted with drinking of old sack, and unbuttoning thee after supper, and sleeping upon benches after noon, that thou hast forgotten to demand that truly which thou wouldest truly know. What a devil hast thou to do with the time of the day?" (1.2.2–7).

Falstaff's voice, insinuating its way over the edges of the scaffold, is an earthy English tongue, usually talking about material things: the pleasures of food and drink, how all bodies are not sites of honour but feel pain, that death is to be avoided at all costs. Falstaff lives wholly amid the concrete in an immediate present. When that present grows uncomfortable, he'd like it to be over. Faced with battle, he laments: "I would 'twere bedtime, Hal, and all well" (5.1.126). Moral values are nothing to him unless they are of practical use: "Can honor set a leg? No. Or an arm? ... What is honor? A word" (5.1.131–5). Alone as he is speaking here, he spurns honour as a mere abstraction. Later he is prepared to use it as a commodity for barter when he claims to have killed Hotspur (5.4.142). Falstaff is simultaneously comic and shockingly unadmirable.[44] What he seems to invite his audience to share with him is a life that is often banal and shabby, even slippery, and that can at times be cruel and mean-spirited. Nonetheless, its unwavering concreteness homes in on playgoers' sense of their own immediate actuality. By that means, Falstaff makes a connection with them. Although he never speaks openly to the audience, his language is familiar, homely. Falstaff may be a self-confessed "vice," yet he is no devil.[45] He talks about a here and now littered with recognizable material presences; a literal and often unlovely platea-like world where people are worried about being physically hurt and dying, where the crisis is not what kind of death comes but that death comes to all.

When Hal addresses the audience, his talk is more disturbing and, curiously, closer than Falstaff's address to the native English tradition of the guild play devil. The prince speaks to the playgoers only once. After he and his Eastcheap buddies plan to fool Falstaff, Hal, alone on stage, seems to declare precisely who he is and what he plans to do. However, in language that is at once muscular and strategic, he refers his declaration to a disconcertingly ambiguous "you":

> I know you all, and will awhile uphold
> The unyoked humour of your idleness:
> Yet herein will I imitate the sun,
> Who doth permit the base contagious clouds
> To smother up his beauty from the world,
> That, when he please again to be himself,
> Being wanted, he may be more wonder'd at,
> By breaking through the foul and ugly mists
> Of vapours that did seem to strangle him. (1.2.199–207)

Every other character stays ignorant of Hal's intentions: his drinking companions, his political enemies, even his father. Only the people in the yard and the galleries are made privy to Hal's assertion of an inner self, but even they are not told in concrete terms what this reformation will entail. If this is open address, it is clearly not open language. The playgoers alone hear that Hal, using his tavern friends for his own purposes, is biding his time until he sees the right moment to reveal himself to everyone as a royal prince. How he will actually do so is a mystery, lost in his riddling speech. Hal's open address is ambivalent, revealing and concealing at once.

Hal's self-definition is more equivocal than Falstaff's characterization of himself as a Vice. In his address, Hal uses images to ally himself to Christ, likening himself to a long-awaited, despaired-of Messiah-son, who when he comes will "pay the debt," "redeeming time when men think least [he] will" (1.2.217). This newly revealed prince will be a figure to be "wond'red at" (1.2.201). Hal's speech also recalls the pronouncements made by God in the guild plays: like God, Hal will allow the world to run till "he please" (1.2.200). But Hal's words hold disquieting "quips and quiddities" (1.2.45), making him a word-monger like the quick-tongued devil Titivillus. His extended image of the beauty of a longed-for sun, at present obscured by thick, noxious fogs, is disturbing. While it suggests Christ, it also echoes Lucifer, longing to shine, or the devil who hides his true self until the time is ripe, assuring audiences: "I am with Yow at all tymes . whan ye to councel me call / But for A short tyme my-self I devoyde" (N-Town, *Passion Play I*, 122–3). Unlike God's self-referential speeches in guild drama, Hal's address harshly polarizes the pronouns "I" and "they." He ("I") is "bright metal"; "they" are "sullen ground" (1.2.212). Difficult to pin down, Hal worries his father by refusing to give him clear answers about his intentions. He mocks Hotspur; he fools his friends. He is witty yet cruelly manipulative, often more unlikable than Falstaff because he is more clever. Throughout the play, he deliberately leads people on, knowing that they misconstrue him. In this speech and throughout the play, Hal plays an equivocal role vis-à-vis everyone.[46]

Hal's one open address even directs snide words at the playgoers. He talks to them like a devil or an impresario, who would control, confuse, and reduce the audience to nothing, as he does in taunting Francis the tapster:

POINS. [Within.] Francis!
FRAN. Anon, sir.
PRINCE. How old art thou, Francis?
FRAN. Let me see – about Michaelmas next I shall be –
POINS. [Within.] Francis!
FRAN. Anon sir, Pray stay a little my lord.
PRINCE. Nay but hark you, Francis: for the sugar thou gavest me, 'twas a pennyworth, was't not?
FRAN. O Lord, I would it had been two!
PRINCE. I will give thee for it a thousand pounds. Ask me when thou wilt, and thou shalt have it.
POINS. [Within.] Francis!
FRAN. Anon, anon.
PRINCE. Anon, Francis? No Francis; but to-morrow, Francis; or Francis, a' Thursday; or indeed, Francis, when thou wilt. But, Francis!
FRAN. My Lord? (2.4.43–68)

Whereas Falstaff urges his listeners not to bother with anything but concrete immediacy, Hal tells them: "I know you all." This is a huge assertion, suggesting that the playgoers are simple, degrading characters and audience alike into nonentities. Hal promotes himself as prince at the playgoers' expense; however obliquely, he positions his listeners in such a way that they, too, get in his way as "base contagious clouds" that "smother up his beauty".[47]

The contrapuntal voices of Falstaff and Hal flowing over the edge of the stage defeat any possibility of singleness of vision in the play, working much like the contiguous open addresses in guild drama. Pykeharnes and Cain in *The Killing of Abel* each reached out to the Wakefield crowds to pull them into a particular world, each trying to exact a contract that would nullify any other. In *1 Henry IV* Falstaff asks the playgoers to think of a literal world, while Hal enjoins them to see the pre-eminence of the strategic. Falstaff's world cannot be the moral centre of the play – but neither can Hal's. Falstaff talks about common fears of death; Hal speaks about killing. In many ways, the prince's open address is more unsettling than Falstaff's nods at his audience. It is significant that Hal's moment alone with the playgoers comes early on in the play. Because of the structural position of his address, the possibility of Hal as a fiend-like presence worms its way throughout, raising doubts about how this prince regards all English people – including those who have paid to see the play.

Troilus and Cressida: *Open Address, Contradictions, and Deflations*

Troilus and Cressida offers one of the best examples of a series of open addresses all jostling for audience attention. Several characters notice the playgoers: the Prologue and Pandarus, for example, both speak openly to the audience, each identifying the contemporary onlookers as contradictory kinds of community.[48] The playgoers are also made into confidants by the many asides, and are the only ones to hear several characters candidly express their feelings.

The play begins with a Prologue who seems confident that he speaks to the audience from a stage capable of displaying the spectacular history of the siege of Troy, a city barred "with massy staples and co-responsive and fulfilling bolts," with contenders all primed to "disgorge / Their warlike frontage" (Prologue, 12–13). He addresses his listeners in the language of epic – exalted and high-flown. He assures them that armies soon to appear will be made up of youthful, lusty soldiers: the Greeks, for example, "fresh and yet unbruised" (14), bristling with "expectation, tickling skittish spirits" (20). However, a curious anxiety creeps into his announcement, though he himself seems unaware of it. His aureate diction is appropriate to great heroes and actions – the Greeks are "princes orgulous" – but it jars on the ear – its sound is awkwardly Latinate, overblown and comic.[49] The Prologue seems to want massiveness, the solidity of end-stopped lines, sculpted perfection; instead his lines are broken, staccato, uncertain-sounding.[50] Accepting the epic convention of beginning *in medias res*, he fulfills his obligation to push his audience seven years into the long, drawn-out war by making it a problem. And it *is* a problem, since the play will stay in the impasse and cynicism of mid-war – the play is not epic; it depicts inaction. So although the Prologue makes a brave effort to present the heroic, his introduction of the epic falls apart before he finishes his speech to the playgoers.

Furthermore, his naive promise of a story of energetic heroism is immediately contradicted when the central action starts. The playgoers see Troilus, not arming himself for battle but taking off his gear – yet again:

> Call here my varlet; I'll unarm again:
> Why should I war without the walls of Troy,
> That find such cruel battle here within?
> Each Trojan that is master of his heart,
> Let him to field; Troilus, alas! hath none. (1.1.1–5)

The inhabitants of both camps, the besieged and the blockaders, are marooned, bored by seven years of war and sexually frustrated. Trojans and Greeks alike are irritable, torpid, watchers of one another – anything but heroes. In the city, Helen, the cause of the war, passes the time by playing with Troilus's beard. Achilles sulks in his tent like a peevish schoolboy, play-acting with his friend Patroclus, mocking his companions, his leaders, and his fellow soldiers. In a nearby tent, Ajax "groans self-willed," his bad humour fuelled by a cynical Thersites.

On the surface, what the Prologue seems to promise is a play with which the audience's world would have no connection: a drama on classical lines, decorous and utterly remote from ordinary life. The stage does resound at times with formal public rhetoric, impersonal aureate words, particularly from the Greek camp. Ulysses, for instance, holds forth at some length in his massive oration on order (1.3.75–137). More often, though, both inside and outside Troy's walls the stage represents a thoroughly non-heroic world where all are petty, their actions mean. The main action is almost concluded before the playgoers see any shows of war; even then, rather than fierce battles they see only skirmishes between individuals and the cowardly murder of an unarmed man. When eventually spurred to act, both sides manifest snappiness, petulance; their aggression is personal, not strenuous and soldierly.

The epic promised by the Prologue was to be a closed world, perfect in its "pastness." But this playworld is anything but closed; it constantly relocates itself in the playhouse, repeatedly stretches into the audience. Again and again the playgoers, made recipients of

asides or short outbursts, become the playworld's intimates. They are
not auditors of epic, watchers of heroic spectacle. Rather, they are
privy to a gossipy, rumour-ridden world in which characters
constantly catalogue each other's physical or psychological deficiencies.[51]

Referring to the main action of the play, Jean Howard notes that
there is a great deal of "looking on" (115). She explains: "Watching
the play, the audience feel they are seeing a world without truly private dimensions, a world in which action has dwindled to self-dis-
play" (116). Howard is right but what is particularly notable is that
prominent among those "looking on" are the playgoers. Over and
over again, they are forced to be both *viewers* and *voyeurs*. For
instance, when Cressida arrives in the Greek camp, they are put in
the position of watching Greek soldiers eye the young woman, and
of watching her gaze at the Greeks. In the four-layered eavesdrop-
ping scene, audiences hear Thersites, who watches Troilus and
Ulysses, who together watch Cressida with Diomed. Inside the walls
of Troy, Cressida stands with Pandarus watching the Trojan heroes on
silent parade. As if adjudicating a local talent contest, she and her
uncle tot up the assets and defects of the Trojan warriors from
"brave" Hector to the common soldiers, the "asses, fools, dolts! chaff
and bran, chaff and bran! porridge after meat" (1.2.241–2). The playgoers watch and listen to it all.

Stuck in a world arrested at a crude, superficial level, young Cressida has none of the warmth of Chaucer's Criseyde. Shakespeare's
Cressida is naive without being innocent, a brittle humourist. She is
a street-smart kid who exchanges explicit sexual puns with her aging
uncle Pandarus. Yet Cressida is also vulnerable, touching. Like a
wary kid in a dangerous city, she too is a voyeur, but an anxious one;
she scans everyone, her main concern to avoid being fooled. Terribly
isolated, she needs to confide in someone. The only someone available to her is the audience:

> Words, vows, gifts, tears, and love's full sacrifice,
> He offers in another's enterprise;
> But more in Troilus thousand fold I see
> Than in the glass of Pandar's praise may be;
> Yet hold I off. Women are angels, wooing:
> Things won are done; joy's soul lies in the doing.
> That she beloved knows nought that knows not this:
> Men prize the thing ungain'd more than it is:
> That she was never yet that ever knew
> Love got so sweet as when desire did sue.

Therefore this maxim out of love I teach:
Achievement is command; ungain'd, beseech:
Then though my heart's content firm love doth bear,
Nothing of that shall from mine eyes appear. (1.2.282–95)[52]

This young woman with no-one to trust in the closed world makes intimates of her audience, showing them two Cressidas, one who will and must follow the "maxim[s]" of love, and another who truly loves. Cressida's confidences, spoken alone from the stage, reach out for the spectators' understanding of weakness, not of heroism, for their recognition of loss, not of victory. They invoke the playgoers' sense of an immediate, familiar world, not their knowledge of the distant literary world of epic.

Open addresses by Thersites forge a different connection with the audience than the speeches of other characters. Thoroughly disillusioned with everyone around him, shutting out the presence of the other characters, the soldier gives the audience a thumb-nail sketch of each participant: Ulysses is a "dog-fox" (5.4.11); Nestor "a stale old mouse-eaten dry cheese" (5.4.10); Ajax an "elephant" (3.2.4), a "mongril cur" (5.4.13); Achilles "a valiant ignorant" (3.3.303); Agamemnon "an honest fellow enough, . . . but he has not so much brain as ear-wax" (5.1.51–2); Diomed a "false-hearted rogue, a most unjust knave" (5.1.88–9), a "Greekish whoremasterly villain" (5.4.7). Self-exiled, Thersites mediates between audience and play, forcing the playgoers to listen to his disgust at everyone involved in this travesty of war: "Vengeance on the whole camp! or rather, the Neapolitan bone-ache for that methinks is the curse depending on those that war for a placket" (2.3.18–20). The seasoned soldier straddles the threshold of the stage, conferring self-awareness on the audience as fellow watchers at a war with no heroes. Fed up with the laziness, selfishness, and pettiness around him, Thersites wishes things to be clear-cut: war to be war, and heroes to be heroes.[53] After watching Cressida and Diomed, Ulysses and Troilus, he sums up the action to the playhouse: "lechery, lechery, still wars and lechery, nothing else holds fashion" (5.2.194–5). Later, observing the fight between Troilus and Diomed, he reduces their duelling to two men "clapper-clawing one-another" (5.4.1), deflating all putative heroes. Like Falstaff and Hal, Thersites is an unlikely moral centre of the play. He does involve his audience in a discussion that values heroism and is realistic about both Trojans and Greeks, but he also imposes on the playgoers a heavy load of brutal invective and drags them into a sour-eyed view of the world. At times, though he has justification, Thersites seems to have some of the medieval Cain's view of the world, taking as

personal slights the actions and inaction of others. Thersites, impatient, intolerant and surly about everything and everyone, wants the
audience to feel the same way.[54]

Whereas Thersites is reminiscent of Cain, Pandarus plays the role of
impresario. The organizer of sexual and theatrical events, he titillates
the onlookers as he invokes their presence in the sex scenes. At the end
of the young couple's love scene, Pandarus offers up a wish for the
young women in the audience: "And Cupid grant all tongue-tied
maidens here / Bed, chamber, Pander to provide this gear" (3.2.20–1).
Here Pandarus performs what the entire play does: shows the playgoers
that they too are witnesses, salacious eavesdroppers, peeping Toms.

The epilogue is spoken by no Expositor or Doctor; rather, Pandarus
the pimp turns to face the audience, offering a closing address anti-
thetical to the opening speech. Instead of the Prologue's feisty call to
arms, Pandarus begs the playgoers for "a goodly medicine for my
aching bones" (5.10.35). The old go-between rails against the audience's world, where a pimp's job is treated with contempt and "the
poor agent is despised." The audience has passed through many
incarnations in the course of the play; here, Pandarus re-invents it yet
again. At the opening, the playgoers were "fair beholders"; now they
are defined as traders and bawds. Pandarus impresses his personal
disenchantment on the people he sees in the seventeenth-century
London playhouse. He ends the play with a mix of smutty jokes,
prose, song, and these verses:

> Good traders in the flesh, set this in your painted cloths.
> As many as be here of Pandar's hall,
> Your eyes, half out, weep out at Pandar's fall;
> Or if you cannot weep, yet give some groans,
> Though not for me, yet for your aching bones.
> Brethren and sisters of the hold-door trade,
> Some two months hence my will shall here be made:
> It should be now, but that my fear is this,
> Some galled goose of Winchester would hiss:
> Till then I'll sweat and seek about for eases,
> And at that time bequeath you my diseases. (5.10.35–56)

The playgoers may have elbowed one another in the yard, or craned
from their galleries to stare at Cressida as she entered the Greek
camp. Straining to catch the dirty jokes over the sound of cracking
hazelnuts, they have been told throughout that they, like the play's
Trojans and Greeks, are eavesdroppers. The whole playhouse has
been addressed by a series of direct speeches, intimate confidences,

gossip, rumour, asides. Staring back at the onlookers, the exhausted Pandarus refuses to see them as anything but London pimps, fellow guildsmen of his hall. No society could be less heroic than the one Pandarus situates in the playhouse. If the playgoers have been labouring to find heroism on the stage, they have not discovered it among Shakespeare's Greeks and Trojans. Now Pandarus fails, in turn, to see it in them. Pandarus leaves the playgoers with a play that ends up back in contemporary red-light Southwark. Like the figures in guild drama, Pandarus makes a connection between remote history and the present, a figural link between a world of Trojans and Greeks and that of Shakespeare's London. What joins the two worlds is not war or heroism or romance. When Pandarus addresses his audience as fellow guildsmen, what links the two worlds is sex. A play that opened with the audience looking in at an apparently heroic stage ends with the stage looking out at a seedy audience.

THE ALTERNATION OF THE CLOSED AND OPEN STAGE

In his tragedies, Shakespeare made use of opposing possibilities of the permanent playhouse: to support both a closed, self-contained stage and an open one like that of popular tradition. Although the focus here is mainly on *Hamlet* (1600) and *King Lear* (1605), a similar pattern of stage use can be found in the other tragedies written around the same time: *Othello* (1604), *Macbeth* (1606), *Antony and Cleopatra* (1606), and *Coriolanus* (1608). All these plays at times ignore the playgoers, as if all that existed in the playhouse were the play-world. At such times, the spectators are on neutral ground; they are people whose identities are erased. At other times, the plays acknowledge through open address that there are people crowding around the platform, sitting in the galleries, within eyeing and spitting distance of the characters. When Shakespeare's permanent stage refuses to see the audience, it signals that they are people whose world is insignificant compared with the society on stage. When it turns its gaze on the playgoers, it signals that they and their world's values are incorporated into the play. This idea is more fully explored in the remainder of this chapter.

Hamlet: *Open Address from a Closed Stage*

The stage world in *Hamlet* ignores the audience most of the time, as if the land of Denmark were barricaded within its scaffold. (Actually, much of the rest of Europe is also contained there, lying somewhere behind the tiring house.) No-one on stage finds it easy to leave. Hamlet is stuck in Denmark, unable to return to university: first, because his stepfather wants him at the Danish court; second, because his mother likes to have him near her; and last, because his father comes back from the dead expressly to order Hamlet to stay in Denmark and avenge his death. Laertes returns to Paris, but even there is watched by Danish eyes.

In Denmark, watching and being watched is endemic. Although there are many secrets on this stage, nowhere is private. For example, Ophelia is never left alone; playgoers see and hear her being harried by all the men in her life. Off to Paris, Laertes catechizes her about their prince's attentions and intentions. Then she is interrogated by her father, before being "loose[d]" to the prince like a heifer to a bull (2.2.162). Intrusions and spying are all-pervasive: Polonius and Claudius eavesdrop on Ophelia and Hamlet; Polonius listens in on Gertrude and Hamlet; Hamlet stares at the king at prayer; a Danish audience watches the "Murder of Gonzago" with Hamlet scrutinizing the spectators – while the London playgoers gaze at everyone. The scaffold is built as a closed space enmeshing everyone with everyone else. Hamlet sums up the playworld Denmark's claustrophobic nature: "the age is grown so pick'd that the toe of the peasant comes so near the heel of the courtier, he galls his kibe" (5.1.140–1).

The compressed and suffocating platform is also unremittingly self-referential and materialistic. Polonius's parting advice to Laertes quintessentializes Danish notions of how to get by in life. His sententious instructions are mundane; he gives no spiritual or even moral advice (1.3.57–77). For instance, the platitude "neither a borrower nor a lender be" (1.3.75) might, out of context, be seen as an expression of the value of self-worth. However, when, soon after, Polonius sends Reynaldo to spy on Laertes and says he expects his son to engage in gambling and "drinking, fencing, swearing, quarreling/Drabbing" (2.1.25), he contradicts his own earlier injunctions. Polonius's values are clearly limited to the practical and useful. The world on stage is governed by codes and conventions but not by ethics, its inhabitants living comfortably enough but existing without spiritual vision. In "this world" of Denmark, as Hamlet says, customs are "flat, stale and unprofitable" (1.2.133). The stage is shut, a claustrophobic, earthbound place, a truly flat world where one can, according to Claudius, "in equal scale [weigh] delight and dole" (1.2.13).[55]

In a space so framed and closed, what is immediately tangible and material becomes the only point of reference. No time other than its own here and now matters to the Denmark on stage; time is beaten "out of joint" to accommodate the desires of the Danish elders, as are joys and sorrows. Death and wedding rites are so closely allied that they virtually exchange places, become "mirth in funeral and ... dirge in marriage" (1.2.12). Gertrude the widow-bride assures her son that mourning the dead very briefly is perfectly normal: "Thou know'st 'tis common, all that lives must die, / Passing through nature to eternity" (1 1.73-4). The Danes in power move quickly. Claudius's suspicion that his nephew knows more than he says provokes his "hasty sending" for Rosencrantz and Guildenstern (2.2.4); later he dispatches Hamlet "with speed" to England and, he hopes, to death (3.1.169). Briefly persuading the king and queen to agree with him, Polonius leaps to the happy conclusion that the prince's eccentric behaviour is caused by "the very ecstasy of love" for Ophelia (2.1.99) – though he says it in such a long-winded way that it nettles Gertrude, that lover of the expeditious, who soon after tells him to hurry up: "More matter with less art" (2.2.95).[56] The outsiders, Rosencrantz and Guildenstern, become trapped in Elsinore's hurry. Claudius explains his urgency to them: "The terms of our estate may not endure / Hazard so near's as doth hourly grow / Out of his brows" (3.3.5-7). Claudius worries with good reason about the hasty and unceremonious burial he gives Polonius; the ordinary Danish people are upset that Polonius was given only an "obscure funeral" and was buried "huggermugger" (4.5.84). The king's messenger, in turn, accuses the same ordinary Danes of regarding only the present moment, of thinking as if "the world were now but to begin, / Antiquity forgot" (4.6.104–5) when they condemn the king and support Laertes.[57]

There are clear signals from the stage that the here and now of the playworld acknowledges no other place and time than Denmark's. The stage asserts a temporal frame that has no contact with the audience's time; it is a place where the past is eradicated, where the future is ignored, and where eternity does not exist.[58] Completely self-involved, this "too solid" stage divorces itself utterly from the reality around it. Only Hamlet is allowed to look outwards. He speaks of a personal sense that there might be something beyond the stage when he assures Horatio, "There are more things in heaven and earth, Horatio, / Than are dreamt of in your philosophy" (1.5.166–7). Later, toying again with the possibility of a wider universe, he describes Denmark as a prison:

HAMLET: Denmark's a prison.
ROSENCRANTZ: Then is the world one.
HAMLET: A goodly one; in which there are many confines, wards, and dungeons, Denmark being one o' th' worst. (2.2.243-7)

Hamlet is trapped in Denmark's secular and parochial here and now. Whenever the possibility of a further dimension arises, the stage on which he stands clamps down on it.

Struggling against the sterility of his stage world, whenever Hamlet is alone with no other listeners but the audience he battles to discover that world which is not Denmark. Isolated from everyone, Hamlet studies those around him: Danes, English players, Norwegian soldiers. In particular, he peers to see whether there is anyone in the playhouse, even "the groundlings, who for the most part are capable of nothing but inexplicable dumbshows and noise" (3.2.10–12). A victim of the stage's closed world, silenced by it, tortured by its contradictory moral values, its promise then withdrawal of spiritual values, Hamlet looks outward – past the edge of the platform, towards the yard and galleries – for understanding, for sympathy, for answers to his questions, to a place where his listeners inhabit a reality complete with all the things missing from the stage world. Although shut off from the stage, the life in the playhouse dominates this play. The living, breathing masses in the theatre, the real pulsating world that Hamlet tries to capture and import to the stage, are the centre of the play. Sadly for Hamlet, he can recognize the solidity, but he cannot touch it. He is snared in a paradox. At the moments when he tries to speak outward to and about the actuality of the people ranged around the stage, he sabotages his own desire with theatricalizing words and gestures.

Hamlet gives the playgoers implicit instructions about the play they are viewing. These refer to playhouse architecture and are largely embedded in the dialogue, in winks and nods to the crowds about their present physical surroundings. For instance, Hamlet speaks these lines:

this goodly frame, the earth, seems to me a sterile promontory; *this* most excellent canopy, the air, *look you, this* brave o'erhanging firmament, *this* majestical roof fretted with golden fire,[59] why it appeareth nothing to *me* but a foul and pestilent congregation of vapours. (2.2.298–303) [my italics]

David Bevington interprets the speech thus:

Its potent symbolism of the cosmos provides an admirable backdrop for Hamlet's speech on the nature of man; its inclusive depiction of the heavens above and hell beneath gives a spatial immediacy to Hamlet's notion that "this goodly frame, the earth" is also "a foul and pestilent congregation of vapours." In the Elizabethan theatre the spectators see a painted heavens corresponding to Hamlet's stirring invocation of "this most excellent canopy, the air ... this brave o'erhanging firmament, this majestical roof fretted with golden fire." (127)

Bevington's view may be taken as an orthodox reading, but I think he is wrong here. In this implicit reference to the playhouse, Hamlet in fact refuses to endorse symbolism. Notice the repeated gestural "this," a positioning word. While this and other gestural words ("look you," for instance) are ostensibly addressed to Rosencrantz and Guildenstern, they also ensure that everyone in the playhouse gazes at the same structures as Hamlet himself. Hamlet says in *this* play the canopy does *not* symbolize heaven; Heaven is in fact just an overhanging roof. Hamlet's speech, therefore, is not an invocation of majesty and excellence, but a reminder to the onlookers that they are surrounded by painted pieces of wood. His instruction to them is relentlessly concrete.

The language of this address forces the audience to see a play-house, not a world. It reverses the old theatrical metaphor that the stage is a world. This perspective is often called "metatheatre," which Patrice Pavis, noting that the term was introduced in 1963, defines as "theatre which is centred around theatre and therefore 'speaks' about itself, 'represents' itself" (210). Referring to this kind of directing of audience attention, Michael Mooney argues that the "phenomeno-logical nature of the [whole] theatrical experience is an essential component of a play's meaning." He continues:

These theatrically self-conscious devices cannot, of course, accurately be called "extradramatic" or "metadramatic": everything that occurs on stage *is* part of the drama. Let us also remember that "audience multiconsciousness" is as basic to drama as the knowledge that an actor performs a role and that there may not, finally, be any such thing as "metadrama." (21)

The point I am making here does not centre on the modern abstract notion of metatheatricality; the play is not theatre about theatre. By reducing his universe to wood and paint, Hamlet's words reinforce the flat world in which he is trapped. They do so by inducing the audience to see the playworld Denmark as reductive. Hamlet also implicitly recognizes the playgoers as themselves. If Hamlet poten-tially sees a stage, he may also be able to see or at least be aware of the audience. His words position static, imprisoning Denmark amidst an organic world, that of the playgoers. The contrast between the two worlds is vital to the play; their division devastates Hamlet. Thus the playgoers are rapt up to the heavens by his gorgeous words, then tumbled brutally back into their places in the playhouse. This goodly frame is a real wooden building; the earth is only the Globe, its echoing boards a promontory jutting into a sea of playgoers. Throughout, Hamlet reminds the playgoers that the building is not a cosmos but a frame structure, created from the Theatre's studs and beams, which Shakespeare had watched being used to build the Globe.

The Denmark of the play, then, is also only a wooden apron stage under a decorated roof, its "Heavens" filled with the playgoers' "steames of strong breath," the stink that Dekker complained of (Gurr, *Playgoing*, 219). Though Hamlet titillates them with hints of the symbolic, he won't let the playgoers disappear into an imagined world; he keeps them located in a real playhouse and in the present moment. Whatever flies upwards from the scaffold's Elsinore hits the playhouse canopy and falls back down onto the platform – like Claudius's prayers: "My words fly up, my thoughts remain below:/ Words without thoughts never to heaven go" (3.3.92–3).

In this play, even the traditional revenge ghost seems to have returned from a world more material than spiritual. Young Hamlet instructs the audience to think of old Hamlet as a solid presence. While the dead king bellows out orders and reminders to his son, Hamlet makes sure the audience knows the "ghost" is not in some ethereal space but under the stage floor: "this fellow in the cellerage" is "hic et ubique," thumping about under the platform (1.5.156–64). He reinforces the notion of ghost-as-body rather than ghost-as-spirit when he praises the below-stage activity as if the ghost were a sapper digging tunnels to bring down the walls: "Well said, old mole, canst work I' th' earth so fast?/ A worthy pioner" (1.5 162–3).

Hamlet *could* make his audience surrender to the illusion his words create, as Tom o' Bedlam does in his deceiving of Gloucester (*King Lear*, 4.6), or as Hamlet himself does with the player who can present "[b]ut in a fiction ... a dream of passion" (2.2.544–5). Indeed, the playgoers may be drawn to the beautiful idea. Nonetheless, Hamlet yanks them all down, moneyed and poor, educated and unlettered, the yard and the galleries, to the concrete reality of being crowded into a thundering wooden frame building, breathing the stinking breath and foul odours of other people.

Why does this matter? Because Hamlet suggests it is better to be than not to be.[60] However wretched one's existence, it is better to be in a London theatre's yard and galleries than on the stage; better to be smelly and real than to be Hamlet. Hamlet is trapped on the wooden platform; the playgoers inhabit a substantial world. He knows that matters.

The Denmark playworld is limited and static. There, Hamlet's friend Horatio is honorable; however, rather than being the unhappy philosopher, Horatio is immune to Elsinore's distasteful world. Hamlet sees his friend

> As one in suff'ring all that suffers nothing,
> A man that Fortune's buffets and rewards
> Hast ta'en with equal thanks ... (3.2.64–6)

The gap between Hamlet and Horatio cannot be bridged. His peer Laertes is an unapproachable squib; his father is more or less dead; his old companion Yorick is very dead; Gertrude is lost to him as a mother and Ophelia as a lover.[61] Shakespeare has constructed for this play a tightly self-referential stage, which no-one, not even the young, escapes, unless through death. Suffocated, alone, Hamlet desperately needs release and relief from the "weary stale, flat and unprofitable" uses of his on stage world. He is silenced and tormented, a prisoner in a closed, basely material world. Hamlet tries to see beyond the Elsinore stage to obtain answers to questions; to gain understanding, sympathy, and reassurance; to vent anger and frustration. For all these reasons he gazes outward over the edge of the platform, towards the yard and galleries where there are listeners who possess what is overtly elided from the stage: a wider actuality under a real sky. He has to talk outwards because there is nobody to talk to inwards. As noted earlier, this is not metatheatricality as it is generally defined – theatre talking about theatre; rather, this is a rallying of the crowds (particularly the "understanders" massed around the stage) to have them thrust their substantiality – their awareness of Southwark's sky above the Globe, the jostling of body against body in the yard – into the play. It is theatre that tries to bring the audience's concrete, physical here and now onto the platform in a vain attempt to save Hamlet from the masquerade that is Elsinore.

Hamlet's second set of instructions, those he gives to the playgoers about themselves, are the much-discussed speeches usually referred to as "soliloquies." These are often viewed as dissociated internal speeches. For instance, Elizabeth Burns writes that "Hamlet does not directly address the audience nor does the presence of the audience seem to be necessary for the effectiveness of such speeches. In fact the full implications of these soliloquies are better grasped in reading"

(54). I disagree profoundly with this view: the withdrawn speaker so cut off that his words are more accessible in solitary reading than in communal listening. As I shall demonstrate, the audience is not only very much being addressed but is essential; any "implications" of the soliloquies – let alone full information in them – are grasped only when Hamlet struggles to explain his problems to a diverse crowd of people who at the moment of his speaking stand or sit shoulder to shoulder in a real world. In my view the playgoers are truly the other half of a conversation.

Anne Righter, with greater awareness of the flexibility of the playhouse stage, describes the Shakespearean soliloquy as one of the "mediating devices by which the audience might be referred to indirectly without disturbing the illusion of the play" (86). I have difficulty even with this view, since Righter's whole argument sets up playworld and audience world as not only essentially but often desirably discrete. In fact, she grants illusion (playworld and stage) primacy over the "the tyranny of the audience."[62] Bernard Beckerman, too, maintains that for the most part the early modern platform supported an autonomous playworld. He locks Hamlet's speeches firmly into a closed theatrical space where they are internal debates not spoken to playgoers but overheard by them:

Most of Hamlet's soliloquies suffer if the actor insists on using them to confide in the audience. They so much embody internal dissension or dismay at what Hamlet sees about him that efforts to externalize them often dilute their impact. In considering soliloquies, then, we should distinguish between those that are distinctly outward directed, to the audience, and those that have a somewhat different focus. (117)

Robert Weimann has made an immeasurable contribution to our understanding of the history of popular English stagecraft, including the continuing tradition of a fluid stage. Nevertheless, his view of how Hamlet's addresses contact the audience is surprisingly similar to those of Beckerman and Righter. According to Weimann, the prince only obliquely acknowledges audience presence:

In *Hamlet* there are still signs of direct address (4.4.47) but these are admittedly quite rare. More characteristic of a play like *Hamlet* is an indirect audience contact that operates through an awareness of the theatrical medium itself. Such is the case when Hamlet compares his own inactivity with the effusions of the player moved to tears by the emotion of his role. (222)

On the far side of the soliloquy/direct address debate, various critics read Hamlet's speeches as making open and explicit contact with the playgoers. J.L. Styan, for example, argues: "The big speech, with the actor confronting his audience ... was always open to the audience and was never a mumbling into beard or bosom in a simulation of naturalistic thinking, as if the spectator were not there" (165). Stephen Greenblatt proposes that Hamlet's speeches are "delivered in direct address to an enormous outdoor public assembly" (87). Wolfgang Clemen contends that Hamlet's addresses (and many other characters' "*solus*" speeches) are sent outward, although, unlike Greenblatt, Clemen offers a vision of intimate rather than public address:

Direct address of the audience is important for the understanding of Shakespeare's soliloquies. The open stage protruding right into the pit, with the audience on three sides, favoured close contact, even intimacy, and a secret understanding between the audience and the soliloquizing actor who was able to project his emotions by means of gestures, physiognomy and stage business. (4)

John Russell Brown goes even further in fusing player and audience experience: "The actors did not address the audience as if it were in another world. There was a reciprocal relationship; the audience could participate in the drama as easily as the actors could share a joke or enlist sympathy" (44). But Brown, I think, is insufficiently clear about the variable nature of the contract between actor and audience: specifically, the shifting dynamics of the connection of stage and playhouse in Shakespeare (and other early modern playwrights – here I think especially of Middleton). The public playhouse dramatists had a staging system in which they could both close off and open up the "reciprocal relationship" between players and playgoers; the scaffold's proximity to its audience could just as well shut out the playgoers as pull them in. However, when and how the dramatists used each of these strategies is what matters.

Robert E. Wood argues along similar lines, that in

soliloquy ... the speaker is ... circumstantially addressing a theater audience [and that] the substance of the address usually bears out the paramount importance of the audience ... To be aware of ourselves as audience, as we are when we are directly addressed, is to be aware not only of our privileged perspective (an awareness that disengages us) but also of our process of synthesis (an awareness that reengages us). (91)

Wood puts forward important points in his ideas of the "paramount importance of audience" and the simultaneity of disengagement and synthesis in soliloquy. Yet his, too, is a wholesale explanation, as if every opening out by actor to playgoers served the same purpose. His description skirts various questions. "To be aware of ourselves as audience" fails to consider, "What kind of audience are we conscious of being?" Was there diversity of awareness among the huge crowds in the public playhouse? Nor does Wood clarify to what degree, by what method, to what effect, each individual play exploits the "talking to the audience," nor the matter of when playgoers are conscious of themselves as "audience" – either as a community in a theatre with no other present identity, or as a crowd of separate individuals thinking of their different lives. Most importantly, Wood leaves unanswered why Shakespeare and other playwrights would want to make their audiences aware of themselves in this way.

In an insightful study spurred by Weimann's notion of *figurenposition*, Michael Mooney describes the reworking of the interplay of medieval theatre's platea and locus by Shakespeare and other early modern playwrights: "Renaissance drama is a theatrical transaction in which an actor may "break through" the "fourth wall" to engage the audience, alternatively standing within the play, as a participant in the drama, and "outside" the play as its commentator or presenter" (21). Commenting on Hamlet's idiosyncratic *Figurenposition*, Mooney argues that "Hamlet speaks in an idiom and from a figural position shared *with the spectators*, who delight in the irreverent mocking of illusion-bound characters ... Only the spectators truly know what troubles him" (89). Two points here are, to my mind, suspect. First, on this particular stage, within the dynamics of this particular play, in either aside or soliloquy, whether through idiom or figural position, Hamlet may indeed constantly seek to "share" with the spectators, and may partially succeed in doing so, but he can never fully do so. Second, the playgoers do not know what troubles him, nor do they ever discover it. Mooney is successful in showing that Shakespeare uses and transforms old traditions, but Mooney's Hamlet is too equal and honest a companion to the playgoers.

None of the studies I have discussed deals adequately with how Hamlet's addresses work on the stage that Shakespeare set up for this specific play in a particular playhouse, or to what effect Shakespeare exploits the changes to stagecraft wrought by writing for the commercial stage. Allusions to the "fluidity" of the Renaissance stage and to player-audience "complicity" are copious in writings on Shakespeare's plays, yet any early modern playwright could invent a stage that freely acknowledges the playgoers or create one that utterly refuses to see them. What critics have rarely explored in detail is exactly when and how each strategy operates, and what kind of opening up to the audience is exploited on the playhouse stage.

My own view is that Shakespeare's dramaturgy is not just stage centred, as many literary and performance critics argue; rather, it is persistently playhouse and playgoer centred. In taking this perspective I mean to avoid the much-touted "metatheatricality" of *Hamlet*, an interpretation that I see as a distraction leading us to concentrate on this play as a debate about theatrical illusion or the arbitrariness of life's experiences. Instead, Hamlet's so-called soliloquies try to siphon the concrete world of the audience towards the stage, as his references to the playhouse also do. In Shakespeare's "theatre of the whole," Hamlet's soliloquies – what Clemen calls his "merciless self-interrogation" (121) – are also open and unremitting interrogations of the audience's immediate experience. In other words, Shakespeare, as a practitioner of a theatre of the whole (like some other practitioners in the early modern commercial theatre),[63] locates the play's meaning not simply on the stage, but squarely and equally in the yard and the galleries. When the stage withdraws from the auditorium, it builds a fake world away from the audience, distant and/or self-contained. But when Hamlet on the scaffold acknowledges the crowds, aspects of their physical presence pressure the play itself. In establishing the proximity of Hamlet to the audience in his second set of instructions, I also take a fresh look at the ways he talks to the playgoers, the means by which he forges – in both senses of the word – a contract with them. Hamlet makes a total of seven speeches in which he instructs the audience to think about their own reality; three of these will be examined here, though my argument applies equally to the others.

Hamlet's open addresses all express concern about the actual world's universal values. He craves the reality lying outside the playhouse walls from which the audience has come in, desiring it to provide answers to his questions. He appeals to the playgoers for release from the prison of Denmark, from his isolation. Like many of the platea figures in the guild plays, such as the shepherds and Noah, Hamlet needs to talk to people in an ordinary world, to verify that they understand him, to hope that they can help. Like the guild drama characters, Hamlet is simultaneously painful and comic, naive and profound. But because he is also a member of the unreal crowd on stage, he has to battle with the platform's edge. Often he is reminiscent of the extrabiblical or dislocated figures who addressed medieval crowds in ambiguous and equivocal words, as if they belonged neither to the

playworld nor to the world of the audience. To some extent the playgoers' living, listening presence fills the human and existential empti-
ness of the "sterile promontory" that terrifies Hamlet, but he is also
riddled with anxiety that they may not really exist.

In my view of Shakespeare's dramaturgy, he is heir to a highly
developed tradition of English stagecraft. His words often make most
sense when spoken using old native strategies of address. Such staging demands not only that the actor playing Hamlet drift about the
metaphorical edges of the Elsinore playworld, but also that he physically move around the platform, look the audience in the eye, strain
his head back to glare up into the galleries, skirt the edge of the stage,
and grab at those in the yard, desperate to find someone who will
respond. To sort out his worries about sex, life, death, revenge, good
and bad behaviour, Hamlet leans outward and tries but fails to grasp
at the audience's reality. Because Hamlet's contact with the playgoers
is active, fluid, and ambiguous, I prefer to use the term "open
address" rather than "soliloquy" or "direct address" for his seven
speeches to the audience.

The first of these speeches to be considered comes when Hamlet
turns to the audience after hearing and watching the travelling player. The world is, first, that of theatrical discourse, and, second, that
of Englishness. As David Mann points out, Hamlet's "references to
the 'late innovation' of children indicates an immediate contempo-
raneity, whilst the remark about 'Hercules and his load too' invokes
the very theatre in which the performance is taking place" (44). Even
though it's old style theatre, it is obviously a world much more
familiar to the playgoers than Elsinore is. Hamlet moves away from
that alien world and towards the playgoers' real world and experience. Upon listening to the English actor, Hamlet turns to the audience and says, "Now I am *alone*." The ensuing open address, his final
gesture towards the departed world of Elsinore, begins with a joke,
a laugh for the crowds in the playhouse. Then he hurls at them a
bombastic speech: "O what a rogue and peasant slave am I." He is
desperate to tell them that the English player they have just watched
is a fake, while he is real, and in real agony. But all he can manage is
to sound like a windbag actor casting about for some response from
the crowd. Hamlet postures and declaims. But he also interrogates
the playgoers trying to provoke answers about how to be real.[64] He
gestures to the space just vacated by a player whom both he and the
whole playhouse have watched: "*this* player *here*" [my italics]. He
reminds the onlookers that he and they have shared an experience.
Hamlet's questions may well push the audience right to the brink of
replying out loud; his words and implied gestures demand eye

contact so insistently that perhaps the Elizabethan playgoers standing around the stage or leaning down to see him may have teetered
on the edge of letting him know what they thought, as York's citizens may have when their neighbours, the pinners, stood close to
them asking them to admire their work, asking them where the
missing hammer was.

> Am I a coward?
> *Who* calls me villain, breaks my pate across,
> Plucks off my beard, and blows it in my face,
> Tweaks me by the nose, gives me the lie i' th' throat,
> As deep as to the lungs? *Who* does me *this*? (2.2.571–5) [my italics]

Here Hamlet instructs the playgoers to treat him like a clown in the
old folk plays or like a ranting Herod – to jeer and pluck at him. He
insists on close physical contact, locking eyes with particular members of the audience, asking them to respond: "Who calls me villain?
... Who does me this? Howard Mills proposes a similar way of reading *Hamlet*'s dramaturgy:

There's a smart technical term for this element of dramatic writing: *deixis*.
Hawkes's survey of new critical approaches gives a succinct summary:
drama exploits the way that "language itself performs actions"; *deixis* is "the
process whereby language establishes the context in which it is taking place
and *deictics* are those words, such as the pronouns I and you and the adverbs
here and now, whose meaning can be pinned down by a specific context"
(Hawkes, 1986: 294). This can obviously be related to many passages
analysed in the present book, from York's or Capulet's twists and turns to
Henry addressing Hal in terms of "you" and "I" versus "him" and "them";
from Hamlet's "On *him*, on *him*! Look *you there*, look how *it* steals away" to
Leontes's "many a man there is (even at this present, Now, while I speak
this)" ("yes, you, sir, you in the second row: are you sure you know what
your wife's up to while you sit here enjoying the play?") Perhaps this "deictic thrust" (Hawkes's phrase) is what we should hear in Hamlet's "Frailty,
thy name is woman!" ("Yes, madam, you in the front row with the low-cut
dress and inch-thick, knee-deep make-up: I mean *you* as well as the rest of
your sort"). (212)

Of course, there is no real threat of death here, that someone might
jump up from the stage or playhouse and really stab or club him. It's
only comic danger. This is an over-processed, over-familiar role. The
worst that can happen is that Hamlet might get treated like a stage
clown, like Tarlton. And that wouldn't be surprising because this is

how he acts in front of the audience, self-deflationary, a conscious but
unwilling joker as he prances around the fringes of the stage, literally sparring with the playgoers, daring individuals among them to
shout or grab at him.[66] Hamlet is desperate in his fear that he is not
fully human. Lashing about in his own fury at himself, Hamlet
becomes a parody of himself, a second-rate actor. He is a grotesque,
a stage fool, and a bad one at that, girdled by the playgoers' substantial and diverse realities, which they cannot lend him.

Hamlet instructs the crowd to answer his questions. In the "To be
or not to be" open address, however, he erases his whole being from
his words, he unselfs himself, and hands the onlookers a debating
point. He does not once use "I". In the opening words, he casts everything in non-finite verb forms:

> To be, or not to be, that is the question:
> Whether 'tis nobler in the mind to suffer
> The slings and arrows of outrageous fortune,
> Or to take arms against a sea of troubles,
> And by opposing end them? (3.1.55–9)

This speech is notoriously open to interpretation.[67] In my view,
many elements – the infinitives, the use of a distancing "that" rather
than "this," and the shaping of the speech as a universal worry –
work to implicate the audience in the address. Hamlet refuses to be
alone in his dilemma. Yet whether to kill oneself, or not, is a question
impossible to answer – at least in the solid world the playgoers have
come in from. It is in this speech that his self-erasure has located it.
He's forcing his listeners into a muddle, asking them to supply what
they can't give – as per Steven Booth's famous observation that this
play is a tragedy of an *"audience* that can't make up its mind" (152)
[my italics]. But it is a real questioning of alternatives. Unfortunately
for the motley crowd, with his neat employment of the distancing
"that" rather than "this" – which puts the question out "there" in the
audience rather than "here" on the stage, with him – Hamlet has put
into their laps two dreadful opposites he defines as the only question
one can ask. And so it is for Hamlet at this moment in the play. But
he drops it into their world and their now.[68]

As always, Hamlet tries but fails to get to the fullness of the audience's reality. He speaks words about familiar, real-life fears, which
connect with the audience like those of the guild drama. For instance,
the shepherds' terrible flat despair spoken to medieval audiences is
echoed by Hamlet's "dread of something after death." But, unlike the
shepherds, Hamlet is indirect with his listeners. I think Hamlet looks

straight at the playhouse crowd during this speech; catches the eye of some reluctant audience member, thereby forcing onto him or her unanswerable but ultimately dangerous questions about the basic laws of an actual universe. He instructs the playgoers directly to confront ultimate life issues: death, salvation, and damnation – yet as he begs for understanding, he repels it. His words are provocative and equivocal – in this he is reminiscent of the medieval devil or nonce play impresario. Most disturbingly, Hamlet wavers on the verge, once again, of making his struggle to grapple with reality into a superficial joke:

> To die, to sleep –
> No more; and by a sleep to say we end
> The heart-ache and the thousand natural shocks
> That flesh is heir to; 'tis a consummation
> Devoutly to be wish'd. (3.1.59–63)

This is just as shocking as what's said by Faustus, another Wittenberg alumnus. Hamlet foregrounds the absence of God from this philosophy when he reworks Christ's last words (*"consummatum est"*) to talk about suicide, then uses "devoutly" to modify a desire for self-murder. Then he shifts from the impersonal non-finite to the communal, using "we" and "us", whistling like a man in the dark, trying to force the people in the playhouse to think as he does. He asks,

> what dreams may come
> When *we* have shuffled off *this* mortal coil,
> Must give *us* pause. (3.1.64–7) [my italics]

Implicit in Hamlet's words is the assumption that everyone in the audience would rather put up with a beast's life because of the dread of something nasty in the woodshed of the afterlife.

> *Who* would fardels bear,
> To grunt and sweat under a weary life,
> But that the dread of something after death,
> The undiscover'd country from whose bourn
> No traveller returns, puzzles the will,
> And makes us rather bear those ills we have,
> Than fly to others that we know not of? (3.1.75–81) [my italics]

He nags at this problem, listing a number of ways all lives are difficult:

For *who* would bear the whips and scorns of time,
Th'oppressor's wrong, the proud man's contumely,
The pangs of despis'd love, the law's delay,
The insolence of office and the spurns
That patient merit of th' unworthy takes,
When he himself might his quietus make
With a bare bodkin. (3.1.69–75) [my italics]

What Hamlet describes in detail is messy real life.

Once again, having pulled it toward him, he pushes the world of the audience away with a disturbing deflation from the ironic loftiness of "quietus" to the homely, concrete "bare bodkin" that Shakespeare would have seen in his father's workshop. Rather than serving to make his meaning plain, this fall to the trivial twists Hamlet's argument from the clear and honest to the untrustworthy. He speaks outwards into the playhouse space, challenging people who live in a complete reality. Straining his eyes to see "that" distant world, he fails, turns his back on the playgoers, and retreats into Danish consciousness:

And thus the native hue of resolution
Is sicklied o'er with the pale cast of thought,
And enterprises of great pitch and moment
With this regard their currents turn awry,
And lose the name of action. (3.1.86–90)

His old, reductive physicality takes over. As it was for the English stage fool, body is everything; intellectual debate and "resolution" cause jaundiced skin (he's joking again). The highest enterprise never leaves that world. "Pitch" is the highest point in a hawk's flight; in Hamlet's world, his Denmark, even the best action has limited flight; it falls back down, is never transcendent – like the playgoers' breath, it is stopped by the canopy.

Unable to get the go-ahead from the playgoers to kill himself, Hamlet asks them, in the third open adress to be considered, whether he can kill someone else. As the prince and the audience watch Claudius on his knees, Hamlet's opening words to the crowd are like a joke spat out of the side of his mouth. In fits and starts, Hamlet rationalizes for the playgoers his reluctance to kill:

Now might I do it [pat], now 'a is a-praying;
And now I'll do't – and so he goes to heaven,
And so am I [reveng'd]. That would be scann'd:

A villain kills my father, and for that,
I, his sole son, do this same villain send
To heaven. (3.3.73–8)

Here, the stress falls on the repeated "now," "so," "I." In combination, the comically abrupt "pat" (applied to murder), the monosyllables, the three short clauses, the broken second line, all make his resolution suspect. Hamlet sounds breathless, unreflective. Deciding that killing Claudius *now* would not suit, he decides to save the murder for later, when Claudius is "full of bread / With all his crimes broad blown" (80–1). Hamlet debates the spectators' anticipated reply: he does and does not want them to tell him to do it. But his words tease them to the point of doing so. There is nothing heroic about this plan. The register, the tone, the diction ("full of bread") are comically deflating. Though the reasons he gives for delaying the murder are sound, his way of presenting them makes his refusal to act seem oddly pedestrian:

When he is drunk asleep, or in his rage,
Or in th'incestuous pleasure of his bed,
At game a-swearing, or about some act
That has no relish of salvation in't –
Then trip him, that his heels may kick at heaven,
And that his soul may be as damn'd and black
As hell, whereto it goes. (89–95)

Hamlet trivializes murder, likening it to a man doing a pratfall: "that his heels may kick at heaven." Hamlet's use of "relish" for salvation – bodily appetite, not the soul's need – is farce. Hamlet works the playgoers, his only auditors, trying to wangle out of them their indulgence for both his reluctance and his resolution. He asks them to feel sorry for him because he's reluctant, but he also asks them to give him permission to murder. Once again he instructs the real world to do what it can't do.

Hamlet's last instruction of the play is given to Horatio specifically, but it is still about the playgoers. When he lies dying, Hamlet offers no explanations. Instead he orders Horatio to "report me and my cause aright / To the unsatisfied" (5.2.338–9). Hamlet looks beyond his friend to "you that look pale, and tremble at this chance, / That are but mutes or audience to this act" (5.2.334–5). Anne Righter describes this as "radically alter[ing] the structure of the stage" (147), sweeping everyone into the playworld, into the court, as Danes. In fact, Hamlet's words do not "radically alter" the structure of the play. Hamlet has searched for this audience all the way through. But they are not Danes – they are what they have always been: English playgoers standing in the Southwark playhouse. It would be hard even for them, who have been closest to him, to tell exactly what Hamlet's cause was, to report him aright. It's impossible that Horatio will be able to do so either.

In much of Shakespeare (and certainly in *Hamlet*), the relationship between characters and audience is as important as the relations among the characters on the stage. In many of Shakespeare's plays some characters stay within the closed scaffold and have no dialogue with the audience, while others speak outwards into the playhouse. Those who do not see the playgoers often inhabit a place that constructs itself as amputated from the real world. In Hamlet's two sets of instructions to the playgoers, about the playhouse and about themselves, Shakespeare has Hamlet make several attempts to step off this scaffold into the yard and galleries, to gather living solidity to himself. Hamlet fails every time. I reiterate: this is not metatheatricality as it is usually understood. If such an awkward term existed, I would be tempted to use "metaplaygoerality"; that is, neither the theatre nor the stage talks about itself. The play as a whole – words and staging strategies – foregrounds the playgoers, makes prominent the presence of living, everyday people. The play's strategies do not operate as Brecht's distancing tactics do, by distancing the audience to generate disengagement and critical evaluation of present society. What is needed is a fresh way of considering Hamlet's so-called self-conscious self-reflexiveness. *Hamlet* is not a play about a play. Its primary device is to make its audience dominate the stage, as the late medieval dramas of the northern cities of England did, to promote not the stage but the surrounding ordinary living reality as the play's major referent.

The pain of Hamlet is not what he says – he hardly stops talking – but what he can't say because he is stuck inside a dehumanized universe. To the end, Hamlet is indirect with his audience. Although he thinks hard and aggressively, he is not deeply philosophical; he is either muddled or equivocal. It is hard to tell which. At certain times, he speaks with the genuine platea voice; at others, he quibbles and jokes like a dislocated figure. He botches actions, he is obtuse, he misses obvious answers. He cobbles together proverbs, tags, theatrical histrionics, in desperate attempts to touch something real. In the auditorium lie the missing parts of the philosophy that he so urgently seeks and that can never be supplied. Out there is the knowledge of "a divinity that shapes our ends, rough-hew them how we will" (5.2.10–11). This play's staging system, its physical "theatre of the whole," is set up so that it is a partial, one-dimensional, flat cosmos. No-one here can "reveal the depths of [the] embodied self" (Mooney, 86) because everyone, even Hamlet, is disembodied by this scaffold. Here lies the tragedy of Hamlet: only he knows that to be fully human it is necessary to leap off the edge of the platform.

Out in the playhouse, then, lie the missing parts of what Hamlet senses he needs to be a self.[69] But they can never be supplied, nor can Hamlet reach a full understanding of what they are or might have been for him. Even his death eulogies seem "unprofitable." The audience may hope Horatio is right, that "flights of angels" will sing Hamlet " to [his] rest" (5.2.360), but they have been shown that this playworld has little sign of angels hovering in its aloft. The playhouse canopy does not offer a way to heaven; it simply screens out the sky and keeps in the bad breath.

At its close the playworld shrinks into wooden boards where Fortinbras gives orders for the disposal of Hamlet's body, for that is all Hamlet has become. Fortinbras's brief final speech is grandiloquent but empty. Hamlet is to be borne out "like a soldier" (5.2 396). He is not one; all that can be said, says Fortinbras, is that he might have been one if only things had been different. What speaks "loudly for" Hamlet is "soldier's music" and "the rite" of war. However, Fortinbras has just said that Hamlet never was a soldier; nor is there any evidence that in the future he would ever have to go to war, let alone be good at it. So the play closes full of sound signifying nothing.

The play is over for the London playgoers. They have been repeatedly instructed by Hamlet to be aware of the deficiencies of the stage's Elsinore, to watch its bounded materiality, and to set against it their present actuality, the full reality Hamlet envies. Only the crowds in the yard and galleries have heard Hamlet's attempts to tell his full story. They are now, as they have been for the duration of the play, the "unsatisfied," a diverse group of people that Hamlet has taunted, harassed, equivocated with, even while pleading with them to understand, to empathize, and to give him the impossible. In the end, these listeners are able to go out of the playhouse to where a real sky overhangs that vital world that Hamlet could glimpse but never reach. He sloughs off his burdens onto the audience, dropping it over the stage edge into their world. The playgoers know the answers to these questions – but they can't make Hamlet hear them.

"I," "You," and "We" in King Lear

In *King Lear* Shakespeare again derives tension from the alternation of the closed and open stage. However, in this play he shifts the threshold twice. *King Lear* begins with a stage dominated by "I," a playing space of closed address inhabited by England's powerful few. Later, the stage represents the outdoor world of England's countryside, where characters address the audience as "you." Then it opens entirely, and characters on it say "we," meaning everyone in the playhouse, actors and audience.

As the play opens, the playworld is England's court. Always ignoring the presence of the playgoers, here characters speak from a stage as impenetrable as the walls girding their castles. Both king and court speak a language intended to exclude everyone who is not one of them. As Lear passes on his "rule, / Interest of territory, cares of state" to a new generation, with massive formality he divides up the "shadowy forests," the "champains rich'd" with "plenteous rivers," and the "wide-skirted meads" of an England that seems to be wholly prosperous and to belong only to the rich (1.1.64–5). To everyone on stage, England is an unpeopled tract, to be parcelled out, then owned by those in power.[70] Lear's elaborate speech alternates with the echolalic code spoken by his daughters Goneril and Regan. They give the old man what he wants to hear, thus getting what they want for themselves. Goneril: "Sir, I love you more than words can wield the matter; / Dearer than eyesight, space and liberty" (1.1.55–6). Regan: "I am alone felicitate / In your dear highness's love" (1.1.75–6). Later, exiling Cordelia, Lear vaunts like any guild play Herod or Pilate: "Come not between the dragon and his wrath. / I loved her most, and thought to set my rest / On her kind nursery" (1.1.121–3). No-one on this scaffold – the king, his two elder daughters, or his sons-in-law – speaks honestly of responsibility or caring for anyone else, particularly for the people who live and work outside the courtly world, among the mapped-out forests, fields, and rivers. "We" on this stage is not just royal and public; it is also utterly singular, a malignant, self-absorbed and excluding "I."

In the opening scene, no-one on stage speaks in open address. Only Cordelia on the scaffold's fringes utters abrupt, alarmed comments as she worries about how to respond to her father's demand for public affirmation of love (1.1.76–8). Her nervous murmurs do not reach any of the other characters on stage; she is heard only by the playgoers. Her words punctuate for them the extravagant closed pronouncements of the others. The tone of her secret conversation with the audience is tentative, uncertain. Yet when Cordelia turns her face away from the audience, looking inwards to the royal world, she speaks with a surprisingly assured "I." Within the playworld, the balanced alternation of "you" and "me" with "I" and "you" in her reply is more at one with its closed formality than were her nervous whispers on its edge. Cordelia is correct but not generous. Her response is taut: "You have begot me, bred me, lov'd me: I / Return those duties back as are right fit, / Obey you, love you, and most honour you" (1.1.96–8).[71]

This closed world quickly drives out all nonconformists. Cordelia and her defender, Kent, are banished. Pushed out by the powerful, they must live in the playworld's interstices, along the periphery of the scaffold, close to the playgoers. In the first two acts of *King Lear*, the edge of the closed stage is inhabited by people who, like the fools of earlier drama, occupy no central position in its social and political world. In the guild plays, it was the extrabiblical characters, often the cheeky servant figures who owed their genesis to folk plays, who offered commentary to the audience on the playworld and conjured up visions of alternative worlds. In *King Lear*, a series of fools – the youthful (Cordelia), the professional (Lear's fool), the vicious (Edmund), the feigned (Edgar), and, later, the genuinely mad (Lear)[72] – talk from the traditional fool's stage space. There, outside the closed elite world, these characters conjure up alternative worlds.

Edmund, Gloucester's bastard son, is at first suffered to exist only on the fringes of society and is alone on stage when he describes his plans to break through the barriers. Like Pykeharnes in *The Killing of Abel*, he professes belief in an aberrant world, a place where his "services are bound" to Nature's "law" (1.2.1–2). Even though he confides in the audience, Edmund's brave new world is as "I"-centred as the court's. Certainly he speaks to the playgoers: but his vision does not embrace them. Instead, his words repel, as he spits out alliterative phrases: "Why brand they us? / With base? with baseness? bastardy? base, base?" (1.2.9–10). Like Pykeharnes, Edmund attacks his listeners. His questions to them are acerbic; he is aggressive, demanding that they see a fashionable weakling in "legitimate Edgar" (1.2.16). This does not happen. Edmund further isolates himself from his only listeners by proposing a new society in which not they but he alone will "grow" and "prosper" (1.2.21). Edmund does indeed grow and prosper in his new world. Both Goneril and Regan fall for the energetic and handsome young man; they vye for his affection, pouring favours on him. And when he succeeds in the court's world, Edmund is absorbed by his own closed "I." He has little time now for his old listeners, the audience; he speaks to them only once more: to crow over his conquest of Goneril and Regan (5.1.57–9).

Like Edmund, Lear's fool chats to the audience from the verges of the stage. As professional fool he has a traditional position in society and on stage: in the court he has verbal license, but no power; as a stage figure he can move between the playworld and the world of the audience. He has repeatedly warned his master that a king can't be expected to give away his royal cake and then expect to eat it, mocking him: "thou hadst little wit in thy bald crown when thou gavest thy golden one away"(1.4.163). Away from his master, alone on the stage, he announces with a fool's inconsequentiality that "This is a brave night to cool a courtezan." Then in four-beat doggerel he predicts the advent of a new world:

> When priests are more in word than matter;
> When brewers mar their malt with water;
> When nobles are their tailors' tutors;
> No heretics burn'd, but wenches' suitors; (3.2.80–3)

Lear's fool predicts a topsy-turvy world where the impossible might happen. He also pokes fun at the abuses and stupidities in the kingdom (and in any society, that of London theatre-goers included). But his "prophecy" sticks at the usual formulaic vision given to stock figures in folk plays. His vision of a new "Albion" is limited; it condemns present society but offers no fresh proposal.[73] Its nonsensical wordplay merely extends his persistent nagging at Lear. Flat, undynamic, the fool's "prophecy" is a closed picture, a standard portrait of legendary England, mythologized as Albion. And unlike the addresses of many stage fools, this one fails to acknowledge openly the presence of listeners, or solicit their participation. It lodges itself on the stage. It is locked in a predictable fool's "I," as closed as any other address on this scaffold. Like Edmund's speech, the fool's address emanates from the edge of the stage, but does not fully travel past it.

Nor does Edgar speak in fully open address when, reborn as a roaming "madman," he too has to speak on the fringes of the scaffold. Living on the margins of society, with no place to stay – neither castle nor village house – he speaks alone on stage, explaining that to "preserve" himself, he will "take the basest and most poorest shape / That ever penury, in contempt of man, / Brought near to beast" (2.3.7–9). Edgar now inhabits not the court but a rural England of "low farms," "poor pelting villages," "sheep-cotes," and "mills." Even this England has its outsiders. Edgar becomes one of the "Bedlam beggars" who wander among the villages using their strangeness to frighten or cajole generosity from countryfolk (2.3. 13–20). Only the playgoers hear Edgar transform his identity into: "Poor Turlygod! poor Tom! / That's something yet: Edgar I nothing am"

(2.3 20–1). Despite his new place on the verges of both stage and society, poor Tom does not see the playgoers. His words sound awkwardly artificial; he uses a quaint rural voice, contorted syntax; he is patently an educated man locked into a stock imitation of the unlettered. And his address still says only "I."

Shifting the stage to open heath from royal castle, Shakespeare forges a closer alliance between scaffold and playhouse. Here Lear says "thee" and "you," not the "you" of public rhetoric, but that of a real person speaking to another human being, as if for the first time he is able to look at another person and really see him. On the heath where both he and his fool are drenched with rain, Lear directs his servant to take shelter from the storm. Earlier Lear has shouted up at the elements in language as excessive as the words he used at court:

> Blow, winds, and crack your cheeks! Rage! Blow!
> You cataracts and hurricanoes, spout
> Till you have drench'd our steeples, drown'd the cocks! (3.2.1–3)

Now Lear sees that the only servant he has left is a person who, like himself, is cold and wet. His voice changes:

> Prithee, go in thyself: seek thine own ease:
> This tempest will not give me leave to ponder
> On things would hurt me more. But I'll go in.
> In, boy; go first. You houseless poverty, –
> Nay, get thee in. I'll pray, and then I'll sleep. (3.4.23–7)

"In, boy; go first": these are vital words. Short, quiet, they characterize the stage moment I call "the drop to the native." This theatrical moment is a complex of staging that draws in the audience. Sometimes it involves a lexical change, a drop to simple native diction, as it does here. It may involve a literal physical image as a figure leans down toward the ground, causing the audience to strain to see, as they did in order to see Christ being stretched on the cross in the York Crucifixion episode, or scratching at the earth in N-Town's *The Woman Taken in Adultery*. Or a character's voice may drop in volume so that the audience must physically lean towards the figure to hear. In the drop to the native the figure on stage is an intense theatrical focus, but he or she is never separated from the audience. Rather, this character is the hub of a wheel whose circumference are the playgoers. Most of all, the drop to the native is a moment that unifies the playworld and the audience's world.

Lear's simple words mark the beginning of the second movement in Shakespeare's use of address in the play. From here on, the stage alternates between the old closed political world and a new open world that recognizes others, a stage that says "you" to the audience, and not just from its edge. When his fool disappears into the hovel, Lear is alone with the audience, not pushed to the verge but holding all the stage. He addresses the spectators in simple English:

Poor naked wretches, wheresoe'er you are,
That bide the pelting of this pitiless storm,
How shall your houseless heads and unfed sides,
Your [loop'd] and window'd raggedness, defend you
From seasons such as these. O, I have ta'en
Too little care of this! (3.4.24-33)

These words involve everyone in the playhouse; the language is intelligible to all. The old-style alliterations generate clarity; they do not bring in bombast. Lear takes his listeners with him into the storm. In the last sentence, Lear's realization of a wider world than he has hitherto known is expressed mainly in simple monosyllables and ends with "this." It is as though he is submitting what he sees to the audience.

Like Edmund, his fool, and Edgar, Lear now proposes a new possibility for England. However, his vision is of an unofficial, unexalted place, where power's fancy words are futile in the face of the need to survive. Moving from thinking about his country only as a map, in his mind's eye Lear sees people beyond himself, the English people missing from the map. At this moment, Lear is overcome by the thought that he, too, is one of those people who may also suffer the discomfort and danger of this storm. He sees himself as a member of a community. Because the stage has earlier been so tightly framed, I think the actor playing Lear may have used the native tradition of platea address here, looking out into the playhouse to see the "you" he speaks of, English people like the playgoers. Perhaps he strained outward to see confirmation of his new vision in their presence. All grandiose words have disappeared; Lear's speech drops into a simple vocabulary, to homely images. A more transparent language, every word must have been understood by both educated and uneducated in the audience. Alone with the playgoers, Lear's drop to the native opens up the stage space. I imagine all playgoers craning to hear his words. Repeating "you" and "your," Lear stands alone on stage, with no-one but the audience round him. It is a deeply significant moment. The people in the playhouse are made the "this" he has taken "too little care of," the England he has treated as abstract symbols on a map. As well as articulating a personal turning point in his character, Lear's speech is a crucial commentary on the whole world of the play. At this moment Lear shifts the edge of his stage outwards by speaking inclusively, not about an abstract, mapped world but about "you." However, he does not yet say "we."

This is left for Edgar to say after Kent and the fool help Lear into the hovel. The young man speaks what is an aside to the audience; it marks the next shift towards the playgoers, wholly involving them. When he told them "Edgar I nothing am," he reported to the playgoers, with some detachment, about an England they had not seen on stage, the countryside and its mad wanderers. Now they, too, actually see Gloucester, and watch Edgar's first sight of him. Edgar turns to them to share his pain at what both he and they see: "When we our betters see bearing our woes, / We scarcely think our miseries our foes" (3.6.105–6). "We" and "our" are crucial words. They push out towards the onlookers in the yard and galleries, yoking them to what they see, refusing to allow the stage to carry the experience alone, locating this agony not just on stage but in the playhouse. It is now that "we" is heard: a "we" that means everyone in the playhouse, characters and audience. This "we" is carried through to the end of the play; castle walls never again shut out the playgoers.

In the final scene, Lear carries Cordelia's dead body on stage. The moment is both comic and horrific. At first Lear is wordless, howling like a wounded animal. Then he uses "you." This time he hectors "you," the people around him who, stunned, watch him holding Cordelia's corpse and who can only stare dumbly at the raging old man. Like those on stage, the audience must know full well that Cordelia is dead:

> O, you are men of stones:
> Had I your tongues and eyes, I'ld use them so
> That heaven's vault should crack. She's gone for ever!
> I know when one is dead, and when one lives;
> She's dead as earth. (5.3.258–62)

Lear's accusation is obliquely aimed at the spectators too. Presumably they also are silent, stunned by Lear's contradictions, by his mad assertion of "I know when one is dead and when one lives," by his flat, dreadful "she's dead as earth," by his abrupt call for a looking glass. Then he denies the death he has just agonized over. Lear is a fool. No-one on stage responds when he asks for the looking-glass to see whether Cordelia's breath will mist it:

> Lend me a looking-glass;
> If that her breath will mist or stain the stone,
> Why, then she lives. (5.3.252–64)

The request hovers in the air like a fool's question, ridiculous, unanswerable. The playgoers know when a corpse is a corpse. Yet perhaps they hope for a miracle as they watch Lear struggling both to acknowledge and to deny Cordelia's death.

Lear is the platform's centre of interest. There is nothing the playgoers can do for Cordelia. Their relationship with her, always slight, is ended. Next Lear insists he can see Cordelia's breath by holding a feather (real or imagined) to her lips. Like Cordelia, he too must be a body low on the stage, stooping over his daughter as he cries: "This feather stirs; she lives! if it be so, / It is a chance which does redeem all sorrows / That ever I have felt" (266–8). The old man crouching over the corpse is the focal point for everyone, for the characters on the scaffold and for the audience in the playhouse. Foolish old Lear watches Cordelia; all others have their eyes fixed on him, attending to the living. As Lear bends over Cordelia, listening for her voice, peering to see her breath, possibly the playgoers – those in the galleries straining down over the rails to see, those in the yard rising up to see onto the scaffold – mimic the watchers on stage, as perhaps the citizens of N-Town did when Christ wrote on the ground. While everyone gazes, news is brought of Edmund's death; Albion resigns; Edgar and Kent are reinstated; but these events are rushed over. The focus never wavers. It remains with Lear until Albion cries out, as he realizes the old man is dying. Lear speaks his final words:

> And my poor fool is hang'd! No, no, no life!
> Why should a dog, a horse, a rat, have life,
> And thou no breath at all? Thou'lt come no more,
> Never, never, never, never, never!
> Pray you, undo this button: thank you, sir.
> Do you see this? Look on her, look, her lips,
> Look there, look there! (5.3.306–12)

Lear speaks only simple English words – no Latinate flourishes, no French "champains." Implicit in them is a desperate request for anyone to say, "Yes, I see her lips move," to make of the tragedy a romance. It is an ending no-one can give him. Surely the playgoers now strain even harder to see and hear him. They are the people whose existence the king denied at the beginning of the play, whose aid he now needs. Lear asks, explains, and thanks in the most direct and ordinary language possible. Dying, he does not bellow or proclaim. The dragon who wouldn't allow anyone close, at this moment wants someone actually to touch him.

Lear's final order, "Look there, look there," includes the audience. The onlookers are necessary to Lear. His last words insist that they look with him at Cordelia. He asks everyone on stage and in the playhouse to see her lips move, to hear her voice. Sadly, only the audience knew her voice was "soft and low," when, at the opening of the play, they alone heard her whispers. I imagine a procession carrying its dead back through the tiring house doors. Locked in private grief, Kent cannot help (5.3.320–1). Edgar is perhaps left alone to speak the epilogue:

> The weight of this sad time we must obey,
> Speak what we feel, not what we ought to say:
> The oldest hath borne most; we that are young
> Shall never see so much, nor live so long. (5.3.324–7)

But his words are inadequate. I agree with Peter Brook's assessment of them as "trite," "a strange ambiguity hidden in [a] naive jingle" (104) and with his description of them as a "disturbing statement – a statement that rings like a half-open question" (105). Yet I think the power of the play's closing actually lies in the words' triteness and inadequacy, and in Shakespeare's refusal to end with a closed certainty. Richard III was left alone, isolated on a closed stage. But Edgar almost speaks for the playgoers, unable to sum up satisfactorily what he and they have seen, unable to propose a brave new world. The audience too has watched the political "I" destroy itself, seen the "dragon" become a "bare fork'd animal." Edgar speaks as one bereft, but he speaks for everyone. Stripped of his colourful adjectives, he is able to find only clumsily rhymed platitudes. "Trite" it may be, yet his speech is moving. The "we" he uses is complex, implying that any hope for the future lies in the community encompassing playworld and real world. If there is any hope of rebirth, any promise of restitution, it lies not only with Edgar. By the end of this tragedy, the play's centre has moved into the whole playhouse, as its dramatic shape has shifted from closed "I," to "you," and lastly to "we." The final "we" asserts Edgar's new identity as ruler. But, unlike Lear's early solipsistic "we," Edgar's "we," like his sing-song commonplaces, places him among ordinary grieving humans, a community that includes the audience.

In guild drama, presence of the audience was vital to the whole play's meaning. Playgoers were "this people," "this world," those who were saved or damned. The final episode of every guild play merged the here and now of doomsday with the here and now of the audience. With equal power, Shakespeare invokes audience presence to create meaning in *King Lear*. He re-opens the playworld to the audience, steadily drawing them in throughout the play until they too are fully included in Edgar's "we."

Hardison links the shape of Shakespeare's tragedies with that of the medieval guild plays, suggesting that "the forms and techniques used in the earliest drama of the Middle Ages are important not only to later medieval drama but to Renaissance drama as well" (292). The tragedies follow the arc of guild play structure by closing with an invocation of the audience. *Macbeth*, for instance, ends with Macbeth denying his human nature and insisting that all human beings, including the playgoers, are merely actors on the playhouse stage. *Hamlet* ends on the sterile promontory, which encompasses the play-house, including the playgoers. In *King Lear* Shakespeare goes even further; he restores the play-audience dynamic of guild drama. By the close of each tragedy, the presence of the audience is an essential element in the meaning of the play. Thus, using the old conventions – talking to the audience, using inclusive language, choosing simple words – Shakespeare arrived at a full rediscovery of open address. In so doing, he invented a stage, this time a fully professional one, capable of saying "we."

CHAPTER FOUR

Open Address in the Romances

In this chapter, I look first at how Shakespeare may first have encountered open address in plays put on in Stratford upon Avon. In Shakespeare's early years, his father John was a man of some stature in Stratford. A glover and leather worker by trade in a town that was the "the acknowledged centre of the gloving trade" (Thomson, 9), John Shakespeare held important civic offices including constable, chamberlain, and bailiff. As Stratford's bailiff, he was one of the few officials entitled to grant licenses to travelling players (Clark, 3). In this capacity, John Shakespeare was among those civic officials who brought companies of players to Stratford and who hosted "two of the most prominent contemporary acting companies, the Queen's Men at the Guild Hall in the early summer of 1569 and Worcester's Men in August of the same year" (Thomson, 10). Perhaps, as Thomson observes, even if "[John Shakespeare's] son was too young then" to see these players, "he was old enough to watch Leicester's Men in 1573 or Warwick's Men in 1575" (10).

Less than twenty miles from Stratford, on the road leading through Kenilworth and Warwick, lies Coventry, then as now a cathedral city and at that time a prosperous commercial centre. Coventry's civic records show the city's guilds heavily involved in a particularly lavish annual play. It would be curious if guild business, civic or religious duties, or even an interest in drama, had not at times taken John Shakespeare to Coventry, possibly accompanied by his young son. Coventry guild play performances took place on wagons that moved through the city (Twycross, 21). However, civic records and the two surviving texts, the shearmen and taylors' Nativity episode and the drapers' Last Judgment, indicate that

Coventry's actors also played in the streets among the crowds. This famous stage direction appears in the shearmen and taylors' pageant: "The iij kingis speykith in the strete," together with the notorious "Here Erode ragis in the pagond and in the strete also" (Craig, 99). In his boyhood, Shakespeare may have stood in a Coventry street, raged at by a sword-wielding Herod (Davidson, 18), or watched guildsmen in "gilded crowns as well as garments of rich brocade or other expensive-appearing fabric" (Davidson, 66) as they bore the Magi's gifts through the city. He undoubtedly grew up among people with stories to tell about Coventry's production, perhaps stories about who among the guildsmen was judged the best of the ranters. His own father would likely have known which Coventry glovers made the "frequently purchased" gloves for Jesus's leather suit (Davidson, 42),[1] or how these craftsmen shaped the skin for the naked body of Christ in the Crucifixion (Davidson, 46). Possibly young Shakespeare gazed at Judaean innocents tossed on spears, as later he made Lady Macduff watch her children killed in sport by Macbeth's henchmen. The Coventry play might have offered Shakespeare first-hand experience of the dramatic potential of open address; perhaps God awed him, John the Baptist admonished him, the devil taunted him, Joseph confided in him, tyrants scorned him.

Furthermore, Shakespeare's likely early encounter with guild plays and their dramaturgy need not be confined to nearby Coventry. While he was young, guild drama, if not still being performed, remained fresh in people's minds throughout England. The critic Bing Bills lists towns that during the sixteenth century still possessed guild plays: "Beverley, Bungay, Chester, Coventry, Hereford, Ipswich, Kendal, Lancaster, Lincoln, Newcastle, Norwich, Preston, Wakefield, York, Worcester, and Louth" (159). According to Bills, "it is vital ... to remember that while the dramas disappeared as early as the 1560's in Elizabeth's reign, a few were still heard of as late as the Jacobean reign approximately fifty years later" (167). In York, the play continued to rumble through the city streets until 1569 (Stevens, 18); Chester's crowds were able to see performances until 1575 (Rose, 17). Wakefield's play, although subjected to Protestant revisions, was produced by the town's guilds as late as 1576 (Rose, 18). In nearby Coventry, the city's play was performed until the summer of 1579 (Davidson, 69).[2] So Shakespeare would have been able to attend performances of guild drama until he was fifteen years old – almost a man.[3]

The first piece of hard evidence for Shakespeare's career in the London theatre is Robert Greene's famous reference to "the upstart crow" in his pamphlet "Greene's Groatsworth of Wit Bought with a Million of Repentance" published posthumously in 1592. Thomson points out that Greene's reference is to a playwright who, "whilst comparatively new to London, has had time to establish himself there" (55). He speculates that in 1590, when Shakespeare was twenty-five, he might already have been an actor (65). By 1592, he was certainly well established, "one of a new breed: a professional actor who had the audacity to write plays that were not immediately distinguishable from those of the university wits. What Greene could not accept was that Shakespeare was the legitimate offspring of a professional theatre that had, by 1590, the confidence to begin living on its own wits" (*Career*, 81).

The twenty-eight-year-old playwright must have known a great deal about guild plays from many sources. First, as noted, his youth spent near Coventry might well have brought him into direct contact with that city's performances. Second, as a young actor making his way before 1590 in provincial theatre, then in London, Shakespeare must have been surrounded by people who knew about the old plays. His fellow actors would have been drawn from all over England; they might have learned their trade acting in or watching their local town's guild drama. Some might well have been those provincial guildsmen who tried their hands at itinerant acting, eventually making their way to the prosperous London market (Bevington, 13).

Shakespeare's frequent references to guild plays make it clear that he remembered civic drama. In *A Midsummer Night's Dream* he gives us the "Athenian" actors and extended jokes about guildsmen and travelling players. In *Antony and Cleopatra*, he makes Cleopatra imagine with terror being displayed by artisans in the streets of Rome, where "mechanic slaves / With greasy aprons, rules and hammers shall / Uplift us to the view" (5.2.209–11). In *Hamlet*, he creates an itinerant company of actors who are obliged to listen to the prince's lengthy exposition on good acting, including his warnings not to "out-Herod Herod" (3.2.14). As a novice actor and playwright, surely Shakespeare talked to everybody about everything to do with his trade, including the old guild plays. If he did not see them for himself, he heard about them from other players and playwrights, as well as from audience members. There is little possibility that Shakespeare was ignorant of this enduring English tradition. Moreover, as I have shown, nonce plays employed many of the techniques of guild plays, particularly the native strategy of open address. No-one doubts that Shakespeare attended Tudor plays, that he knew the dramatic strategies of nonce

performances thoroughly, and that he used them on his professional stage.

I argued in the previous chapter that Shakespeare's career may
well be understood not simply in terms of dramatic genres, but also
in terms of his plays' techniques for connecting with audiences. In
what follows, I will demonstrate that Shakespeare made another
return to the native dramatic tradition late in his career, drawing
more explicitly on the strategies of guild plays and their consistent
open address. The final four plays – *Pericles* (1607), *The Winter's Tale*
(1609), *Cymbeline* (1610), and *The Tempest* (1611) – mark not a great
break from his earlier practices but rather Shakespeare's growth in
embracing more fully the familiar dramatic tradition.

PUBLIC AND PRIVATE PLAYHOUSES

For three of these plays (*Cymbeline*, *The Winter's Tale*, and *The Tempest*), Shakespeare worked with two theatres. In the summer of
1608, the King's Men, a consortium of shareholders that included
Shakespeare, leased the Blackfriars playhouse to use as winter playing quarters.[4] Originally a Dominican priory, Blackfriars had been
in use as a private playhouse from 1576 to 1584. Although the building was located within the bounds of London, it had retained its old
status as an ecclesiastical liberty. Part of the property had been
leased to Richard Farrant, Master of the Children's Revels, until his
death in 1580, then to Paul's company. Until 1608 these "little eyas-
es," the Children of the Chapel and of Paul's, catered one day a
week to elite audiences with elaborate, often satirical, plays (Gurr
and Orrell, 47). In 1596, James Burbage had bought a second section
of the building, containing a hall, a stage, at least two galleries, and
seats on the floor (Clark, 101–2). After 1608, for six days a week
through nearly eight months of the year, Shakespeare's company
played there (Gurr, *Playgoing*, 166),[5] retaining the Globe for summer
playing (Styan, *Stagecraft*, 14). All four of Shakespeare's last plays
were performed at the Globe, while only the three named were performed at Blackfriars.

Admission costs were substantially higher at Blackfriars. Everyone went to the Globe; only those who could afford at least six-
pence went to the private theatre. Gurr comments: "Merchants
and wealthier citizens could afford the indoor playhouses (Beaumont's Grocer is tricked into paying more than £1 in all for his
pleasure at the Blackfriars), but distinctly few of the apprentices
and servingmen could" (*Playgoing*, 75).[6] Since Blackfriars had a

smaller auditorium, the relationship of stage and audience was somewhat different in the two theatres. The sides of its stage were bordered by boxes ("lords' rooms"), so at Blackfriars wealthy patrons were close to the play, while at the Globe the penny understanders stood close to the scaffold (*Playgoing*, 27). Foakes suggests that this change in the social composition of the audience nearest the stage altered the manner of playing, and led to a taste "not only for refinement, comfort, and sophistication, but also for a kind of naturalism" (31). Another reason for what Foakes calls "naturalism" could have been the comparative sizes of the playhouses.[7] While the Globe's capacity was up to 3000, Blackfriars could accommodate fewer than 1000 playgoers, although, because of the higher admission costs, it made more money over a year than the Globe.[8] There were other differences: the whole of Blackfriars was roofed, not just its stage. Continuous playing was impossible at Blackfriars and, because the stage had to be lighted and the candles trimmed, it became a convention at the private playhouse to divide the play into acts, with musicians entertaining audiences with entr'acte music from a large gallery above the stage. They also played quieter instruments than were used at the Globe (Gurr, *Stage*, 160). The drums, hautboys, and bagpipes of open air playing were replaced at Blackfriars by violins, flutes, and recorders, instruments more appropriate to indoor performance in a smaller theatre.[9]

In spite of the staging differences between the private and the public playhouses, Shakespeare's work played in both venues. Shakespeare did not write romances for Blackfriars; he simply wrote romances. Plays he had written years before for the big platform in the public playhouse appeared successfully on the smaller indoor private stage. Since Shakespeare's plays worked as well there as at the Globe, clearly the new playhouse did not wholly dictate how he wrote his last plays. Moreover, the first of these four plays, *Pericles*, was written for and performed at the Globe before the King's Men acquired the Blackfriars' lease, and may never have appeared at the private theatre. At the end of his career, Shakespeare was a master playwright. Neither private nor public playhouse confined him; together they offered him new possibilities. He could now afford to write one play a year and could risk big theatrical gestures – a "resurrection" for *The Winter's Tale*, for example, and a *deus ex machina* for *Cymbeline*. He could take chances and experiment. His last plays saw Shakespeare making new aesthetic choices about his dramaturgy.

SHAKESPEARE AND THE ROMANCE GENRE

The English playgoing public had long shown a liking for a certain kind of play, the highly conventional romance. Various kinds of dramatic romances had gone in and out of fashion during the Elizabethan and Jacobean periods.[10] There were folk romances based on old vernacular tales, such as the anonymous *Mucedorus* (1590), which proved popular enough to be revived for public performance in 1610 (Gibbons, 209). There were domestic romances about home-grown folk heroes such as *George a Greene, The Pinner of Wakefield* (1590), which were reincarnated in Thomas Dekker's *The Shoemaker's Holiday* (1599), a play celebrating London's guild companies (Kastan, 153).[11] There was chivalric romance which, along with classical mythology, formed the basis for the Elizabethan and Jacobean court entertainments, the ceremonious masques that by allusion and allegory flattered their aristocratic audiences (Butler, 127–61).[12]

Romance elevated the familiar to a new status.[13] Every romance, whether folk, courtly, or domestic, transformed the ordinary or natural into something not necessarily but usually belonging to a better world.[14] Many romance characters inhabited a nowhere and nowhen, and were quite unlike ordinary human beings, being single-sided rather than complex characters: wholly valiant, peerless, innocent, or vile. Events were rarely under their control. They drifted or were transported from place to place by happenstance, through a universe where "ordinary time, place and causality [were] suspended or reordered" (Gibbons, 234).[15]

When he wrote his first romance, *Pericles*, for performance at the Globe, Shakespeare was availing himself of the interest in the popular genre. His Jacobean audiences would had some idea of what to expect from the heavily codified world of romance. The playworld would be entertaining and perplexing, flat and stylized, intended to puzzle, amuse, and distance rather than to connect directly to the sense of the everyday.[16] Playgoers could predict that, by the close of a romance, good people would triumph, bad people would die or be punished, the noble and pure would remain noble and pure, and comic characters would always be funny. The fashionable genre depicted a world that was often elite, and always, in the end, comforting – a world where things came out all right. In other words, the stage romance's conventions deal indirectly or allegorically with mundane lives in the streets outside playhouses. Yet Shakespeare's romances, like the medieval guild plays, persistently acknowledge and draw on the immediate living presence of audiences. In doing so they intertwine the otherworldly stories with the stuff of everyday life.

In the previous chapter, I discussed the link Hardison saw between the hope for a new world offered by Shakespeare's tragedies and the hope proferred by the guild plays.[17] Romance offers the possibility that what people want to happen can really come to pass. The guild plays have the stuff of great romance. Their overall narrative is one of hope, relentlessly brought by their authors into the medieval world as familiar but distant Bible stories were linked with the playgoers' everyday lives. Shakespeare does much the same in his romances, shifting the genre, making romance's outlandish places, miraculous events, and strange characters lock step with the world of the audience. He presents a blend of classes, genres, styles. Like the guild plays, Shakespeare's last plays are a mixture. Calling them tragi-comedies, Madeleine Doran notices in them "the inherited tradition of mixture in the medieval drama of the serious and the ludicrous, the pitiful and the farcical" (210). To this "inherited tradition of mixture," I add the mingling of play and playgoers, the integration of the world of the audience and the play-world. Shakespeare's last plays are of both Blackfriars and the Globe; Shakespeare integrates into them socially mixed audiences, not just elite playgoers. Like the guild plays, Shakespeare's romances unremittingly talk to and draw in the real world of *diverse* playgoers.[18]

Shakespeare worked last, then, with a fashionable genre that seemed to thrust a shield between the world on stage and the audience's world. He took the conventions of romance and shattered the disengagement and isolation of the stories by opening them to the vagaries of the real world of his audiences. He tangled romance with a dynamic world where people have to toil but don't always succeed; where material things are important; where what one does, as well as what one is, matters; where people get only part of what they aim for. It is in these plays of strange and amazing events that Shakespeare turned back most explicitly and fully to old guild drama strategies, particularly persistent open address. Much of the rest of this chapter is a discussion of three of the plays: *Pericles*, *Cymbeline*, and *The Tempest*.

Pericles: *Ancient Gower's Open Address*

Pericles is about a hero on the run. The play shifts from country to country, tossing its hero about on stormy seas, robbing him of his wife and daughter, and finally restoring them to him. It also tracks its hero's psychological journey, his flight from himself to his recovery of personal identity.[19]

Shakespeare puts on his stage an old-style expositor, very like
those who led medieval playgoers through the guild plays, to aid the
audience in following this episodic narrative. Like them, old Gower
openly addresses the playgoers. He performs many functions, one of
which is to remind his Jacobean audience repeatedly that this will be
a play in the old style. He explicitly connects the story to old oral
romances, those tales that were "sung at festivals / On ember eves
and holy [ales]" (Prologue, 1.6–7).[20] Gower intimates that he is from
an ancient tradition, whereas the members of the audience are "born
in those latter times, / When wit's more ripe" (Prologue, 1.11–12). He
is "ancient Gower" (Prologue, 1.2), an author come back from the
dead expressly to "sing a song that old was sung" (Prologue, 1.1).
The resurrection of Gower for this task turns a man who once lived
into a figure of romance himself. Like medieval writers, he turns to
an old Latin tag to sum up his thoughts about his tale, and possibly
about himself: "*et bonum quo antiquius eo melius*" (the older a good
thing is, the better) (Prologue, 1.10). Throughout the play, Gower
introduces old-style theatre to a modern audience (as Hamlet did).
Significant events, such as the departure of Pericles and Thaisa from
Simonides's kingdom, are acted out in dumbshow, while Gower
comments on them for the audience (Prologue, 3.14). Gower's words
are also in the old style; for example, in describing how "dovelike"
Marina makes Dionysa's daughter look like a "crow," he tells the
audience

Be't when they weav'd the sleided silk,
With fingers long, small, white as milk;
Or when she would with sharp needle wound
The cambric, which she made more sound
By hurting it. (Prologue, 4.19–23)

The old man rambles on, with more four-beat "drasty rhyming" and
a "medieval" vocabulary, apologizing for "the lame feet of [his]
rhyme" (Prologue, 4.48). Throughout the play, Gower lets his audience know that old traditions are at work.

The most important of these is Gower's persistent use of open
address. He appears eight times to talk directly to the spectators. As
their guide, he signals to them many times what this play will be.
Referring to them as "you" or sometimes "we," he actually sees the
playgoers and tells them he shares their space. Gower's open address
is the audience's primary link with the stage; again and again, he
draws the romance into a world like that of the playgoers. He is their
teacher, indicating how the play opens to their world, his "here,"
"this," and "now" repeatedly positioning the play close to them.[21]

He assumes that they see what he sees, saying "here her we place" (Prologue, 5.11), "this Antioch, then" (Prologue, 1.17), and "this time we waste" (Prologue, 4.1).

Gower tells the audience he is the resurrected author of *Confessio Amantis*, on which the story of *Pericles* is based. He therefore has a double ancestry. The first is a theatrical one in the form of those earnest guides in the guild plays who led medieval audiences from episode to episode. The second is a historical one in the form of a real man, the medieval writer trusted by Chaucer, "moral Gower," to whom Chaucer dedicated his "litel bok" *Troilus and Criseyde*.[22] Unlike the other characters in this romance, then, Gower was once a real person. As a mere man, Gower's claims for his own place in the play are modest. He defines his role as moral guide rather than as stage impresario or as creator of the tale. He is one who simply "stands in the gaps to teach you / The stages of our story" (4.4.8–9). Nevertheless, Gower is utterly reliable as a guide. Earlier, we have seen other guides in Shakespeare's work: *Troilus and Cressida* is introduced by a Prologue who proposes an epic, *Henry V* by a Chorus who, intervening at every act, glories in England's past and confidently promises the spectators tht they will see a heroic king. Neither is reliable. The Trojan War that appears on *Troilus and Cressida*'s stage is no epic; King Henry V is as often mean-spirited as heroic. Gower lacks these guides' theatrical self-confidence; he trundles along nervously and heavily. But he is trustworthy. Gower is both the man esteemed by Chaucer as "moral" and the honest guide from the guild drama who stood on the platea, a member of the audience's world.

Whereas old Gower always speaks directly to his listeners, Pericles speaks to them indirectly. Trying to escape Thaliard's vengeance, Pericles is shipwrecked; he makes his entrance soaking wet. Like Lear, he shouts at the hostile elements that have "bereft a prince of all his fortunes" (2.1.9). Nearby three fishermen compare fish to men, saying that "the great ones eat up the little ones" (2.1.28). Listening to them, Pericles speaks in words meant only for the audience. His speech echoes what Gower has said:

> How from the finny subject of the sea
> These fishers tell the infirmities of men;
> And from their watery empire recollect
> All that may men approve or men detect!
> Peace be at your labour, honest fishermen. (2.1.47–51)

Like Hamlet's exchange with the gravediggers, the scene locates itself in real life and work, among the frailties of human beings. In this brief speech Pericles reminds the playgoers of what Gower constantly tells them: that as well as romance there is ordinary human life here. All through the play, the elaborate paraphernalia of romance is on the stage: its riddles, jewels, spices, altars, tests. But also on stage are the infirmities of a real world. Simonides warns Pericles, "jewels lose their glory if neglected / So princes their renown if not respected" (2.2.14). Built into the romance are markers of the importance of the concrete and material, reminders of the close presence of a world where jewels tarnish if not cleaned, that is, where a prince's fame is maintained only by being honoured.

At the close, Gower offers the playgoers a summation of what they have seen on the stage. The main action concluded, he first notes in his epilogue what has happened to the romance hero and villain, Pericles and Antiochus. These figures, whose progress through life was always predetermined, to whom things just happened, both meet an appropriate ending. Then Gower makes sure that his hearers have not missed the story of those who were not able simply to drift through the narrative living a romance existence. Helicanus, a "figure of truth, of faith, of loyalty," and "reverend Cerimon" (5.3.92–3) like Gower himself have had to struggle, to get through life by their own actions. Finally, on a disturbing note, he describes the fate of Cleon and his wife, killed by their own people, of whom he says, "The gods for murder seemed so content / To punish them; although not done, but meant" (5.3.99–100). The broken syntax seems to offer less assured moral judgment than what Gower passed earlier. Here it is not simply the acts and facts of a person's life that are judged, but also each person's intentions. This is far from the superficialities of the usual romance story, where only the demonstrable can be considered.

All the way through, "moral Gower" has been troubled about how to do a difficult job well. He has had to manage the Globe playhouse. He has had to adapt romance time and space to Jacobean time and space. Harder yet, he has had to align romance events and values with those of an actual London. While the other characters live insulated within their closed romance world, old Gower is faced with the task of trying to bring two worlds together. His speeches are not used only as jokes or employed to distance the audience from a largely incredible narrative.[23] Quite the reverse. Like the guides in the guild plays, Gower is on stage to point up what playgoers might expect romance to gloss over: all the things of an ordinary, infirm world. Like poor old Noah, who got on with building an ark in spite of a "wery bak," old Gower does his job as well as he can.

Most of all, Gower's deictic language places him close to the living world of the audience. Gower can talk to the spectators because he can really see them. He lived as they live. He represents a real body, an aged one that grows tired in the course of the play, a body that in the actual world really died. Shakespeare's Gower prevents the romance from deflating to flat villainy or elevating to heroism the characters on stage. Whenever it seems about to do so, Gower makes the playgoers' reality correct the play. By acknowledging audience presence openly, Gower lets the play elude the usual finished closedness of romance. At the very end, he confirms that the stage where he stands is open to the playgoers, deriving meaning from their lives when he says directly to them: "Here our play has ending" (5.3.102). Gower's closing words anticipate what Shakespeare achieves in his last three plays: an open stage, very much akin to early achievements in English drama.

Cymbeline: *Open Address and the Material World*

Cymbeline tells of a legendary England where people are cyphers, their identity residing wholly in their heroism, their innocence, or their villainy. To portray this ancient Britain, Shakespeare uses elaborate, at times bizarre, staging effects. The trap in both the Globe and Blackfriars becomes a grave for the play's heroine and for a headless villain. The machinery above the stage cranks down an eagle with Jupiter sitting upon its back. *Cymbeline*, then, is not an ordinary history, but the story of some amazing, impossible past made more so by startling, obtrusive theatrical effects.

All the paraphernalia could create a disjunctive relationship between play and audience. Nevertheless, *Cymbeline*'s characters behave like ordinary people on the platea of guild plays: as if none of them sees any difference between their world and that of the audience, openly confiding in, lamenting to, or challenging the playgoers. As Clemen points out: "*Cymbeline* has the largest number of soliloquies of any Shakespeare play, and the greatest number of long ones" (73).

Again and again, characters in *Cymbeline* make the kind of direct contact that Bernard Beckerman considers fitting for rare use only. Used repeatedly, he argues, "direct address" turns playgoers off because it makes them feel "coerced" (121); he suggests that its use should be limited since it easily "degenerates into grandstanding" (121). Beckerman is half right, half wrong. He is right in that audience address in *Cymbeline* is often coercive and certainly "grandstands." The characters' speeches are "stagey"; they often talk in stock phrases or in a theatrically stereotypical style. Yet the bond set up between

play and audience is that of an eminently un-romantic ordinary
world. Beckerman misunderstands the goal of the play's relentless
open address, which revolves the romance world to make it gaze
steadily at the world of the audience. All the conventions of romance
are invoked, yet by its repetitive open address Shakespeare draws
the play into a real material culture. To illustrate the workings of this
strategy, I will look next at the way three men talk to the audience
about the play's heroine, how the heroine talks about her life, and
how the king describes England.

In *Troilus and Cressida*, Shakespeare muddies the shining face of
heroism and removes literary epic to Southwark's brothels. War turns
out to be about sex. Although the characters talk interminably about
war, all the playgoers see is sex. In *Cymbeline*, it seems the reverse is
true. Posthumus, Jachimo, and Cloten all desire Imogen. The three
men seem obsessed; they repeatedly envisage having sex with Imogen, and they tell the playgoers so. Yet no sexual activity takes place.
Through these and other exchanges with the audience, Shakespeare
makes the play propose the romance convention of sexual danger, of
sexual innocence tested, and simultaneously thwart the usual expectations of the genre. Each time the play seems about to follow the predictable high road to sexual tests and perils, Shakespeare redirects it
onto the many by-ways of the material world.

As dramatic romance convention often dictates, the innocent
heroine is subjected to what might turn out to be rape. In order to
win his bet with Posthumus that Imogen can be seduced, Jachimo
hides in a trunk in her bedchamber. Imogen lies asleep; no-one on
stage witnesses Jachimo as he creeps around her room, speaking
only for the audience. The playgoers are made Jachimo's sole confidants while he absorbs "some natural notes" of Imogen's vulnerable sleeping body. But romance is subverted for the audience. The
scene is not eroticised. In fact, Jachimo spends more time detailing
an "inventory" of the furnishings in Imogen's bedchamber – "the
pictures ... window ... the adornment of her bed ... the arras" and so
on (2.2.25–6) – than observing her body. Rather than a scene of
seduction or potential rape, the scene is more like a celebration of
conspicuous consumption. Jachimo's words speak more of lust for
Imogen's expensive belongings than for her body. Finally looking at
her sleeping figure, he notes: "On her left breast / A mole cinque-
spotted, like the crimson drops / I' the bottom of a cowslip"
(2.2.36–7), a sexual detail that he quickly converts into a legal one,
"a voucher, / Stronger than ever law could make" (2.2.39–40). In his
address, lust is transformed into avidity and acquisitiveness. Following the conventions of romance, he longs: "That I might touch ...

But kiss, one kiss!" (2.2.16). Unlike the guildsmen in *A Midsummer Night's Dream*, Jachimo does attribute the conventional lilies and rubies correctly, describing Imogen's skin as "fresh lily / and whiter than the sheets" (2.2.15–16), her lips as "Rubies unparagoned" (2.2.16). But he *doesn't* kiss her: instead, he is satisfied to leave her lips kissing each other, and to compare her skin and her lips to her material goods, her bed linen and jewels. The whole scene is diverted into voluptuous materialism.

Clemen nevertheless claims that the scene is intensely erotic: "When, with the utmost care, he lifts off her bracelet, with the twofold 'Come off, come off' and the epithet 'slippery' (for the bracelet [34,35]), the moment is full of suspense and sensuousness, for this time the risk of Imogen's awakening is very real indeed" (78). My view, however, is that the scene's eroticism is subordinated to or depends heavily on its materialism. Its sensuousness relies more on Jachimo's lascivious delight in the feel of jewellery in his hand than on his potential sexual attack on Imogen's body. In fact, any double meaning seems turned inside out. Jachimo steals not Imogen's virtue but only her bracelet, evidently relishing the theft of an object. In this scene the erotic serves to intensify Jachimo's lingering on the room's opulence, not vice versa; luxury moves away from its earlier sexual meaning towards its modern sense of material splendour. Moreover, Imogen's likelihood of waking up is slighter than Clemen suggests; the event is in the realm of romance. With her bracelet clutched in his hand, Jachimo plans to tell Posthumus that he has "pick'd the lock" of her honour (2.2.41). Jachimo stops there; he is materially "satisfied." Her "treasure" is no metaphor (2.2.42). In Jachimo's open address, what might have been metaphorical has become literal.

The second man to want sex with Imogen is her step-brother Cloten, who is obsessed by thoughts of rape. He tangles up sexual lust with lust for money, gambling, and social status. Cloten's visions of rape are extravagantly ugly, sadistic, and ridiculous. But despite being a violent and thick-headed fool, Cloten knows the power of money. Straightforward bribery can get him into Imogen's chamber: "If I do line one of their hands? 'Tis gold / Which buys admittance (oft it doth), yea" (2.3.66–8). Alone on the stage, he fantasizes that, disguised in her husband Posthumus's clothes, he will violate his step-sister. Confident in his new status as stepson to the king, Cloten scorns the "low Posthumus" and plans to "conclude to hate" Imogen (3.5.78). Cloten forces on the audience a self-indulgent, grotesque narrative, in which he is as much fixated on Posthumus's clothes as on his step-sister's body:

With that suit upon my back will I ravish her; first kill him, and in her eyes; there shall she see my valor which will then be a torment to her contempt. He on the ground my speech of insultment ended on his dead body, and when my lust hath din'd (which, as I say, to vex her I will execute in the clothes that she so prais'd), to the court I'll knock her back, foot her home again. (3.5.137–44)

Later, dressed as Posthumus, Cloten openly exults to the audience about his appearance. He can see no difference between his physique and Posthumus's: "The lines of my body are as well drawn as his" (4.1.9) – a mistake Imogen also will make. Cloten's address is conventional to some degree. In it are the expected romance signals about the villain planning to violate the heroine. However, Cloten, like Jachimo, is constantly diverted by the material. He lusts after Posthumus's clothes; he is even more obsessed by social status. As much as he wants to rape her, he wants Imogen to acknowledge that he, Cloten, belongs to a better class than her husband and dresses and looks just as well.

Posthumus, banished at the outset of the play, will prove to be the branch from which modern Jacobean England sprang. But while exiled in Italy, this father of the nation is capable of betting on his wife's body, wagering on her fidelity. Gulled by Jachimo, he comes to believe Imogen is unfaithful. Alone on the stage, he rages to the playgoers, forcing them (or "coercing" them, as Beckerman has it) to listen to his views on women as a whole: "Is there no way for men to be, but women / Must be half-workers?" (2.5.1–2). Like Mr and Mrs Noah, Posthumus tries to stir up support for his personal perspective.[24] He snarls to the crowds that men are all good, women are all evil. Even his own mother "who seem'd / The Dian of that time" (2.5.7–8), he now argues, must have been by nature sexually unfaithful. His sweeping generalizations directed outwards presumably include every female in the playhouse.

Banished, deceived, Posthumus undergoes many tests. Later he will prove a courageous fighter. However, in his talks with the audience, he is always drenched in self-pity. No hero, he grumbles about how, after their marriage, Imogen would refuse to have sex with him: "Me of my lawful pleasure she restrain'd, / And pray'd me oft forbearance" (2.5.10–11). Recounting his memories lashes him to sexual fantasy. As inarticulate as Othello in his jealousy, Posthumus is able only to stammer out a few words at first: "O, all the devils! / This yellow Jachimo, in an hour – wast not? – / Or less – at first?" (2.5.13–15). He then tortures himself by imagining a lurid sexual adventure between Jachimo and his wife:

> Perchance he spoke not, but
> Like a full-acorn'd boar, a German [one],
> Cried "O!" and mounted ; found no opposition
> But what he look'd for should oppose and she
> Should from encounter guard. (2.5.15–19)

Posthumus races out of a sexual nightmare worthy of Cloten (or Iago) into preposterous generalities, cataloguing at length for the men and the women in the audience every female evil there could be, blaming women for all that is wrong with him and all men, and finally resolving to make public his hate for women. He will

> write against them,
> Detest them, curse them; yet 'tis greater skill
> In a true hate, to pray they have their will:
> The very devils cannot plague them better. (2.5.32–5)

Posthumus "out-Herods Herod," with threats that go over the top into burlesque. Rather than a hero displaying romantic agony, he is a young man in a raging tantrum, flailing about because he thinks his wife has got the better of him. Alone with the playgoers, he has invented a minidrama in which Imogen willingly has had sex with another man, doubly galling since she has withheld it from him.

Posthumus talks more about other women – his mother, women in general, the women in the audience – than about his own wife. Perhaps because he is distraught, he shows very little knowledge of Imogen or of her body. The real Imogen disappears as much from Posthumus's address as she does from Jachimo's when her body is blocked out for him by the sight of the goods in her room, as she does when Cloten sees only himself transformed by Posthumus's clothes. The actual woman is absent from what all three men tell the audience. Moreover there is no real sex in what they say. And in Posthumus's address, there is no real marriage. Posthumus does not know his wife. His raging against all women forces the romance into a contentious physical world, where men compete with women, where husbands fight their wives for control but fail to know them as real individual women.

Posthumus's wife is as absorbed by the material as the men who lust after her. Early in the play, Imogen wishes herself away from the corrupting influence of the court: its power, money, and goods. The first time she speaks alone on stage, she longs for a simple life, a romance heroine's existence in an archaic pastoral world: "would that I were a neatherd's daughter / And my Leonatus our neighbour shepherd's son" (1.2.149–50). Later, lamenting that her life is difficult, she makes the extraordinary statement: "Had I been thief stol'n / As my two brothers, happy!" (1.6.6–7). The false note here is that of romance. Imogen implies that her brothers are happy because they were "thief-stol'n," that they are safe in a romance where things will come out all right. But her troubles are real, and no one knows how real things will end. Later Imogen is astonished to discover that the simple life of poverty does not necessarily make for wholly good people. She is shocked that two "poor folks" misdirect her as she makes her way to Milford Haven (3.6.8). She is also not above using her status to get her own way. Imogen begs the servant Pisanio to kill her because "Against self-slaughter / There is a prohibition so divine / That cravens [my] weak hand" (3.4.76–7). She may plead weakness; however, Imogen is actually putting Pisanio to the test. As his social superior she has power over him and she asserts it to protect herself from the sin of "self-slaughter." Imogen would play the martyred saint, or Isaac to Pisanio's Abraham:

> Prithee dispatch,
> The lamb entreats the butcher. Where's thy knife?
> Thou art too slow to do thy master's bidding
> When I desire it too. (3.4.95–8)

However, the guild plays' Isaac is more real than Imogen's dramatics. In most of the guild plays, a terrified little boy is made to beg his father to kill a sheep instead of him. The meek "lamb" in this play herself issues orders like a "master."

Imogen's problems stem largely from her own false assumptions about money, status, and appearance. When Cloten's headless body is laid in the grave beside her, she wakes from her drugged sleep with no notion that the corpse is not her husband's. She says, to the audience only – there is no-one else around other than the corpse:

> A headless man? The garments of Postumus?
> I know the shape of's leg; this is his hand,
> His foot Mercurial, his Martial thigh,
> The brawns of Hercules; but his Jovial face-
> Murther in heaven? How? 'Tis gone. (4.2 307–12)

When Imogen lay asleep in her bedchamber, Jachimo catalogued her body as he ran his eyes over her. Now, possibly running her hands over Cloten's corpse, certainly as close to it in the grave as she was to Posthumus in her marriage bed, Imogen talks about this body as if she knows it intimately.[25] Yet, although they see her touch the body, the playgoers hear Imogen back away from the personal. She trusts to the body's clothes – to material, external things – to tell her who is lying beside her. The onlooker knows that her sex with Posthumus was dutiful, not passionate; she had no intimate knowledge of his body. Ironically, Imogen earlier complained that living as cavekeeper and cook to honest creatures gave her a sense of unreality that was like "a bolt of nothing shot at nothing" (4.2.300), where "Our very eyes / Are sometimes like our judgements, blind" (4.2.301–2). Now fully aware of being awake, able to tell that the corpse exists tangibly outside her brain (4.2.306–7), she touches the body with words if not with hands, labelling its limbs with the names of classical gods. Lee Bliss rightly observes the blend of "despair and comedy" in the scene: "When Imogen awakes next to the headless body she identifies as her husband's, *Cymbeline* insists on both the tragic intensity of her despair and the grotesque comedy of her mistake, since she in fact mourns over the corpse of the dead villain, Cloten" (254). What Bliss does not note is that Imogen's "mistake" is physical, material. Imogen does not know her own husband's body, even when she actually feels the thighs of the body beside her. She relies on its clothes to make an identification, then distorts its flesh into myth. Her eyes and hands both mistakenly assure her that the dead man is her husband.[26] Imogen is so fixated on the external, so ready to judge by clothes and by status, to depersonalize, that she fails to recognize that this is not the body she has slept with, made love to, spent her married life with. Like her husband Posthumus, she knows little about the real individual she is married to.

This play has another body, and another mistake. Guiderius and Averagus, mourning Imogen's apparent death, spoke this charm over her body in an earlier scene:

Fear no more the heat o' the sun,
Nor the furious winter's rages;
Thou thy worldly task hast done,
Home art gone, and ta'en thy wages:
Golden lads and girls all must,
As chimney-sweepers, come to dust. (4.2.258–63)[27]

The chant is a simple one. This is not conventional, stylized poetry about life and death. It contains no mythological labelling or depersonalizing, no elegant tropes, no luxurious distractions. The song speaks neither of romance nor of obsessive materialism. Like Lear's when he embraces the "poor houseless ones," the voices of Guiderius and Averagus drop to the native. Their diction is simple, not learned or elegant; the verse, in the old style, is a four-stress line. The simple words tell of a real world, the world of the audience, where death alone exempts real bodies from tyranny, fear, and pain. They are sung for the audience. Sadly, although the chant ends with a wish for "quiet consummation," its overall vision is of a world of the dead – not the world of the living that the jailer hopes to inhabit, where "we were all of one mind and that mind good" (5.4.203).

From the opening to the close of *Cymbeline*, there is never "one mind" on stage. Each character is at cross purposes with the others. After the jailer's speech, no one speaks again in open address to the audience until Cymbeline's final words. Things happen very quickly in the final recognition scene when, in accordance with romance tradition, everyone's true identity is established. The wicked (Cloten and the Queen) are destroyed. Those who are able to reform do so; Jachimo, for instance, regrets his lies, renounces his non-British identity, and is forgiven. Belarius, who has hidden the princes from their father for twenty years, tells Cymbeline who the fine young men are, repents, and is forgiven. A soothsayer reports that Posthumus is the new stock from which modern Britain will spring and flourish. The king's sons are reinstated as princes, their heredity confirmed by a birthmark. In turn, the brothers discover that the young lad whom they liked so much and thought was dead is, in fact, not only still alive but their sister. King Cymbeline happily, but somewhat oddly, declares himself "[a] mother to the birth of three." Yet the refrain "come to dust" haunts the ending.

All the recognitions that bring the play to its close are uncomfortable. Even as identities are being uncovered, the smooth face of romance is sullied by reality.[28] At the British court, all is not harmony; class still divides people, as do sex, power, and money. The hero and heroine of romance, Imogen and Posthumus, fail their final tests. Although he had wanted her dead, Posthumus bewails the loss of "Imogen, / My queen, my life, my wife" (5.5.225–6). Imogen, still dressed in a man's clothes, tries to attract his attention but can only manage "Peace, my lord, hear, hear" (5.5.227). Then Posthumus, assuming she is a servant speaking out of place, knocks her down, saying, "Shall's have a play of this? Thou scornful page / There lie thy part" (5.5.228–9). Thus Imogen discovers what life is like without status or money: one has no right to speak. As usual, the level-headed servant Pisanio is the only one paying attention to reality. He calls for help for Imogen and chides his master: "You ne'er kill'd Imogen till now" (5.5.231). Neither Cymbeline nor Posthumus copes well with the revelation. Both are made dizzy, literally staggered by their astonishment: the king cries "Does the world go round?" (5.5.232); Posthumus is overcome by "these staggers" (5.5.231). Only Pisanio physically tends to Imogen, as he first tries to "wake" her, then asks her how she fares. When Imogen sees the anxious face of Pisanio, who she thinks has poisoned her, she asserts the full weight of real social authority: "Dangerous fellow, hence! Breathe not where princes are" (5.5.237–8). Rank and wealth matter; the play returns repeatedly, particularly at its close, to a world where reconciliation can only ever be provisional, where problems remain to be worked out.

Even the final new identity revealed to the audience, the picture of "our" England generated by the chronicle, is not one of unalloyed joy. The king ends the play with a general proclamation for "all our subjects" to celebrate, for London to turn out to see its own triumph. Cymbeline addresses his fellow Britons, the audience in the London playhouse, as "we":

> Laud we the gods;
> And let our crooked smokes climb to their nostrils
> From our blest altars. Publish we this peace
> To all our subjects. Set we forward: let
> A Roman and a British ensign wave
> Friendly together: so through Lud's-town march:
> And in the temple of great Jupiter
> Our peace we'll ratify; seal it with feasts.
> Set on there! Never was a war did cease,
> Ere bloody hands were wash'd, with such a peace. (5.5.477–85)

As Cymbeline faces the playgoers with what is ostensibly a speech of peace and plenty, his words are full of tensions and contradictions. Britain's incense goes up "crooked," rising to the mundanely physical "nostrils" of a god who the audience must remember is simply a mechanical bird up in the rafters. Although Roman and British flags wave together and Posthumus and Imogen are celebrated as father and mother of the English nation, as the play ends, both nations' hands are still covered with the blood of those who died in the war. Although peace is established, Britain still pays tribute. The court will turn to celebration, but it will do so with "bloody hands." The play ends where the dead remain dead. Again, open address draws two worlds together. In the real world, even the most beautiful and heroic will grow weary and old, and "as muk upon mold ... widder away" (Towneley, *Noah and the Ark*, 62–3). In this England, there are no romance endings, not even for "golden lads and girls"; there are only the endings of real people who, "as chimney sweepers, come to dust" (4.2.262–3).

The Tempest: *Open Address and the Great Globe Itself*

Although in *The Tempest* Shakespeare's stage represents a literally insulated world, a remote island, the familiar England of the audience is present everywhere. When, for example, Caliban, who "needs must curse" at his treatment by Prospero, describes the island, he talks about somewhere quite unlike the exotic lands of romance convention; Shakespeare has dragged his stage out of the distant Atlantic or the Mediterranean and dropped it into rural England. Alone on the stage, Caliban tells how he is tripped up, not by foreign porcupines but by English hedgehogs, and the snakes that wind about and hiss at him are England's only type of venomous snake, the adder (2.2.13). The audience's countryside reappears in the masque celebrating the betrothal of Ferdinand and Miranda. This formal entertainment is performed by amazing figures who, Prospero claims, are "spirits, which by mine art / I have from their confine called to enact / My present fancies" (4.1.120–2). Yet the lines spoken by Iris, Ceres, and Juno describe a familiar agricultural landscape rather than any foreign scene. Ceres describes fertile English earth producing abundant crops such as rye, barley, fetches, oats, pease, and hay, a landscape dotted with "nibbling sheep." But this is not the real England. It is a pastoral vision: the perfect rural England of romance, a land of plenty and harmony where everything grows.

Spirits playing English reapers join in a dance. Then, at the very moment that the masque seems to epitomize the vision of a perfect England, Prospero aborts the performance with a huge gesture. Like God bringing a guild play – and with it, the world – to an end, he dismisses the masque. Curiously, though, the entertainers don't flit spirit-like off stage. Instead, after "their graceful dance ... to a strange, hollow, confused noise," the spirit-actors "heavily vanish" (stage directions after 4.1.138). Prospero's god-like gesture, in fact, is precisely that of a stage manager clearing the stage. The masque was not a vision; it was a human entertainment toppled from the remote to the ordinary, from an elite dramatic form celebrating an unreal pastoral England to actors thumping across wooden boards. As in *Cymbeline*, the closed perfection of a romance England is subverted, this time by very substantial actors lumbering off stage.

Prospero's role as magician, ruler, impresario, disappears with the masque. He is only a man, distressed by real things, which, he says, have troubled him. No god, he is infirm; he must walk "a turn or two" to still his "beating mind" (4.1.162–3). Prospero links the vanishing of the masque to events in the real world, explaining to both Ferdinand and the playgoers:

> The cloud capp'd towers, the gorgeous palaces,
> The solemn temples, the great globe itself,
> Yea, all which it inherit, shall dissolve,
> And like this insubstantial pageant faded
> Leave not a rack behind. We are such stuff
> As dreams are made on; and our little life
> Is rounded with a sleep. (4.1.152–8)

Prospero's speech contains many paradoxes. In the main, they lie in how he stands in relation to the playhouse. The playgoers have also witnessed the pageant, a type of entertainment that traditionally invites its spectators to see images of themselves on stage. Prospero offers Ferdinand and the audience weighty images: "cloud capp'd towers," "gorgeous palaces," "solemn temples." These are the stuff of romance. But then he drops to real things: to "the great globe itself," which as well as being a poetic image is solid and real – so solid that the playgoers may see its wooden walls surrounding them as he speaks. For the people in the playhouse, the spirits did not "dissolve" as Prospero asserts; the performance was not at all insubstantial: its actors vanished "heavily." However, the vision conjured by the masque has indeed disappeared like mist. The perfect England of romance was an "insubstantial pageant"; it vanished.

Now Prospero wants to talk about a world where perfection and endlessness are not possibilities. He draws the masque of a perfect world into imperfect real life, among "stuff," the things of a solid, substantial world. Prospero's words about sleep do not offer a saucy challenge to the audience, as did Puck's outrageous suggestion that those who didn't like the play can pretend they napped. This is Prospero telling all those on stage and every member of the audience who "we" are, and to what end "we" all must come. Nevertheless, he remains something of the ruler-magician he has been throughout. His speech does not ask for confirmation or collaboration from his listeners. Prospero dictates who "we" are. His "we" has much of Cymbeline's or Lear's self-absorption about it. He defines himself as "our" leader, not as "our" equal, in words still carrying some of his earlier insular certainty, reserving to himself the right to define life and death. But his play is not yet over.

The final scene firmly challenges romance notions of reconciliation. As in *Cymbeline*, all is not harmonious at the close. In the "brave new world" (5.5.183), Stephano and Trinculo are still drunk, "reeling ripe" (5.1.280); Prospero acknowledges "demi-devil" Caliban (5.1.272) as his property, dismissing his "thing of darkness" (5.1.275) from the stage. Caliban, disenchanted with the "dull fool" Stephano (5.1.298), still fears Prospero. Antonio speaks only once, and then to speculate about the marketability of Caliban. Miranda and Ferdinand squabble, albeit lightly, about cheating at chess. After seeing his daughter married in Naples, Prospero plans to return to isolation, to "retire [him] to Milan" where "Every third thought shall be [his] grave" (5.1.311–12). His autobiography repeats itself, but with a difference. Now Prospero will pull away from the world, not to disappear into the occult but to confront real time.

Prospero then withdraws from the play itself. In his famous epilogue, he talks openly to the playgoers, telling them that he is no longer either god or magician: "Now my charms are all o'rthrown, / And what strength I have's mine own, / Which is most faint" (Epilogue, 1-3). He hands over his power to the audience:

> Now tis true,
> I must be here confin'd by you,
> Or sent to Naples. Let me not,
> Since I have my dukedom got,
> And pardon'd the deceiver dwell
> In this bare island by your spell,
> But release me from my bands
> With the help of your good hands
> Gentle breath of yours my sails
> Must fill, or else my project fails,
> Which was to please. (Epilogue, 3–12)

Prospero doesn't talk now about his magic; he lists what he has done in an ordinary human world: performed a political act and a moral one, retrieved his dukedom and forgiven his brother. He is left without a kingdom, without anything he created: instead of an island, a wooden platform. Power in this world, he says, lies with the audience; only their clapping hands will let him leave the stage:

> Now I want
> Spirits to enforce, art to enchant,
> And my ending is despair,
> Unless I be released by prayer,

Which pierces so, that it assaults
Mercy itself, and frees all faults. (Epilogue, 13–18)

He depends on the playgoers in an ordinary human way. This is the Prospero Caliban hinted at, the Prospero who is human, the Prospero Caliban remembers who "stroke[d] me and made much of me, [would] give me water with berries in't" (1.2.332–3), who gave Caliban not simply drink for survival but a gift, the sort of gift the shepherds in the guild plays give the infant Christ: a spoon to hold forty peas, a ball to play with, a pretty bob of cherries – a sign of mutual affection.

Prospero is not a god, neither of the island nor of the stage; he is no longer even a magician. Unlike God, he can't bring a world to an end. Prospero has been arrogant and isolated, has made himself a "bare island." Nevertheless, he has also been a man who inspired loyalty in Gonzago; who still loves his daughter, yet now must relinquish her because she is a mature woman; who likewise loved Ariel and let him go; who in the past looked after Caliban. He has in turn been helped to survive by others: saved from death by Gonzago; from starvation by Caliban, who showed him "all the qualities of th'isle, / The fresh spring, brine pits, barren place and fertile" (1.2.337–8). Now this man wishes for community. He does not wish Gonzago's utopian vision of a "commonwealth" (2.1.48), or the elaborate world of the masque. He wants a real world. Like Lear, he is old and tired; like Lear, he looks to the audience to help him. Prospero asks to be part of the playgoers' world, not a world of romance, nor one compelled by a magician, but a world where all people have is each other, where indulgence must be freely given. This is the "we" Prospero asks to be admitted to, and where he and his audience all must end.

Confronting the island-stage is the audience's actuality. At this moment Prospero abdicates as master of a theatrical performance. He no longer owns the stage. It belongs also to the playgoers, upon whom he is dependent. At the close of his speech, Prospero reaches right out to the world in the Globe or Blackfriars, speaking openly to the audience. Here, for the last time, is Shakespeare's drop to the native – that intensely focused moment – with the kind of stage address that involves the playgoers with words to which they may have listened with their whole bodies. In childlike, four-beat broken lines, the rhyme falling on simple monosyllabic words, Prospero begs his audience: "As you from crimes would pardon'd be, / Let your indulgence set me free" (Epilogue, 19–20). The signals are there, as they were in guild drama, for everyone to pay close heed. What Prospero says will be unambiguous, something everyone among the playgoers can understand. Prospero does not bring the play to an end alone; he asks the audience to help him. His words, this ending, are acts of community fusing play and audience. This is the closest Shakespeare comes to a dramatization of community like that of the medieval guild plays. We applaud because we are all dependent on one another, are all inhabitants of the same world – players, playwright, audience. At this moment, *The Tempest* becomes "our play."

"HERE NOW WE MAKE AN ENDE"
(Chester, *The Shepherds*, 695)

"HERE OUR PLAY HATH ENDING"
(*Pericles*, 5.3.102)

Notes

INTRODUCTION

1 The Towneley play is named after the former owners of the manuscript. It is generally believed to have been performed in Wakefield, a rural centre in west Yorkshire.

2 Throughout, quotations from Wakefield's play are from George England, ed., *The Towneley Plays*. 1897 (London: EETS, 1952); from the York play, from Richard Beadle, ed., *The York Plays* (London: Arnold, 1982); from the N-Town play, from K. S. Block, ed., *Ludus Coventriae or the Plaie Called Corpus Christi* (London: Oxford University Press, 1922); and from the Chester play, from R. M. Luminiansky and David Mills, eds, *The Chester Mystery Cycle* (London: Oxford University Press, 1974).

3 A.C. Cawley identifies "Gudeboure" as Goodybower (that is, Godith's cottage or dwelling), pointing out that there are many references to Goodybower and its quarry in Wakefield documents. Goodybower was renamed Brook Street in the nineteenth century (93–4).

4 David Bevington's *Medieval Drama* is my source of dates for medieval drama and his *From "Mankind" to Marlowe* the source of dates for Tudor drama.

5 For a full discussion of stage space and time, see Manfred Pfister, 246–95.

CHAPTER ONE

1 Lincoln, Norwich, and King's Lynn have all been proposed as possible sites for N-Town's play; Lincoln seems to be the favourite. For discussion of the possible homes of the N-Town play, see Tydeman, 136 and Cameron and Kahrl, 134–8.

2 In his examination of the characteristics of the four extant complete plays, Martin Stevens "insists on recognizing the cycle form as a generic

entity" (ix). For a close examination of the four texts, see Stevens, 326–7.

3 For N-Town's play, see Stevens, 189–90. For a description of medieval open-air staging, both processional and place and scaffold, see Twycross, "Theatricality" 38–64. For a more detailed discussion, see Tydeman. Also see Wickham, *Theatre*, Wickham, *Stage* Vol. 1, Southern, *Round*, and Southern, *Staging*.

4 For a lengthy examination of York's processional staging procedures, see Nelson, *Stage*; Nelson, "Some Configurations"; and Meredith and Tailby, 69–90.

5 Robert Weimann makes a vital argument about the connections and "interplay" between loca and platea. However, he also regards the platea as neutral ground (79).

6 Twycross offers a clear definition of loca in English and European medieval drama:

> There are a variety of technical terms for the scaffolds: *scaffold, stage, house*, and *tent*, which implies a temporary construction of "stretched" (*tentum*) cloth, either a booth stage or a pavilion as set up for the contenders in tournaments. Presumably they could be as simple or elaborate as funds and taste allowed. Their inhabitants call them *houses, castles, towers, halls*, or *bowers*, which gives a sense of their function. They represent identifiable locations, such as Jerusalem, Marseilles, the castle of Magdela or the Mount of Olives, or the unnamed "seats" of earthly potentates such as Herod, Pilate or Caesar Augustus, or of psychological and moral forces such as the World, the Flesh and the Devil, enemies of God who dwells in the Heaven scaffold. ("Theatricality," 60)

7 For a detailed discussion, see Higgins. Coldewey points out that for the trade and manufacturing guilds the burden of putting on the plays was often a heavy one. In cities such as York or Chester fines were levied in the case of a guild's failure to come up with the money for Corpus Christi performances: "In Chester, as in York, the guilds cooperated with the city. Cooperation, however, does not necessarily mean enthusiasm. In fact the fines may not have been necessary in the first place because guild members were not always prepared to spend time and money in support of these enterprises" ("Contexts," 86). Coldewey also notes, however, that the plays brought in good business for the towns in which they were performed (86–7).

8 For a detailed account of which guilds took on specific episodes, see Higgins, 78–84. Also see Davidson. Tydeman describes how English guild plays were financed:

> In Britain a variety of methods was employed to support drama: the means most often referred to is the tax variously known as

"pageant-pence" or "pageant-silver" levied on all the members of a guild participating in the performances or processions of Corpus Christi or some other feast day. The records of the York Glovers of about 1476 state that native-born guildsmen paid 2d. annually towards the guild's pageant, while "straungers" were assessed at 4d. In 1525 the Coventry Weavers received "of the masters for the pagynt money xvj s iiij d," while the Smiths in "6 Edw [1552–3] reseyved of the craft for pageant pencys iij s iiij d," and the Cappers in 1562 accepted "of the fellowship for pageant xxxij s iiij d." On 18 June 1519 the Lincoln Common Council recorded that "it is Agreid that every man And woman within this Citie beyng Able Scahll be Broder & Syster in Scaynt Anne gyld & to pay yerely iiij^d Man & wyf at the lest." At Chester the Smiths' Company in 1554 was levying 2s. 4d. annually from each of its guildsmen and about 1d. from each of its journeymen, and in 1575 one Arthur Tailer, a dyer, went to prison rather than contribute to the pageant-money. Such levies doubtless went some of the way towards meeting the necessary expenses of performance, bearing in mind that pageant-carts, stage properties and costumes could often be preserved and used again in subsequent years, although sometimes it was a matter of pride that fresh apparel and furnishings should appear each year. (226–7)

9 Davidson describes the production of costumes for the play by medieval textile and clothing industries (57–81). Meredith and Tailby list English and European records of which guilds supplied the plays, special effects, properties and costumes (101–47).

10 Chester's Early Banns, 1539–40, ascribe the episode of "cristes monday where he sat with his Appostles" (*The Last Supper*) to the "bakers & mylners" (REED: Chester, 32).

11 For instance, the York City Memorandum Book of 10 April 1541 records that the goldsmiths provided crowns and gowns for the Magi episode (REED: York, 334).

12 Recorded in the House Books for 27 June 1482 is the following:
    thys same day it was agreid that Iohn harper shall sell a vessill of white wyn that he has with owt ony thyng paying thar for to the Vintners pagent so that the said Iohn herper sell the said wyn for x d A galon. (REED: York, 130)

13 Richard Beadle notes the play's "copious and demonstrative use of technical terms" from medieval shipbuilding. He argues that "these are some of the means whereby the dramatist creates a link between the daily labour of the York shipwrights and the parts played by God and their remote ancestor Noah on the drama of salvation" ("Shipwrights' Craft," 58).

14 In 1422 York's painters and stainers combined with the pinners and lat-
teners to produce the city's Crucifixion episode. According to the
Memorandum Book for 1482,

> it is graunted unto the said Craft of pynners that the same craft of
> pynners and Wyredrawers from this present day forward be on Craft
> that is to say þat all that makes pynnes or draweth wyre or makes
> ffisshe hukes or Shobokilles [shoe buckles] yerelie tobe contriborie of
> And to the upholding of þer pageaunt. (REED: York, 128)

According to Stevens, the pinners made "pins, fishhooks, mousetraps,
and other small metallic objects" (30).

Tydeman discusses how towns and guilds organized, recompensed,
and disciplined their actors (184–222). Chester's Early Banns (1539–40)
state that the city's play is to be mounted not only for the

> Augmentacion & incresse of the holy and catholyk ffaith of our
> sauyour cryst Iesu and to exhort the myndes of the comen peple to
> gud deuocion and holsom doctryne ther of but Also for the comen
> welth and prosperitie of this Citie. (REED: Chester, 33)

15 Crouch examines the history of York's stationholders and their customers from 1399 to 1499, concluding that over the hundred-year
stretch the "paying audience was ... largely composed of the city elite,
the master artisans, and their households" (101). For Twycross's
description of York's patterns of station leasing from the end of the
fourteenth century to 1572, see "Places," 10–33.

16 Coldewey observes that

> the plays also were an advertisement for a town's wealth, power,
> status, and stability. These readily translated, as the Chester record
> tell us, into 'profitte,' 'common welth and prosperitie' (REED:
> Chester, 33, 115). Along the same lines should be mentioned what
> has often been noticed before, that the plays could act as shop
> windows for a guild's wares and services; hence the peculiar, some-
> times humorous, sometimes grotesque, pairing of guild and
> pageant: the Bakers with 'The Last Supper' (York), the Mercers and
> Spicers with 'The Coming of the Magi' (Chester), the Ironmongers
> and Ropers with 'The Crucifixion' (Chester). But whatever benefits
> accrued to a guild from such advertising and publicity, it should be
> clear by now that the willingness of its members to undertake the
> chores of supporting the plays, of self-imposed regulation, and any
> other duties required by the town, depended very much upon that
> guild's power to preserve its monopoly and to serve the welfare of
> its individual members. To be Pageant Master at York was a duty
> for a junior officer in the Merchant's Guild; it carried with it no
> status and the officer had to advance his own money whenever nec-
> essary, clear evidence that guilds were willing but not overly keen

to involve themselves in the civic theatrical enterprise. ("Contexts," 87)

17 Twycross points out that plays were performed each year during the period 21 May to 24 June, the time of the longest daylight, although York's long processional play may have ended by torchlight (38–9). See also Tydeman's summary of views on how York's play was organized (115–20).

18 The grocers' guild lists among the expenses for its staging of paradise payments for oranges, figs, almonds, dates, raisins, prunes, and apples (REED: Norwich, 343).

19 Like Lady Macbeth, Herod treasures hierarchical seating at his celebration, and, as at her feast, his finicky arrangements disintegrate when Death comes to dinner and wreaks havoc.

20 Weimann suggests that the "delicacies ... did not remain on the stage but were passed out amongst the audience" (95). Rosemary Woolf, on the other hand, finds the tone in these scenes of peasant feasting "harsh and satirical" and compares them to Breughel's "Land of Cockayne" and its "atmosphere of coarse repulsiveness [imposed] on the never-never land of abundant food" (186–7).

21 For texts of folk plays, see Tiddy's *The Mummers' Play*. The Revesby play, in particular, is of interest, with its repeated calls for silence, nonsense dialogue, verbal inversions, and subversive characters such as Pickle Herring and Fool. Weimann traces in detail the continuations and transformations of many aspects of native English folk drama (mummings, Robin Hood plays, sword plays) in the guild plays.

22 Richard Southern describes the characteristics of mummings and amateur plays in England (*Seven Ages*, 40–103). Also see Wickham, *Theatre*.

23 Southern writes that "a typical opening line of the Hero in the Mummer's Play is 'Here am I, St. George, an Englishman so stout ... '" This seems to be what Trowle has in mind. It is interesting, too, that as well as being a participatory and spectator sport, wrestling or fighting (followed by restitution) is an integral part of folk drama (*Seven Ages*, 51).

24 Owst quotes from a fifteenth-century sermon:

A common game in use nowadays is that which the soldiers played with Christ at his Passion: it is called the bobbid game. In this game, one of the company will be blindfold and set in a prone position; then those standing by will hit him on the head and say –

"A bobbid, a bobbid, a biliried:
Smyte not her, bot thu smyte a gode!"

And as often as the former may fail to guess correctly and rede amys, he has to play a fresh game. And so, until he rede him that smote, he will be blindfold and hold in for the post of player. (510)

25 Tydeman notes that similar mimed massacres and sword games were
   popular as early as the tenth century in Twelfth Night celebrations.
26 The story of the "snow baby," is used by the first detractor to slur Mary:

> in Ffeyth I suppose þat þis woman slepte
> With-owtyn all coverte whyll þat it dede snowe
> And a flake þer of in hyre mowthe crepte
> and þer of þe chylde in hyre wombe doth growe.
>
> (N-Town, *The Trial of Joseph and Mary*, 273–6)

Woolf comments:

> This sceptical scoffing is based upon the story of the snow-child ... It
> is the story of a merchant who, returning to his wife after a long
> absence, finds her with a small baby. His wife, frightened by his
> anger, then makes the excuse that one day when she was thirsty she
> drank some snow and thus conceived. Five years later the merchant
> took the child on a voyage with him and gave him as surety to
> another merchant. Returning alone, he explained to his wife that the
> snow child (*nivis-natus*) simply melted away when sitting in the hot
> sun. The author of *Ludus Coventriae* has moulded this fabliau plot to
> provide the detractors with insolent, taunting fantasies. (176)

Woolf notes that the story was "current in Latin poetry between the
tenth and twelfth centuries ... and later in French fabliaux" (176).
   See also Towneley's *Shepherd's Play I* for the familiar story of the Wise
Men of Gotham.
27 For discussion on the associations of these gifts, see Ross, 180–98 and
   Helterman, 73–115.
28 For further information about Heaven's staging, see Davidson, 91–7,
   and Meredith and Tailby, 92–5. Davidson offers detailed descriptions
   about how actors were raised to and lowered from Heaven's raised
   structure (81–101).
29 This entry also notes the delivery of elaborate stage properties to the
   pageant master, including such things as yellow wigs as diadems for
   the apostles, gilded masks and a Heaven hung with red and blue
   clouds, gold stars, and sunbeams and rainbows.
30 This is based on the twelve stopping places in York's play listed in
   Crouch.
31 Davidson notes that "kings would have required gilded crowns as well
   as garments of rich brocade or other expensive-appearing fabric" (66).
32 In Lincoln the city's aldermen lent silk gowns to costume the kings
   (Kahrl, 53).
33 Squires argues that the N-Town play highlights contemporary abuses of
   law, including those of the ecclesiastical courts where bishops partici-
   pated wearing hoods and hats like those clothing the play's Annas,
   Caiaphas, and the two doctors (207–11).

34 References to his balls being repaired appear on 202, 220, 223, 229, 236, 241, 245, 161; to his club being repaired: 79, 181, 202, 288, 291 (REED: Coventry).

35 Later Lady Macduff will see a similar slaughter of "all [her] little ones" (*Macbeth*, 4.2).

36 Chaucer speaks of his summoner's use of ecclesiastical court Latin:
> And eek ye knowen wel how that a jay
> Kan clepen "Watte" as wel as kan the pope.
> But whoso koude in oother thyng hym grope,
> Than hadde he spent al his philosophie;
> Ay "Questio quid iuris" wold he crie. (General Prologue, 642–6)

37 Tydeman points out that although "many medieval performances were presented without charge being made to spectators some people paid for a good view of the play from windows in houses that overlooked the performances or by hiring seats on scaffolds. In York, the city authorities accepted bids for scaffolds along the play's route which could then be rented out to audience members" (232).

38 God's open address from his locus brought the modern medieval world into his; Christ's platea address allied him with the audience's ordinary life. Mary too stood on the platea when she marvelled to the audience at the annunciation, or lamented her son's death at the Crucifixion. Mary's traditional words of praise in Towneley's *The Salutation of Elizabeth*, with their mix of Latin and simple native English, were spoken from the platea:
> Magnificat anima mea dominum;
> My saull lufys my lord abuf,
> And my gost gladys with luf,
>   In god, that is my hele;
> ffor he has bene sene agane,
> The buxumes of his bane,
>   And kept me/ madyn lele. (49–54)

Or consider the Chester Mary's agonized and graphic cries on the platea space below the cross:
> Alas, whye nyll my liefe forlorne
> to fynd my sonne here be beforne,
> tugget, lugget, and all totorne
> with traytors nowe this tyde,
> with nayles thrast and crowne
> of thorne. (*Passion*, 249–53)

39 Elliott explores the comic structure of the play. He argues that "pathos is abundantly present but never for its own sake; rather it serves to heighten the peripeteia from sorrow to joy ... Moral conflict is fully developed but never into tragic tension" (171). Thomas Rendell

examines stage spectacle in the Abraham episodes, proposing links with other plays; for example, the binding of Isaac foreshadows the binding of Christ at the Crucifixion (221–32). These are important figural associations. However, I think the most immediate (and possibly most urgent) relationship the plays suggest is that between Abraham and ourselves as suffering human beings.

40 Isaac is no cypher. He displays a child's anguish and terror. In Brome's *The Sacrifice of Isaac* (a single play that may have belonged to a play cycle) he tries to interest his father in a sheep grazing nearby. In Chester and Brome he fears the blade, asking to be blindfolded.

41 Rosemary Woolf takes a different view. She considers that some of the "amplification" made by the redactors of the Abraham plays was done at the cost of "dramatic and typographical consistency" (152). She glosses over the doubts expressed by Abraham. In particular, she does not note that they are spoken directly to the audience and therefore, I would argue, carry great weight. Her view is that

> the dramatists ... show in Abraham reasoned obedience tempered by natural human feeling. Since he is a type of God the Father he can feel no conflict nor judge the situation as a tragic dilemma. The dramatists are concerned only to show what the cost of obedience can be. Just as Noah had done, though in far less testing circumstances, Abraham instantly expresses obedience to God's will. (147)

42 In the N-Town play, Mrs Noah puts up no objections and joins her husband in a long prayer of obedience to God's will. This episode omits the building of the ark, substituting the story of blind Lamech, an archer who mistakenly kills Cain.

43 Helterman, on the other hand, suggests that by the end of the episode "the operation of parody [Mr and Mrs Noah's behaviour] allows the audience to identify with this family, in which domestic hierarchy and a sense of community welfare have been established" (94).

44 Woolf thinks Mrs Noah stretches audience credulity too far, and that she is overdrawn in an attempt to cope with the "implausible action" of someone choosing to stay behind in a flood (143).

45 Punch and Judy shows and traditional pantomime in England still exploit this relationship between actors and audience. A recent history of pantomime by Gerald Frow is titled *"Oh, Yes It Is!"* The phrase is obviously so well known that it can serve as the name for a book, yet it is not used in the book and no explanation for the title is given.

46 The old Roman road running from Chester to London.

47 Various sumptuary laws regulated the quality of clothing permitted to different ranks of society, from royalty to labourers, restricting certain fabrics, colours, and styles to specific groups. For instance, in 1363 laws designated that the lowest strata of society, farm labourers and those

whose worldly belongings amounted to under 40 shillings, should dress in undyed cheap cloth. In 1463 a sumptuary statute allowed only those who served in a royal household or who were sergeants, gentlemen, and esquires worth 40 shillings per annum to wear damask. Later still, under Henry VIII, this fabric, which could be either linen or silk, was confined to those whose estates were valued over £100 (Davidson, 114, 116). See also Youings: "[T]he sumptuary laws of late-medieval and Tudor England were concerned with the prevention not of social mobility but of social emulation" (110).

48 The devil also encourages the audience to admire his fine Holland cloth shirt, not yet paid for, and to want a linen waistcoat like his, even though owning one would impoverish them.

49 Pinners are defined as "manufacturers of pins and other small wire articles" in REED: York II, 922.

50 Stevens argues that "the city of York itself in all its complexity, is really the subject of the cycle." Of the social criticism inherent in the play, he writes:

> York ... is a major city – a provincial capital, a regional if not international trade center, as well as the seat of an archdiocese – and to the extent that the cycle implicitly reflected life in the city and brought into conjunction its diverse and unrelated institutions, it is a more highly charged instrument of social criticism than any of the other cycles. (77)

For a discussion of the history of York's craft guilds, their make-up, and the often contentious relation of guilds with one another and with the civic authorities, see Palliser. See Swanson on changes in the power structure and regulation of the city's guilds, in particular in the control exerted over York's manufacturing artisans in the fifteenth century.

51 In counterpoint to the addresses to the audience of all patriarchs and prophets are familiar Latin tags, words that people in the audience would be most likely to associate with each figure. For Isaiah: *Populus qui ambulabat in tenebris vidit lucem magnam.* (The people who walked in darkness have seen a great light.)

52 According to Rodney Hilton, the tapster was a very significant figure in everyday medieval life:

> It may be worth speculating that women may have played a role beyond the purely economic in the development of the ale-house whether as brewstesses or as tapsters. Such places were common in early fourteenth century London and by the end of the fourteenth century were to be found in other towns, large and small. Ale-houses were places for drinkers, but they were also places for sociability, for talk, perhaps subversive talk. If we knew more about these places we might discover that the presiding genius was "mine hostess" rather

than "mine host." The medieval ale-house, in the particular setting of the household economy, where women in the workshop, women stall-holders, women selling n the street were not as separated from the male worker as in modern times, might well have been a place where women had influence, quite different from the predominantly male working class pub of modern times. Who kept the ale-house where Glutton was tempted to stay on his way to church in Langland's *Piers Plowman*? It was Betty the brew-wife. Who was sitting there? Watt the warrener and his wife; Tim the tinker and his two lads; Hick the hackneyman; Hewe the medlar; Claryce of Cockes Lane; the church clerk; Peres the priest with a woman, Purnele of Flanders; Rose the dishmaker; all sitting with craftsmen, retailers (including a garlic monger) and various rogues. (214–15)

53 The stage direction in N-Town's *Passion Play I*, for instance, calls for several loca: "skaffoldes" for Annas, Caiaphas, Pilate, and Herod, as well as Heaven and Hell; a "cownsel hous" where the Jews plot Christ's death; and Simon the Leper's house where Christ celebrates the Last Supper.

54 I am grateful to John Baxter for pointing out the episode's revision of the biblical narrative and for sharing his insight into how it emphasizes the concrete nature of Christ's action.

CHAPTER TWO

1 Some players in the guild drama received payment for their performances. The Herods and Pilates were notoriously the best paid. Occasionally, as in New Romney in 1560, a professional "devyser" or producer was called in to help organize the play. However, guild plays were predominantly amateur; acting was more commonly rewarded with a good breakfast before the performance than money. See Tydeman, 203–7.

2 Using the royal "we," Theseus reminds Hermia that Athenian law rather than he will condemn her if she refuses to obey her father's wish that she marry Demetrius:

Or else the law of Athens yields you up
(Which by no means we may extenuate)
To death or to a vow of single life.
(*Dream*, 1.1.119–21)

3 Phythian-Adams concludes:

With certain notable exceptions, by the late fifteenth and early sixteenth centuries even the more important towns and cities were under pressure; so much so indeed, that the period 1520–1570, the culminating years of the period, might well be regarded as a time of

acute urban crisis. The two major elements in that crisis were, exter-
nally, the threatening growth of rural competition and, internally, the
costly disincentives to urban residence. The result seems to have been
a trend towards what could be described as de-urbanization from
which, apart for the exceptions noted, the leading market towns
appear to have been economically but not demographically the main
beneficiaries. (183)

Swanson also describes changes in the fortunes of the guilds in late
fifteenth-century York, a city that supported a massive play cycle (53).

4 Coldewey examines the declining prosperity of cities and their trade
guilds during the sixteenth century:

Many factors contributed to the demise of the cycle plays, and these
varied widely in individual towns and cities. But it is fair to say,
given the steady deterioration of their mutually beneficial arrangements, along with the widespread decline, side by side, of towns and
guilds in the face of the demographic and economic crises, that the
demise of these plays might be forecast from a time well before the
reformation. In any case it must be stressed that an important and
continuing element to be reckoned with in both the rise and the
demise of these craft plays was economic. (89)

On the widespread economic decline see also Phythian-Adams,
Desolation; Phythian-Adams, "Ceremony"; and Dobson, 265–86.

5 Both Wickham and Gardiner assert that from Henry VIII's reign on the
plays were suppressed by the state and by the Protestant church
(Gardiner, 47–8; Wickham, *Stage* vol. 1, 117). Bills, on the other hand,
argues that "the notion of a conscious campaign against [the guild]
plays, beginning with Henry and culminating with Elizabeth is not
credible" (167). Bills considers that religion "was only one factor, and a
late one at that" in the disappearance of the plays. A more significant
cause was the "serious economic trouble" that towns with guild plays
experienced just before the Reformation (159).

6 Further to this, Ian Lancashire writes:

On the other hand, the Roman Catholic Mary Tudor had much more
to fear from itinerant playing troupes than from the town drama, and
her control of these companies tightened: in 1555 she ordered hereti-
cal books (including Bale's) burned, and the next year she forbad performances by these troupes throughout the kingdom. London in 1554
and 1557, Hatfield Broad Oak in 1556, and Canterbury in 1557 felt
special acts of repression. One incident illustrates her attitude. In
1553, some months after Mary came to the throne, certain players
from Coventry were jailed, apparently on religious grounds, but one
of the most stubborn of these, John Careless, was let out briefly so
that he could take part in the town's own play, after which he

returned himself into custody. Other towns too benefited from Mary's decentralized controls on their activities. Canterbury briefly revived its St Thomas pageant in 1554–5, New Romney planned to revive its pre-Reformation Passion play in 1556, Wakefield's Corpus Christi play appeared (first?) in 1555, Southwark brought back its Palm Sunday prophets in 1555, and for the first time in perhaps 150 years London was able to see a Passion play, at the Grey Friars, in 1557. (*Texts*, xxix–xxx)

7 York's play was performed for the last time in 1569; Chester's in 1575; Wakefield's in 1576. The last recorded performance of a guild play was in Coventry, in 1588 (Tydeman, 241–2).

8 See Bevington, "Popular"; Bevington, *Tudor Drama*; Bevington, *From "Mankind"*; Lancashire, *Texts*; Southern, *Seven Ages*; Southern, *Staging*; Tydeman, *The Theatre*; Weimann, *Shakespeare*; Wickham, *Theatre*; Wickham, *Stage* Vol. 1.

9 Bevington comments that *Play of the Weather*

requires ten players, all of whom gather before Jupiter's throne in the closing scene ... Two of the roles are women's parts, and the role of the young boy is assigned to 'the lest that can play,' implying that the rest are also boys. All the indications point to boys' courtly drama. No adult troupe of this size is known to have traveled publicly in England before the 1570's, or to have commanded the talents of three or more qualified boys. (*From "Mankind,"* 40)

All references to the play are to Bevington's edition.

10 For example, E.K. Chambers quotes Sir John Paston's letter of 16 April 1473 in which Paston "laments 'the loss of a man Woode, whom he had kept thys yer to pleye Seynt Jorge and Robyn Hod and the Shryff off Notyngham'" (134).

11 Peter H. Greenfield describes a small semi-professional company brought in to entertain and impress the Duke of Buckingham's Gloucestershire neighbours:

The Christmas festivities of 1507–08 clearly aimed at impressing and wooing the Gloucestershire gentry. The nearly 500 guests included not only the duke's client gentry, but several who were considerable landowners in their own right: Maurice, Richard, and James Berkeley, Sir Robert and Anthony Poyntz, and William Kingston. The duke's hospitality was lavish. On Epiphany alone his guests consumed (among other things) 678 loaves of bread, 259 gallons of ale, 33 bottles of wine, 36 rounds of beef, 12 mutton carcases, 4 pigs, 400 eggs and 200 oysters. To aid digestion, entertainment was provided by two minstrels, six trumpeters, the four waits of Bristol, and our friends, the four "lusores domini de Writell." (176)

12 Gurr quotes the Act:

> All and everye persone and persones beynge whole and mightye in Body and able to labour, havinge not Land or Maister, nor using any lawfull Marchaundize Crafte or Mysterye whereby hee or shee might get his or her Lyvinge, and can gyve no reckninge howe he or shee dothe lawfully get his or her Lyvinge; & all Fencers Bearewardes Common Players in Enterludes & Minstrels, not belonging to any Baron of this Realme or towardes any other honorable Personage of greater Degree; all Juglers Pedlars Tynkers and Petye Chapmen; whiche seid Fencers Bearewardes Comon Players in Enterludes Mynstrels Juglers Pedlers Tynkers & Petye Chapmen, shall wander abroade and have not Lycense of two Justices of the Peace at the leaste, whereof one to be of the Quorum, when and in what Shier they shall happen to wander ... shalbee taken adjudged and deemed Roges Vacaboundes and Sturdy Beggers. (*Stage*, 28)

13 Bevington shows how the dramatists of this time cope with limited resources, stage properties, costumes, and actors, adjusting their plays to meet these physical exigencies by constructing plays with patterns of doubling parts and episodic structure (*From "Mankind"*, 106).

14 Bevington finds no clear evidence of boy actors in the casting lists of popular plays until *Cambises*, *The Marriage of Wit and Wisdom*, and *Mucedorus* (*From "Mankind"*, 78).

15 Bevington lists fifty-eight plays for the period 1474–1583. They vary in auspices, subject matter, and style. Some, such as *Fulgens and Lucrece* (ca 1497), are humanist dramas of ideas; others are popular moralities or court plays (*From "Mankind"*, 65–7).

16 Examples are *The Castle of Perseverance*, but more particularly *Everyman* and *Mankind*. (All references to these three plays are to Bevington's editions.)

17 See Potter, 105–12. Even so, no substantial morality plays such as *The Castle of Perseverance*, the performance of which must have involved many amateurs in its huge cast, were mounted in the sixteenth century.

18 Rastell's play offers explanations of new scientific ideas, and also promotes the commercial settlement of the Americas. (All references to this play are to Richard Axton's edition.)

19 Where Rastell's play shows excitement at new discoveries and an urge to promote exploration, Fulwell's is more conservative. It urges the importance of education, stressing study and application and representing these in a comical but repressive manner.

20 Potter comments on the adaptation of the morality play: "Its original didactic purpose of calling the sinner to repentance had evolved into socio-political purposes in the plays of Medwall, Skelton, Lindsay,

Bale, and Udall" (112). However, as he also notes: "Overtly political drama, which had flourished amid the controversy of the Reformation struggle during the reigns of Henry, Edward, and Mary Tudor, quickly expired in the moderate environment of the Elizabethan compromise. *King John* and *Respublica* were among the last of the polemical kind" (112).

21 Examples of costly productions are the boy company court plays *Wit and Science* (ca 1530–48), *Respublica* (1553), *Jacob and Esau* (1553–8), and *Apius and Virginia*.

22 Tydeman compares hall performances in the late fifteenth and early sixteenth centuries to the "lavish production mounted in court circles, in colleges and in the Inns of Court." About the former plays he remarks:

> Frequently unrewarding to read, these plays often blossom into life in the warmth of actual presentation. Few depended for their effect on built scenic structures such as mansions, or on grandiose stage devices; when we consider the limited means, both financial and technical, available to the itinerant performers mostly associated with these pieces, we shall understand why their forte was improvisation and "doing without." (81)

23 Lancashire discusses the staging of *Youth*:

> *Youth* was written, like most interludes, for indoor performance at a hall banquet, "among all this cheer" (205), as Youth says, where a riddle about mustard and salt fish (120) would be topical. Humility's entrance from evensong (570) suits a banqueting hour, and what stage conditions can be inferred from a text with only one stage direction (389.1) are consistent with a hall play. The staging "place" (640), a term meaning "manor house" as well as "acting Area" offered the interluders a space that, visible to the audience "beforn" (547), must have been at ground level, since Youth enters brushing through the spectators (40–1, 589), and since Riot, as he comes in talking to them, overlooks and discovers Youth in a way that suggests he blends with the crowd. (215–19)

24 Like the guild plays' tyrants, Freewill has a mixed vocabulary, a smattering of upwardly social English, with a large amount of scatological English. He also addresses the audience directly:

> Cock's passion, my noble is turned to a stone!
> Where lay I last? Beshrew your heart, Joan!
> Now, by these bones, she hath beguiled me!
> Let see: a penny my supper, a piece of flesh ten pence,
> My bed right nought; let all this expense –
> Now, by these bones, I have lost an halfpenny! (171–6)

In *Youth* the spectator-badgering is largely carried out by the young protagonist's riotous companions. Youth, led by Riot and Pride into a careless and licentious lifestyle, also picks on the potentially vulnerable among the spectators:

Aback, gallants, and look unto me,
And take me for your special!
For I am promoted to high degree.
By right I am king eternel –
Neither duke ne lord, baron ne knight,
That may be likened unto me;
They be subdued to me by right,
As servants to their masters should be. (*Youth*, 589–96)

25 There are many other examples of ways in which evil characters bait their audience to gain their ground. Fools, too, make close contact with the crowds. Spectators at performances of *The Marriage of Wit and Wisdom* are made the recipients of a nonsense proclamation. An announcement by the morally upright Search is reconstituted and distorted by Idleness:

SEARCH First, cry "Oyez" a good while
IDLENESS Very well. *SD: he cries too long.*
Then SEARCH Cry shorter, with a vengeance.
IDLENESS Oyez! Oyez! Oyez! Oyez! *SD very often*
SEARCH Art thou mad. Canst thou keep no mean. (494–8)

The proclamation continues at some length:

Then SEARCH Say, "One, the king's Most Royal Majesty"
IDLENESS King John gave a Royal to lie with Marjorie
SEARCH "Doth charge you, all his true people"
IDLENESS "A barge flew over a steeple"
SEARCH "They watch elsewhere and see in the town"
IDLENESS "That every patch that a man wears on his knee
        Shall cost a crown." 514–9)

26 As Weimann points out, the intermingling of classical and native material has an important effect on the meaning of the play as a whole, with the minor plot impinging on and providing rich counterpoint to the nobility debate (107).

27 Bevington suggests that Medwall may have needed to be cautious in his dealings with his elite audience (*Tudor Drama*, 50). Jones, however, disagrees with the view "that the humble chaplain-dramatist was simply being tactful (or toadyish) in his presentation of an unpalatable lesson to a wellborn audience":

Surely this would seem overcautious on his part, since the lesson that virtue is the foundation of true nobility was scarcely a radical one. Perhaps it became more commonplace with the development of humanism in England, but it was already a well-worn topic when Medwall picked it up. In any case it is less than tactful to say that the lesson you are presenting "shall stond with treuth and reason," that "every man that favoreth and loveth vertue" will prefer such truth to false flattery, and then to imply that your audience might after all prefer flattery to this "playne trouth." ("Stage World," 140–1)

28 Weimann discusses the servant-Garcio figures: their travesties of action and language, particularly their sexual punning (133–51).

29 Later we hear *Henry V*'s Chorus apologize for the "rough and all-unable pen" of the playwright (Epilogue).

30 It is the kind of jolt we get when Pykeharnes cheerfully introduces the first murderer, or when the Chester tapster follows the patriarchs on stage.

31 Gurr discusses the first uses of the term "audience":

The Oxford English Dictionary records "audience" and "auditory" from the 1370s, and "auditor" from the 1380s, when Chaucer used it. While "audience" tended to hold the judicial connotation of a hearing, in both the king's court and in lesser lawcourts, "auditor" meant simply a listener. We have to look beyond OED to locate the terms used specifically for playgoers. In about 1533 a stage direction in the closet interlude *Love* describes a stage trick with fireworks which survived for more than a century:

Here the vyse cometh in ronnynge sodenly aboute the place among the audiens with a hye copyn tank on his hed full of squybs fyred. (*Playgoing*, 90)

32 Hamlet is very concerned with this image. He instructs the players: "the purpose of playing ... both at the first and now, was and is, to hold, as 'twere, the mirror up to nature; to show virtue her own feature, scorn her own image, and the very age and body of the time his form and pressure" (*Hamlet*, 3.2.20–4).

33 Titivillus is heard roaring somewhere off stage, but if the playgoers want to see him, "a man with a head that is of great omnipotence"(460), they must hand over money – preferably not groats, but "red ryallys" (Bevington, *From "Mankind"*, 464).

34 Gurr remarks that these romantic narratives were "evidently the staple of amphitheatre [public] playhouse at first" (*Playgoing*, 116).

35 Bernard Spivack, who looks only at the impresario figure's morality play origins, describes him as the Vice:

The Vice, by natural extension of the theatrical side of his allegorical nature and homiletic enterprise becomes ... the play maker whose histrionic deceits and beguilements create the action of the play as 'game' or 'sport' for the play goer. (191)

Anne Righter comments on the way this versatile stage figure survives from Tudor drama to the later Elizabethan stage:

It was with the brilliant unscrupulous figure of the vice that the age-old connexion of the actor with the deceiver seems first to have entered English drama. Even before he had acquired a capital letter and command over all other evil forces in the play, the Vice possessed a quality which associated him naturally with the actor. (55)

36 In Wakefield's *The Killing of Abel* Pykeharnes also denies any moral world.

37 Robert C. Jones examines how the Vice figure's contract with the audience provokes the spectators to make moral judgments:

We are made to see that our very responses to the play are actual manifestations in ourselves of the better and worse impulses in man that are being represented on-stage; and we can accordingly place our delight in the vices as something in us to be guarded against. This technique is perhaps the fullest theatrical realization of the possibilities of instruction through entertainment in the moral plays. That it serves the instructive purposes of the play does not make the entertainment itself any less lively. ("Vice," 52)

CHAPTER THREE

1 For the brief account of the growth of London's commercial playhouses I am indebted to Bentley; Gurr, *Stage*; Gurr, *Playgoing*; Gurr and Orrell; Hattaway, *Popular*; Thomson; Tydeman and Wickham, *Stage*.

2 In 1558 Elizabeth I herself licensed an acting company. Her patent "specified the permissible scope of the company in unambiguous terms, and came to serve as a model for all patents granted subsequently:

Elizabeth by the grace of God quene of England, &c. To all Justices, Mayors, Sheriffes, Baylyffes, head Constables, under Constables, and all other our officers and mynisters gretinge. Knowe ye that we of oure especiall grace, certen knowledge, and mere mocion have licenced and auctorised, and by these presentes do licence and auctorise, oure lovinge Subjectes, James Burbage, John Perkyn, John Lanham, William Johnson, and Roberte Wilson, servauntes to oure trustie and welbeloved Cosen and Counseyllor the Earle of Leycester, to use, exercise, and occupie the arte and facultve of playenge Commedies, Tragedies, Enterludes, stage playes, and such other like as they have alredie used and studied, or hereafter shall use and studie, aswell for the recreacion of oure loving subjectes, as for oure solace and pleasure when we shall thincke good to see them, as also to use and occupie all such Instrumentes as they have alreadie practised, or hereafter shall practise, for and during our pleasure. And the said Commedies,

Tragedies, Enterludes, and stage plaves, to gether with their musicke, to shewe, publishe, exercise, and occupie to their best commoditie during all the terme aforesaide, aswell within oure Citie of London and liberties of the same, as also within the liberties and fredomes of anye oure Cities, townes, Bouroughes &c whatsoever as without the same, thoroughte oure Realme of England. Willynge and commaundinge yow and everie of yowe, as ye tender our pleasure, to permytte and suffer them herein withoute anye yowre lettes, hynderaunce, or molestation duringe the terme aforesaid, anye acte, statute, proclamation, or commaundement heretofore made, or hereafter to be made, to the contrarie notwithstandinge. Provyded that the said Commedies, Tragedies, enterludes, and stage playes be by the master of oure Revells for the tyme beynge before sene & allowed, and that the same be not published or shewen in the tyme of common prayer, or in the tvme of great and common plague in oure said Citye of London. In wytnes whereof &c. wytnes oure selfe at Westminster the xth daye of Maye. (Gurr, *Stage*, 30–1)

3 Innyards in the north of London, such as the Bull Tavern at Bishopsgate or the Bell in Gracechurch Street, continued to act as theatre spaces until the 1590s. See Gurr, *Playgoing*, 15. Tydeman comments:

some of the inn-yard theatres of Elizabethan London involved more than temporary installations, and ... permanent stages together with stands for the accommodation of spectators were erected at the Red Lion and Boar's Head Inns at Whitechapel at least, the Red Lion construction being being recorded in the Court-Book of the Carpenters' Company for 1567. But dramatic performances at London inns date back at least ten years before this, the earliest records alluding to plays at the Boar's Head and the Saracen's Head in Islington in 1557. (245)

4 Gurr calls the building of the Red Lion "the watershed" for all those involved in London theatre: for entrepreneurs, who collected the box office receipts, as well as for the playgoers, who had a fixed venue to attend (*Playgoing*, 15). The Red Lion seems to have held a large stage surrounded by galleries (Foakes, 3).

5 Gurr and Orrell, 16. The Hope was the last of the open air theatres, and soon became a bear-baiting amphitheatre. The building contract stipulated a trestle stage, one that could be easily taken down to allow for entertainments other than plays (Hattaway, *Popular*, 22).

6 Thomson describes the move:

On 28 December, under cover of darkness, [Richard Burbage] was with his mother, his brother, a financial backer and friend called William Smith, a carpenter-architect called Peter Street, and about a dozen labourers, outside the empty Theatre. That night, despite attempts to interrupt and prevent them, they began to dismantle it. They carried the timbers, the best preserved of them anyway, down Bishopsgate Street and into the walled city. The Thames was still frozen on 28 December, and it may be that the timbers were slid across. It would have saved the toll on London Bridge, or the considerable cost of several trips in a Thames ferry. (17-18)

7 A venue owned by the entrepreneur Christopher Beeston, which became famous both for its plays about London's citizens and for its jigs. For an account of Beeston's playhouses, the Red Bull and the Cockpit, see Gurr, *Playgoing*, 170–7.

8 Thomson comments that:

> Either openly, or by inference, *The Isle of Dogs* criticised the government of the country, and of the City of London too. It was, we presume, the immediate cause of the Lord Mayor's complaint to the Privy Council. It certainly provoked the council not only into concord with the Guildhall, but also into instructing the Middlesex justices to investigate the writing and performing of "a lewd plaie that was plaied in one of the plaiehowses on the Bancke Side, contanynge very seditious and sclanderous matter." (4)

9 In 1596 James Burbage bought Blackfriars, a former monastery, a liberty inside the walls of the city. Burbage converted the building to a theatre; however, in November of that year the area's residents successfully petitioned the Privy Council to ban its use as a public playhouse (Thomson, 15–16).

10 Nevertheless, as Thomson cautions, in any theatrical enterprise the owners had to take risks and the development of the playhouse business suffered from setbacks. The Globe's success, for instance, as well as being a story of "business acumen and artistry" is also one of "small disasters smothered" (35). Gurr notes that the market fluctuated; in the period 1596–1606, for example, "supply exceeded demand" (*Playhouse*, 18).

11 According to Gurr, "modern estimates of the capacities of the public playhouses converge on about 2,500 as a maximum figure." Of the numbers visiting the playhouses he says: "In 1595 the estimates suggest that the two acting companies were visited by about 15,000 people weekly. In 1620, when 6 playhouses were open, 3 of them the smaller private houses, the weekly total was probably nearer 25,000" (*Stage*, 196).

12 Gurr and Orrell record that the Swan's stage was about 4 feet 8 inches high and the Red Lion's, "the only case where the height of an Elizabethan public stage is precisely known," was 5 feet (118).

13 Even so the acting companies needed to foster a good relationship with the entrepreneurs:

When a company first set up in London it almost always lacked the resources to finance itself, and had to borrow money from an impresario to get started. Travelling in the country required few plays and few costumes, because the venue was constantly changing. In London the one stable venue meant that it was the plays and properties which had to change constantly, and that was expensive. So the companies usually mortgaged their expectations of future prosperity to secure the resources which would make their prosperity possible. In London in the mid-1590s that meant using one of the two impresarios who owned playhouses and the resources that went with them. Philip Henslowe, who owned the Rose playhouse on Bankside, was one ... The other impresario, builder and owner of the Theatre playhouse in Shoreditch, was James Burbage. (Gurr and Orrell, 72)

14 Gurr and Orrell observe:

The sharers in the cooperative enterprise put an exact valuation on their shares. If a player took himself out of the company he was paid the agreed value, and a replacement sharer would have to buy his way in. Share prices were high. The Pembroke's Men to whom it is thought Shakespeare may have belonged in about 1592 valued their shares at £80 each. That is rather more than Shakespeare paid for the second largest house in Stratford in 1597. A share in the rival company to Shakespeare's in 1599 was put at £50. The value of a Chamberlain's Men's share in 1594 was probably the same. (70)

15 For a description of the repertory and procedures of London companies on tour, see Bentley, 177–205. Bentley considers that touring, an "inescapable part of the life of London players," was "nearly always an unpleasant and comparatively unprofitable expedient for London misfortunes, and as the metropolitan companies became more prosperous they resorted to the road less frequently" (179).

16 Gurr quotes Henslowe's inventory of properties for March 1590 (*Stage* 171); he points out, however, that a large proportion of playhouse budget went on sumptuous costuming:

For example, Alleyn's accounts list some quite startling totals for clothing by present-day priorities: £20 10s. 6d. for a "black velvet cloak with sleaves embrodered all with silver and gold," more than a third of Shakespeare's price for a house in Stratford. No wonder Henslowe had a rule against players leaving the playhouse wearing his apparel. (*Stage*, 178)

Gurr also lists Alleyn's wardrobe holdings for 1598 of "clokes," "gownes," "Antik sutes," "Jerkings and dublets," "frenchose" and "Venetians"; 83 garments in all, many of them made of velvet, satin, or silk, several decorated with gold lace or embroidery (*Stage*, 178–81).

17 Under Elizabeth, for example, the London companies performed the same repertoire at court that they mounted in the public playhouses (Gurr, *Stage*, 11). For a brief discussion of court drama under the Stuarts, see Butler.

18 Gurr argues that "the visitations of the plague ... were the most severely limiting phenomenon the players encountered" (*Stage*, 77).

19 The Dutch traveller Johannes de Witt made his famous sketch of the Swan in 1596 and recorded his impressions:

> There are four amphitheatres in London of notable beauty, which from their diverse signs bear diverse names [the Theatre, Curtain, Rose, and Swan]. In each of them a different play is daily exhibited to the populace. The two more magnificent of these are situated to the southward beyond the Thames, and from the signs suspended before them are called the Rose and the Swan. The two others are outside the city towards the north on the high way which issues though the Episcopal Gate, called in the vernacular Bishopsgate. There is also a fifth [the Beargarden], but of a dissimilar structure, devoted to the baiting of bears, where are maintained in separate caged and enclosures many bears and dogs of stupendous size, which are kept for fighting, furnishing thereby a most delightful spectacle to men. Of all the theatres, however, the largest and most magnificent is the one of which the sign is a swan, called in the vernacular the Swan Theatre; for it accommodates in its seats three thousand persons, and is built of a mass of flint stones (of which there is a prodigious supply in Britain), and supported by wooden columns painted in such excellent imitation of marble that it is able to deceive the most cunning.
> (Quoted in Nagler, 117)

The Swiss traveller Thomas Platter described his visits to London public playhouses:

> Every day at two o'clock in the city of London two and sometimes three comedies are performed, at separate places wherewith folk make merry together, and which ever does best gets the greatest audience. The places are so built that they play on a raised platform, and every one can well see it all. There are, however, separate galleries and there one stands more comfortably and moreover can sit, but one pays more for it. Thus anyone who remains on the level standing pays only one English penny: but if he wants to sit, he is let in at a further door, and there he gives another penny. If he desires to sit on a cushion in the most comfortable place of all, where he not only sees everything well, but can also be seen, then he gives yet another English penny at another door. And in the pauses of the comedy food and drink are carried round amongst the people, and one can thus refresh himself at his own cost. (Quoted in Nagler, 117–8)

20 Gurr quotes Sir John Davies who in about 1593 was clearly trying to
   include all comers in his epigram "*In Cosmum.*" He uses the crowd
   struggling out of the playhouse at the end of a play as a metaphor
   describing the confusion of thoughts falling over one another when
   Cosmus struggles to express them all:

   > For as we see at all the playhouse dores,
   > When ended is the play, the daunce, and song:
   > A thousand townsemen, gentlemen, and whores,
   > Porters and serving-men together throng,
   > So thoughts of drinking, thriving, wenching, war
   > And borrowing money, raging in his minde,
   > To issue all at once so forwarde are,
   > As none at all can perfect passage finde. (*Playgoing*, 65–6)

   Often London audiences had little notion of exactly what they would
   see on the platform. Playbills put up around the city advertised the
   time and place of performances, announced whether the play would be
   a tragedy or comedy, but did not necessarily inform the public about
   the play's title or subject matter (Hattaway, *Popular*, 46).

21 Gurr and Orrell describe the "hectic level" of the repertory system operated by Henslowe, with "nearly forty plays in their stock in any one
   year, performing them with a frequency that ranged from six times in
   one month to a single performance – a fate that befell nearly half of
   Henslowe's plays" (80).

22 For detailed discussion of regulations and censorship in the period, see
   Bentley, 145–97.

23 An anonymous play performed by the King's Men at the Globe around
   1606. Other plays on contemporary subjects – domestic dramas –
   include *Arden of Feversham* (1590), *A Woman Killed with Kindness* (1603),
   and *The Witch of Edmonton* (1621).

24 His tedious taxonomy includes "tragedy, comedy, history, pastoral,
   pastoral-comical, historical-pastoral, tragical-historical, tragical-comical-
   historical-pastoral, scene individable, or poem unlimited" (*Hamlet*,
   2.2.396–400).

25 For the inventories of costumes, properties, and expenses received or
   incurred, see Henslowe's *Diaries* 319–21.

26 Gurr observes:

   > The Rose was demolished in 1606, though in a sense it grew up again
   > in 1614, when Henslowe and Alleyn decided to replace their other
   > main business venue, its neighbour the Beargarden, with a new mul-
   > tipurpose playhouse-and-gamehouse, the Hope. The Hope was some-
   > thing less than the last of its kind, for it was designed from the start
   > as a dual-purpose playhouse and bull- and bear-baiting house with a
   > removable stage. (*Stage*, 119)

27 Michael Hattaway, who, like Gurr, considers that evidence points to audiences as a mix of social classes, imagines the gathering in the public playhouse to be active, noisy, but not necessarily disruptively rowdy:

> The audience was not ... as some early scholars would have us believe, an unruly, ignorant mob. Nor is it likely, however, that it attended to the play in hushed reverence as a modern audience might do. The mere fact that the public playhouse performances generally took place by daylight meant that the spectators were on show to one another. Gallants took tobacco as they sat conspicuously on the stage (the habit was established by 1596), orange- and beer-sellers plied their trade before the play began and possibly during the performance; and certainly complaints about the distractions of nut-cracking among the audience are fairly common in the plays. Books and pamphlets were also hawked in the auditoria. (*Popular*, 46)

28 I have drawn the move to commercial playing in a way that I realise greatly oversimplifies its history, smoothing out what was a complicated, uneven, and often contentious process. As well as the authors cited in my text, Michael Bristol, Jean Howard, David Scott Kastan, and Michael Shapiro have informed my discussion.

29 Righter, on the other hand, considers that the acknowledgment of audience presence (particularly in the Tudor period) precluded self-sufficiency, "inhibited the growth of English drama towards the creation on the stage of a three-dimensional image of human life which reflected reality, as represented by the spectators, and yet stood aloof from it, like a dream" (44). She argues that Elizabethan dramatists turned away from the native English tradition and thereby "found in Roman comedy a means of overthrowing the tyranny of the audience, a liberating sanction of the self-contained play" (43).

30 Dates for Shakespeare's plays as listed in Braunmuller and Hattaway, 419–46, are listed below. Asterisks indicate approximate dates.

> *1 Henry VI* *1590
> *2 Henry VI* *1590
> *3 Henry VI* *1590
> *Two Gentlemen of Verona* *1590
> *Taming of the Shrew* *1591
> *Comedy of Errors* *1591
> *Richard III* *1591
> *Titus Andronicus* *1591
> *Love's Labours Lost* *1594
> *Romeo and Juliet* *1595
> *Richard II* *1595
> *A Midsummer Night's Dream* *1595

The Merchant of Venice *1596
1 Henry IV *1597
2 Henry IV *1597
Merry Wives of Windsor 1597
Much Ado About Nothing *1598
Henry V *1599
Julius Caesar *1599
As You Like It *1599
Hamlet *1600
Troilus and Cressida *1602
Othello *1604
King Lear *1605
Macbeth 1606
Antony and Cleopatra *1606
Pericles *1607
Coriolanus 1608
The Winter's Tale *1609
Cymbeline *1610
The Tempest *1611

31 Dessen, writing about the three plays as theatre, describes the first play
    in the trilogy as exhibiting "perhaps the most flexible Shakespearean
    use of 'place'"(89) and, using several examples from all three plays,
    shows that the stage action is constructed in such a way that it "makes
    the central point unmistakable" for the audience (Conventions, 36).

32 Francis Berry calls this kind of stage talking "monoplaned language,"
    very like the style of Marlowe's Tamburlaine, where most speeches seem
    to soar above the playgoers' heads (Berry, 33). All that Berry says of the
    young Marlowe's Tamburlaine applies to Shakespeare's early efforts.
    Describing how Tamburlaine connects to its audience, he writes: "The
    psychological distance between audience and stage-spectacle is a con-
    stant," and while acknowledging the magnificence of its language he
    nevertheless observes that "the verse is delivered within a narrow
    range of vocal tone and pitch" (32). Berry's central argument about
    Marlowe's early way of using his stage applies equally to Shakespeare's
    early writing. In the early plays Shakespeare, like Marlowe, uses no
    frontal movement; in other words, the play stays firmly on the stage
    rather than reaching out to audiences. Berry finds a flatness in
    Tamburlaine:

    No doubt that in a performance of Tamburlaine in the Elizabethan
    theatre, as in a modern revival, there would be movements from
    down-stage to up-stage (and vice versa), but such movements would
    be purely practical rather than visual fulfilments or equivalents of the
    language. The effective, and illustrative, movement is on or near the

apron, is from left to right or right to left, is processional except when it is punctuated by Tamburlaine's declamations to a frozen stage-audience. (32)

33 This play also offers dramatic display (even more sensational and bloodthirsty fare than in the *Henry VI* plays), and again follows a heavily patterned and emblematic dramaturgy. Where the *Henry VI* plays delight in battles and skirmishes, big public action, the violence in *Titus Andronicus* is grisly murder, graphically represented. Shakespeare uses the stage's resources; for example, he exploits the trap for "the blood-stain'd hole" (2.3.210) where Basianus's corpse is dumped.

34 Brennan examines the way Shakespeare uses the off stage to affect audience understanding of the central action:

> Plays are not composed simply of characters enmeshed in sequences of action performed in the presence of an audience. They are a complex weave of actions and reactions, of events that we see and events we hear about performed offstage, and of the differing reactions of characters to events they have acted in on and off stage. An action which occupies only a handful of lines may generate reactions which occupy many hundreds of lines. Reports and the reactions they provoke are vividly recurrent opportunities of presenting the audience with differing versions of the truth and the conflicting viewpoints that are at the very heart of Shakespeare's method of dramatization. (15)

35 I am much indebted to Dessen, *Viewer's Eye* and *Conventions*, for information on Elizabethan theatrical practice, particularly the stage's flexibility of localization and the patterning of gestures, properties, stage groupings as "linking analogues."

36 Like that of Dessen, Styan's stage-centred criticism in *The Shakespeare Revolution* and *The Elements of Drama* has had a deep influence on my thinking about the movement of bodies on the Elizabethan platform.

37 As early as 1589 for *The Jew of Malta* Marlowe had shifted from a processional, largely exclusive playhouse style to an inclusive form.

38 Vickers observes of Shakespeare's characters who make us their intimates:

> If the character is forceful, however, as are Iago, Richard III, Macbeth, direct address to the audience involves us immediately with the full range of their intentions, before, during, and after their execution. As I have observed elsewhere, this involvement leads to an intimacy which we would willingly avoid, if we could. There is no-one in the world whose confidence I would rather less care to share than Iago's. (78–9)

39 It's hard to overemphasize the dramatic weight carried by a stressed first word, particularly by a "now" that opens the play.

40 Later the audience will disappear from Macbeth's vision, too. Gradually
during the course of the play, Macbeth withdraws inside a self-enclos-
ing self, until before his battle he becomes nothing but

> a walking shadow, a poor player
> That struts and frets his hour upon the stage
> And then is heard no more: [life] is a tale
> Told by an idiot, full of sound and fury,
> Signifying nothing. (5.5.24–8)

41 Falstaff tells Hal: "If I do not beat thee out of thy kingdom with a
dagger of lath, and drive all thy subjects afore thee like a flock of wild-
geese, I'll never wear hair on my face more" (2.4.136–9). At first sight,
Falstaff seems to behave like an amalgam of the guild plays' devils
clowning servants, and the nonce plays' impresarios. For a discussion
of Falstaff's inheritance from the Tudor Vice, see Spivak and Potter.
Empson examines Falstaff's many-sidedness in *Pastoral*, (102–9). In
Essays he remarks, "there is a quick answer to the idea that the old
brute has no heart ... If he had no heart, he would have had no power,
not even to get a drink, and he had a dangerous amount of power" (66).

42 Wagner, Faustus's servant in Marlowe's *Dr Faustus*, shares a similar
rapport with the playgoers, a companionable, "down-home," "we're-
all-in-it-together" relationship.

43 In his pockets he keeps lists of what makes life good: "Item, capon for
2s. 2d., Item, Sauce, Item, Sack two gallons 5s. 8d. Item, Anchovies and
sack after supper 2s. 6d. Item, Bread obolus" (2.4.535–41).

44 E. Talbot Donaldson draws parallels between Chaucer's Wife of Bath
and Shakespeare's Falstaff. Both are, he says, "though utterly charming,
perfectly horrible people." He continues by commenting that both characters are, however, "associated with passages of unrivaled emotional
effectiveness, passages that are as splendid tributes to human vitality as
any I know" (137–8).

45 Clemen argues that Falstaff has a "complex personality operating on
many different levels" (38). He finds it impossible to assert a single
source for Falstaff's persona and way of engaging the public:

> Falstaff's alternative view of the heroic events of the war have prece-
> dents in the popular theatre. This popular tradition provided
> Shakespeare with the figure of the Vice, that mischievous and
> immoral joker who commented on the dramatic action from a critical
> distance and maintained his links with the audience by addressing
> them directly. The construction and arrangement of Shakespeare'
> stage were particularly favourable for this, but with Falstaff, as so
> often, Shakespeare goes far beyond all possible precedents and tradi-
> tions. Whether one looks at the traditional Fool, at the Lord of
> Misrule or at the *miles gloriosus*, it is apparent that Falstaff is a more

complex, multi-faceted character, and is above all more human than any of the possible prototypes. (43)

46 Willard Farnham is more generous to Hal. He regards the speech as an example of Hal's conscience at work and the honest words of a man of honour (83–4).

47 Hal also mocks the patently heroic:

[T]he Hotspur of the north; he that kills me some six or seven dozen of Scots at a breakfast, washes his hands, and says to his wife 'Fie upon this quiet life! I want work.' 'O my sweet Harry,' says she, 'how many hast thou killed to-day?' 'Give my roan horse a drench,' says he; and answers 'Some fourteen,' an hour after; 'a trifle, a trifle.' (2.4.102–8)

48 Unlike *Henry V*'s Chorus, Prologue offers the audience no apologies for deficiencies of staging.

49 This is a diction that fits him badly, like Herod's stumbling French in the guild play.

50 John Baxter observes that in *Lear*: "The heroic couplet, holding out the promise of order in its closed couplet form, becomes an instrument for measuring precisely the violation of that order" (166).

51 Kott writes: "War has been ridiculed too. Helen is a tart, Cressida will be sent to the Greek camp and will become a tart. The transfer of Cressida to the Greek camp is not only part of the action of the play; it is also a great metaphor" (79).

52 Donaldson observes about this speech:

[T]he rhyming couplets could be taken as memorized advice from her mother, recited by a girl of no experience—straightforward self-preservative advice based on the not wholly misguided assumption (in Troy at least) that what is to be found in man is lust in action. In his matching soliloquy, just before the lovers meet, Troilus looks forward to an opportunity to "wallow in the lily-beds / Propos'd for the deserver" of Cressida's favors (3.2.12–13) – a not unlustful program of action. Cressida's maxims are, like most maxims, ungenerous but sensibly prudent; they were recognized as maxims by the printer of the Quarto of the play, who surrounded three of them with the quotation marks accorded to gnomic sayings in Elizabethan play texts. (91)

53 In *Antony and Cleopatra*, the other play where war and sex contend, Enobarbus also longs for Antony to get on with being a soldier.

54 Kott claims "Only the bitter fool Thersites is free from all illusions" (82).

55 Dennis Kennedy describes a production of *Hamlet* in East Germany before the 1989 collapse of the German Democratic Republic:

I saw Siegfried Höchst's production at the Volksbühne in East Berlin, which treated Denmark as a literal prison from which almost everybody was trying to escape, just as almost everybody was trying to escape at that moment from East Germany. The stage was enclosed with three rows of wire fencing, and when Laertes was given permission to return to France in the second scene, he was handed a green document that looked suspiciously like the passports issued by West Germany. The audience howled with delight. (136)

56 The countries around also suffer from their controller nation's need to do everything *now*. Young Fortinbras, forbidden to fight the Danes, races off to fight the Poles instead, all for a "little patch of ground" (4.4.18).

57 In Towneley's *Herod the Great*, a messenger brings the king much the same message:

> Bot romoure is rasyed so, that boldly thay brade
> Emangys thame:
> Thay carp of a king:
> Thay seasse not sich chatering. (76–9)
> (But there are so many rumours doing the rounds,
> That they keep yelling out
> Amongst themselves about some king.
> They wouldn't stop their stupid nonsense.)

58 As if a corpse was never a man, after killing him Hamlet degrades Polonius further, saying, "I'll lug the guts into the neighbour room" (4.3.19–21). Hamlet, too, is contained by the materiality of the world. He carries around "this picture./ The counterfeit presentment of two brothers" (3.4.53–4); obliges his mother to look in her mirror to see her offence in her physical reflection, rather than urging her to picture it spiritually.

59 "Hamlet evidently alludes to the Globe's stage roof [here]. 'Frets' in contemporary plasterwork were moulded ribs which divided the whole area of a ceiling into panels or compartments. The intersections of the ribs were marked by bosses which were often gilded, and could well have been fashioned to represent stars." (Gurr and Orrell, 117)

60 I am indebted to Hamlet for the words, but very grateful to Anne Higgins for knowing when to say them.

61 Later in the main action in the shut-in world of Denmark, Hamlet begs Rosencrantz and Guildenstern to treat him as a friend, as an equal who shares a past with them. He says: "let me conjure you, by the rights of our fellowship, by the consonancy of our youth, by the obligation of our ever-preserv'd love, and by what more dear a better proposer can charge you withal, be even and direct with me, whether you were sent for or no! (2.2.283–8). But they, locked by Claudius in a prison of their own, can't supply what he needs. Even his closest friend and confidant Horatio is cut off from him. Although Hamlet says that Horatio is someone with whom he can talk: "thou are e'en as just a man / As e're

my conversation cop'd withal" (3.2.54–59), this praise seems to me barbed. Horatio is merely the best Hamlet can find in Denmark.

62 "The Tyranny of the Audience" is Righter's title for the second chapter of *Shakespeare and the Idea of the Play*, where she discusses Tudor inter-ludes, morality plays, and hybrid plays.

63 I think particularly of the playhouse dynamics of *Women Beware Women*.

64 Michael Bristol observes that in the central action Hamlet often plays the part of the licensed jester, "his jokes and paradoxes acting as real criticism of the madness around him" (9). Responding to this statement, Hattaway writes: "But all too often Hamlet seems to be using the con-ventional role of madman not only as a psychological safety valve but also as an excuse for cruel and unnatural behaviour" (*Hamlet*, 91). Both these observations on Hamlet's behaviour could equally well apply to the stance he takes towards his audience.

65 The English player sheds tears in his performance; Hamlet himself wishes he could weep real tears and wants to make contact with people in the audience who can really cry. But all he succeeds in doing is reminding them of a comic world of amateurish false beards, like that in the popular Tudor play *Like Will To Like*, where a stage direction says, "Here entereth Ralph Roister and Tom Tosspot in their doublet and their hose, and no cap nor hat on their head, saving a nightcap, because the strings of their beards may not be seen" (346). Another example comes from Bottom in *A Midsummer Night's Dream* who "will discharge [a part] in either your straw-colour beard, your orange-tawny beard, your purple-in-grain beard, or your French-crown-colour beard, your perfit yellow" (1.2.93–6).

66 Gurr quotes another theatrical reference to bodkins, from the Induction to the anonymous *A Warning for Fair Women*:
> How some damnd tyrant, to obtaine a crowne,
> Stabs, hangs, imprisons, smothers, cutteth throats,
> And then a Chorus too comes howling in,
> And tels us of the worrying of a cat,
> Then of a filthie whining ghost,
> Lapt in some fowle sheete, or a leather pelch,
> Comes skreaming like a pigge half stickt,
> And cries Vindicta, revenge, revenge:
> With that a little Rosen flasheth forth,
> Like smoke out of a Tabacco pipe, or a boyes squib:
> Then comes in two or three like to drovers,
> With taylers bodkins, stabbing one another,
> Is not this trim? is not here goodly things?
> That you should be so much accounted of. (*Playgoing*, 213)

Hamlet's bodkin is also a comic weapon of revenge (3.1.75).

67 Melissa Furrow suggests that Hamlet's persistent use of infintives in this speech may represent his impotence, observing

> Hamlet goes out of his way to avoid constructions that force him to link his own suicide with his own self. He never uses the pronoun *I* in this speech. When he uses the pronoun *we*, he is thinking of us all. More often, he avoids personal pronouns ("*Who* would bear ... puzzles *the* will") and finite verbs, which require a personal object ("To be or not to be" rather than "Should I kill myself"; "To die, to sleep / To sleep, perchance to dream" rather than "If I died it would be like sleeping, but if I slept, perhaps I'd dream.")

She continues:

> All the action of the play depends on Hamlet ... Yet in this critical speech, a speech made by Hamlet in crisis, Hamlet himself is missing. It is as if the whole play centred on a single point and it were discovered to be a void, as if the heart of the mystery were hollow.

John Baxter suggests another approach: that the point may not be that the spech is impersonal or that Hamlet somehow goes personally missing in it. Rather, given that the address is in the mode Polonius calls "poem unlimited," the question is a general one and not a limited case.

J. V. Cunningham describes the rhetorical strategy of "poem unlimited" as Shakespeare uses it in "Plots and errors: *Hamlet* and *King Lear*." See particularly 216–17.

68 Charles Dickens recognized how Hamlet provokes the audience, and perhaps it might have been so in the Globe. In *Great Expectations* the members of a rowdy Victorian audience offer advice to Hamlet: "Whenever that undecided Prince had to ask a question or state a doubt, the public helped him out with it. As for example; on the question whether 'twas nobler in the mind to suffer, some roared yes, and some no, and some inclining to both opinions said 'toss up for it'; and quite a Debating Society arose" (275).

69 Clemen describes Hamlet's "self-dramatization" as inviting the actor to explore the part's theatrical potential, for the text contains indications both of gestures and movements and of changes in tempo. Often, however, self-dramatization means overstatement. At times Hamlet seems to work himself up to extremes of mood, to cascades of words. (121)

70 Terence Hawkes describes the shocking "material impact of the map placed before Lear – a whole pre-literate and spiritually conceived culture shockingly reduced to and treated as a physical diagram" (124).

71 Kathleen McLuskie views Cordelia's intervention as a "saving love"

which "is the central focus of emotion in the scene. Her resistance to her father gains audience assent through her two asides during her sisters' performances" (99).

72 Bristol observes that the fool is closer to the audience than other characters in the play: "[T]he clown who mingles with the dramatis personae of a dramatic text is not simply a character in a play. He traverses the boundary between a represented world and the here-and-now world he shares with the audience" (*Carnival*, 140).

73 See Weimann on fools' topsy-turvy visions (20–30).

CHAPTER FOUR

1 The Coventry cappers paid 1s. 4d. for actors' gloves in 1542 (Davidson, 1).

2 See also Phythian-Adams, "Ceremony" 238–65. In that last year of playing, the smiths "hired or borrowed a gown from the Taylors and Shearmen's guild" (Tydeman, 210).

3 Particularly when one considers that by the age of nineteen he was married and a father.

4 Other members were Richard and Cuthbert Burbage, John Heminges, Henry Condell, William Sly, and Henry Evans.

5 The Children of the Chapel performed Ben Jonson's and John Lyly's plays at Blackfriars. They gave the first performances of Jonson's *Cynthia's Revels* (1600) and *The Poetaster* (1601). Almost all of Lyly's work was performed here by boy companies, who played *Alexander and Campaspe* and *Endimion, the Man in the Moon*.

6 Gurr describes the reaction of the playgoing public to the more pricy theatres:

> Circumstantial evidence ... suggests that a mob of apprentices which smashed the Cockpit in 1617 were driven by the removal of its plays beyond their capacity to pay for them. Jonson mentions a 'shop's foreman' paying sixpence at Blackfriars for a place in the top gallery, but this minimum price could bother even a gentleman. Ann Halkett's decision to arrange parties of ladies to go to the plays was spurred by her overhearing some gentlemen complain how much it cost them. (*Playgoing*, 75)

7 Foakes argues:

> At the public theatres the groundlings stood nearest to the stage, and spectators paid more to sit further away in the galleries; at the private playhouses, as in modern theatres, the expensive seats were those closest to the stage. At the public theatres, actors would literally play to the galleries, if they played to the most esteemed part of their

audience, and in open-air theatres that would require bold and strong
delivery of lines. At the private theatres, where for the players the
most important part of the audience was seated nearest the stage, a
more low-keyed and intimate style was possible. (31)

Foakes bases his argument on the shaky assumption that actors played
to, and playwrights wrote primarily for, the rich in these audiences.
This is the kind of logic belied by Shakespeare's open stage. I have
argued that open address acknowledges diversity in the audience. In
fact, the drop to the native, so vital a part of open address, sets up a
dynamic between actor and audience, the very reverse of that asserted
by Foakes. The speaker on-stage does not stretch out to shout and
gesture up at the galleries; instead, all the people in the playhouse are
obliged to strain towards the speaker.

8 It cost a minimum of 6d. to enter Blackfriars; a "gentleman's box"
alongside the stage cost five times as much: 2/6 (Gurr, *Playgoing*, 27).

9 Blackfriars had an orchestra of "organs (that is, pipes, lutes, pandores –
the ancestor of the modern banjo) violins and flutes" (Gurr, *Stage*, 27).

10 Robert Hanning observes that "the defining attribute of the romance
form is its plot, which organizes incidents ranging widely in space and
time around the life of the hero without any larger controlling narrative
context, action, or system (such as fate, providence, or national destiny)"
(196). About the characters who inhabit romance, he comments:

The diverse identities used by romance to explore the nature of per-
sonhood include natal (identity of parent and inherited title or situation), qualitative (identity by the intermingling of virtues and vices),
circumstantial (who the world judges us to be in a given situation),
assumed (strategic disguises), and desired or destined (who we want
to be or become again). In a romance world of chance and adventure,
where there may be immature stages in a process of growth, the hero
cannot always control his identity; yet the unstated principle of the
genre is that *in time* his qualitative identity will enable him to regain
his natal, or gain his desired, identity, passing in the course of his
quest through various circumstantial (and sometimes assumed) identities. In other words, identity in romance is at once a *given*, a *process*,
and a *goal* – a past, a present, and a future. (202–3)

Some of the aspects of early romance that Hanning describes survive in
Shakespeare's last plays. However, Shakespeare wrote within a later
context and responded to another tradition. By the Jacobean period,
romance – particularly in its dramatic form – had lost some of its shape.

11 Kastan describes Dekker's "strategy of idealization" (153) of
Elizabethan London in his play *The Shoemaker's Holiday*:

"[I]t is a realistic portrait only of Elizabethan middle-class dreams – a
fantasy of class fulfillment that would erase the tensions and contra-

dictions created by the nascent capitalism of the late sixteenth century. The comic form offers itself as an ideological resolution to the social problems the play engages" (151–2).

12 Butler examines Elizabethan to Stuart court masques describing how romance fiction celebrated noble audiences.

13 Brian Gibbons discusses the prevalence of this kind of celebratory entertainment in Coventry:

> Chivalric romance, which is so prominent an element in the Kenilworth entertainments, was widely circulated in various forms and was extremely popular among non-aristocratic classes. A Coventry citizen, Captain Cox, the chief actor in the Kenilworth Hock Tuesday play, had a collection of chivalric romances, and though his owning so many books might have been exceptional, it is clear that the spirit of the Coventry players accords with the similar type of entertainment offered on the professional stages in London in the 1570s and 1580s. (215)

Kenilworth was on the road between Coventry and Stratford, about six miles from the former and fourteen from the latter. The young Shakespeare may well have seen the Kenilworth entertainments.

14 Gibbons argues:

> The essence of romance is an encounter with events so strange that the hero is challenged to the limits, yielding an experience so radical that it produces a transformation. Although erotic love is an important element in heroic romance, and the chivalric ideal personifies virtue as woman, the central concern of heroic romance goes beyond: ... it is the energy of heroic aspiration, the transcendence of limits, which is the centre. (234)

15 Dutton argues that Shakespeare's last plays are best categorized as tragi-comedies in which characters are notoriously unable or unwilling to communicate, often seeming less than full individuals. the language becomes incoherent, inanely repetitive, or self-reflective. the plays are defiantly strange and disorienting in terms of the audience's expectations, so that the audience vicariously shares something of the perplexity of the characters. the drama is also often self-consciously theatrical and draws attention to its artifice. (15) Tragi-comedy, then, if not "otherworldly" like romance, is at least "another-worldly," not the everyday.

16 As in the plays of Shakespeare's followers Beaumont and Fletcher (for example, *Philaster*, written expressly for Blackfriars).

17 Madeleine Doran argues that the conventions of romance turn on hope for the miraculous: "'Oh, the pity of it' of tragedy becomes 'oh the wonder of it'" in romance (211).

18 Although I discuss only three of the last plays, my argument also applies to *The Winter's Tale*, where open address insistently alerts the

audience to its world, particularly to the passage of real time. The
most obvious example is the figure of Time himself who, telling the
audience openly that the play slips over sixteen years, makes the
playgoers aware of the temporal rules of their existence. In the
central action, Leontes especially would deny time's natural course,
wishing to erase the complexities inherent in maturity and experience
(for example, his aside at 1.3.108–19). The old shepherd encapsulates
the play's reflection on the contradictions of natural time when he
tells his son, "Thou met'st with things dying, I with things new-
born" (3.3.114). In the play as a whole, whenever romance time –
either pastoral or literary – seems to hold sway, some marker from
the real world pulls it back. At Hermione's "resurrection," Leontes
and the audience confront the necessary and natural ravages of real
time. The living woman has aged sixteen years and shows it.
Leontes wonders to Paulina: "Hermione was not so much wrinkled,
nothing / So aged as this seems" (5.3.28–9). In this final scene, the
audience is invoked by open address from Paulina and Leontes.
Paulina gives a general order: "Then, all stand still. / Those that
think is unlawful business / I am about, let them depart" (5.3.95–7).
Leontes follows with: "No foot shall stir" (5.3.98). In other words,
the playgoers are ordered to join in Leontes's act of faith. But,
unlike Leontes, they know that they participate in "an art / Lawful
as eating" (5.3.101–2), since their sense of real time and of what
is actually possible in the real world have been kept alive
throughout.

19 In *Confessio Amantis*, the source of Shakespeare's story, its protagonist,
Amans, like Pericles, needs to understand the past in order to understand himself.

20 In *Pericles*, Shakespeare also draws on the old genre of the saint's life (a
type of romance): Marina's purity is unsullied by her time in a brothel.
Marion Lomax comments on the appropriateness of Gower's resurrection by Shakespeare for this play: God's desire to create a perfect world
intrudes into Book VIII of the *Confessio Amantis*, of which the tale of
Pericles is the central part (76). Of Gower she says, "It is appropriate
that the basic structure of the play should be provided for by a dead
man who has been reborn" (97).

21 Chester's expositor also uses repeated and emphatically positional language. In *The Sacrifice of Isaac*, for example, he explains, "This deede yee
seene done here in this place" (463).

22 "O moral Gower, this bok I directe / To the" (4.1856–7).

23 Gurr suggests that, at Blackfriars, Shakespeare had an "audience long
accustomed to the sophisticated games of the 'theatre of estrangement'"
(*Playgoing*, 168).

24 Brown calls attention to the way that "humour is dispersed throughout the action, but the relaxed enjoyment of comedy is seldom unalloyed" (102). This is particularly true of this play's use of open address, at once inviting and repelling sympathy.

25 Kirsch says "[T]he play deals with [Imogen] very strangely. In a scene that is studiously prepared for, she awakens by the headless body of Cloten, who is dressed in Posthumus's garments, and mistaking him for her husband, she sings an aria of agony. It is a moving and convincing one, but we cannot help being conscious that Imogen also is very ready to be exploited by frauds" (45). John Russell Brown, however, notes the absurd and fantastic nature of some of Imogen's "nightmare-dream":

> For Imogen the experience is specifically like a "dream." The apparent reality as expressed here –
>> Pisanio might have kill'd thee at the heart,
>> And left his head on.
> – is so absurd that very few actresses have dared to use all the words provided. Bernard Shaw recognized that Shakespeare has successfully created the "dim, half-asleep funny state of consciousness" but he nevertheless advised Ellen Terry to cut "A headless man" from her performance. (102)

26 As Emrys Jones aptly puts it, "while an audience inevitably titters" (207), Imogen's misjudgments continue. She mistakes loyal Pisanio for her husband's murderer, inventing a conspiracy in which money ("malice and lucre") is again a driving force (4.2.323–9).

27 John Baxter observes that this song

> registers simultaneously the elements both of tragedy and of romance that are characteristic of the play as a whole, and their conjunction is reflected somewhat in the very structure of the verse. The tetrameter lines of the first three stanzas create a mood of tragic resignation, the recognition that death is universal and inevitable and that both these facts must be accepted. The rhythm, which hovers between trochaic and iambic meters in the first four lines of each stanza, comes out more solidly iambic in the couplet refrain, which drives home this recognition. By contrast the trimeter lines of the fourth stanza, together with the use of feminine endings, seem to transpose the tragic note to another key, invoking protection and solace. These lines are more ritualistically incantatory and more strongly endstopped than most of the preceding. The song is sometimes called a dirge, but in a sense this term applies only to the first three stanzas. The fourth stanza seems to be disarmed, as if by the magic of romance. ("Chastity," 319)

28 Robert Ornstein, referring to what he calls "the silliness of the denoue-
    ment" of *Cymbeline*, describes the ending as "artistically indefensible."
    He states that "in parodying Fletcherian tragicomedy, Shakespeare
    makes a joke of his own play" (212). I think, however, that while
    Shakespeare makes comic the usual conventions of romance ending,
    he also offers an alternative ending that is at once funny, serious, and
    disturbing.

Bibliography

Adams, Joseph Quincy, ed. *Chief Pre-Shakespearean Dramas*. Boston: Houghton Mifflin, 1924.

Adams, Robert. "The Egregious Feasts of the Chester and Townley Shepherds." *Chaucer Review* 1986. 21.2. 96–107.

Anderson, M.D. *Drama and Imagery in English Medieval Churches*. Cambridge, Cambridge University Press, 1963.

Apius and Virginia. *Tudor Interludes*. Ed. Peter Happé. Harmondsworth: Penguin, 1972. 271–318.

Artaud Antonin. *The Theatre and Its Double*. Trans. Mary Caroline Richards. New York: Grove Press, 1958.

Aston, Elaine, and George Savona. *Theatre as Sign System: A Semiotics of Text and Performance*. London: Routledge, 1991.

Auerbach, Erich. *Literary Language and Its Public in Late Latin Antiquity and the Middle Ages*. Trans. R. Manheim. New York, Pantheon Books, 1965.

– *Mimesis*. Trans. W.R. Trask. Princeton: Princeton University Press, 1973.

– *Scenes from the Drama of European Literature*. Gloucester, MA: Peter Smith, 1973.

Axton, Marie, and Raymond Williams, eds. *English Drama: Forms and Development: Essays in Honour of Muriel Clara Bradbrook*. Cambridge: Cambridge University Press, 1977.

Axton, Richard. *European Drama of the Early Middle Ages*. Pittsburgh: University of Pittsburgh Press, 1975.

– "Popular Modes in the Earliest Plays." *Medieval Drama*. Ed. Neville Denny. London: Edward Arnold, 1973. 13–40.

Baker, Herschel. "*Henry VI*, Parts 1, 2, and 3." *The Riverside Shakespeare*. Ed. G. Blakemore Evans. Boston: Houghton Mifflin, 1972. 587–93.

Bakhtin, M.M. *Rabelais and His World*. Trans. Helene Iswolsky. Cambridge: MIT Press, 1968.

Bale, John. *Kynge Johan. Specimens of the Pre-Shakespearean Drama*. Vol. 1. Ed. John Matthews Manly. 1897. New York: Dover, 1967. 525–618.

Baxter, John. "*Cymbeline* and the Measures of Chastity." *Shakespearean Criticism Yearbook 1993*. New York: Gale Research Inc., 1994. 319–27.

– *Shakespeare's Poetic Styles: Verse into Drama*. London: Routledge, 1980.

Beadle, Richard. "The Shipwrights' Craft." *Aspects of Early English Drama*. Ed. Paula Neuss. Cambridge: D. S. Brewer, 1983. 50-61.

– ed. *The York Plays*. London: Arnold, 1982.

– and Pamela King, eds. *York Mystery Plays: A Selection in Modern Spelling*. Oxford: Clarendon, 1984.

Beckerman, Bernard. *Shakespeare at the Globe, 1599–1609*. New York: MacMillan, 1964.

– *Theatrical Presentation: Performer, Audience and Act*. New York: Routledge, 1990.

Beer, Gillian. *The Romance*. London: Methuen, 1970.

Belsey, Catherine. *The Subject of Tragedy: Identity and Difference in Renaissance Drama*. New York: Methuen, 1985.

Ben Chaim, Daphna. *Distance in the Theatre: The Aesthetics of Audience Response*. Ann Arbor: UMI Research Press, 1984.

Bennett, Susan. *Theatre Audiences: A Theory of Production and Reception*. London: Routledge, 1990.

Bentley, Gerald Eades. *The Professions of Dramatist and Player in Shakespeare's Time 1576–1642*. Princeton: Princeton University Press, 1984.

Berry, Francis. *Poetry and the Physical Voice*. London: Routledge, 1962.

– *The Shakespearean Inset: Word and Picture*. Carbondale: Southern Illinois University Press, 1971.

Bethell, S.L. *Shakespeare and the Popular Dramatic Tradition*. London: Staples Press, 1944.

Bevington, David M. *From "Mankind" to Marlowe: Growth of Structure in the Popular Drama of Tudor England*. Cambridge, MA: Harvard University Press, 1962.

– *Medieval Drama*. Boston: Houghton Mifflin, 1975.

– "'Maimed Rites': Violated Ceremony in *Hamlet*." *Critical Essays on Shakespeare's Hamlet*. Ed. David Scott Kastan. New York: G.K. Hall, 1995. 126–38.

– "Popular and Courtly Traditions on the Early Tudor Stage." *Medieval Drama*. Ed. Neville Denny. London: Edward Arnold, 1973. 91–108.

– *Tudor Drama and Politics: A Critical Approach to Topical Meaning*. Cambridge: Harvard University Press, 1968.

Billington, Sandra. *Mock Kings in Medieval Society and Renaissance Drama*. Oxford: Clarendon Press, 1991.

Bills, Bing D. "The Suppression Theory and the English Corpus Christi Play: A Re-Examination." *Theatre Journal* 32 (1980): 157–68.

Blake, Herbert. *The Audience*. Baltimore: Johns Hopkins University Press, 1990.

Bliss, Lee. "Pastiche, Burlesque, Tragicomedy." *The Cambridge Companion to English Renaissance Drama*. Eds A. R. Braunmuller and Michael Hattaway. Cambridge: Cambridge University Press, 1990. 237–62.

Block, K.S., ed. *Ludus Coventriae or the Plaie Called Corpus Christi*. London: Oxford University Press, 1922.

Booth, Stephen. "On the Value of *Hamlet*." *Reinterpretations of Elizabethan Drama*. Ed. Norman Rabkin. New York: Columbia University Press, 1969. 137–76.

Bradbrooke, M.C. *Themes and Conventions of Elizabethan Tragedy*. Cambridge: Cambridge University Press, 1935.

– *The Rise of the Common Player*. London: Chatto and Windus, 1962.

Braunmuller, A.R. "The Arts of the Dramatist." *The Cambridge Companion to English Renaissance Drama*. Eds A. R. Braunmuller and Michael Hattaway. Cambridge: Cambridge University Press, 1990. 53–90.

Brennan, Anthony. *Onstage and Offstage Worlds in Shakespeare's Plays*. London: Routledge, 1989.

Bristol, Michael. *Big-Time Shakespeare*. London: Routledge, 1996.

– *Carnival and Theater: Plebeian Culture and the Structure of Authority in Renaissance England*. New York: Methuen, 1985.

Brody, A. *The English Mummers and their Plays*. Philadelphia: Pennsylvania University Press, 1970.

Brook, Peter. *The Empty Space*. Harmondsworth: Penguin, 1968.

Brown, John Russell. *Shakespeare's Plays in Performance*. New York: Applause Theatre Books, 1993.

Bulman, James C. *Shakespeare, Theory, and Performance*. London: Routledge, 1996.

Burns, Edward. *The Chester Mystery Cycle: A New Staging Text*. Liverpool: Liverpool University Press, 1987.

Burns, Elizabeth. *Theatricality: A Study of Convention in Theatre and in Social Life*. London: Longman, 1972.

Butler, Martin. "Private and Occasional Drama." *The Cambridge Companion to English Renaissance Drama*. Eds A.R. Braunmuller and Michael Hattaway. Cambridge: Cambridge University Press, 1990. 127–60.

Cambises. *Specimens of the Pre-Shakespearean Drama*. Vol. 2. Ed. John Matthews Manly. 1897. New York: Dover, 1967. 159–210.

Cameron, Kenneth, and Stanley K. Kahrl. "Staging in the N-Town Cycle." *Theatre Notebook* 21 (1967): 134–8.

The Castle of Perseverance. *Medieval Drama*. Ed. David Bevington. Boston: Houghton Mifflin, 1975. 796–900.

Cavell, Stanley. *Disowning Knowledge in Six Plays of Shakespeare*. Cambridge: Cambridge University Press, 1987.

Cawley, A.C. "The 'Grotesque' Feast in the Prima Pastorum." *Speculum* 30 (1955): 213.
- "The Staging of Medieval Drama." *The Revels History of Drama*. Vol. 1. Eds. A.C. Cawley, Marion Jones, Peter F. McDonald, and David Mills. London: Methuen, 1983. 1–66.
- ed. *The Wakefield Pageants in the Towneley Cycle*. Manchester: Manchester University Press, 1958.
Chambers, E. K. *The English Folk Play*. Oxford: Oxford University Press, 1933.
- *English Literature at the Close of the Middle Ages*. 1945. Oxford: Clarendon Press, 1976.
- *The Medieval Stage*. 2 vols. Oxford: Clarendon Press, 1903.
Chartier, Roger. *The Cultural Uses of Print in Early Modern France*. Princeton: Princeton University Press, 1987.
Clark, Sandra, ed. *Shakespeare Dictionary*. Oxford: Hutchinson, 1986.
Clemen, Wolfgang. *Shakespeare's Soliloquies*. London: Methuen, 1987.
Clopper, Lawrence M., ed. *Records of Early English Drama. Chester*. Toronto: University of Toronto Press, 1979.
Cohen, Walter. *Drama of a Nation: Public Theater in Renaissance England and Spain*. Ithaca: Cornell University Press, 1985.
Coldewey, John C. *Early English Drama: An Anthology*. New York: Garland, 1993.
- "Some Economic Aspects of the Late Medieval Drama." *Contexts for Early English Drama*. Eds Marianne G. Briscoe and John C. Coldewey. Bloomington: Indiana University Press, 1989. 86–7.
- "That Enterprising Property Player: Semi-Professional Drama in Sixteenth-Century England." *Theatre Notebook*. 31 (1977): 5–12.
Cook, Anne Jennalie. *The Privileged Playgoers of Shakespeare's London 1576–1642*. Princeton: Princeton University Press, 1981.
Courtney, Richard. *Shakespeare's World of War*. Toronto: Simon and Pierre, 1994.
Craig, Hardin. *English Religious Drama of the Middle Ages*. Oxford: Oxford University Press, 1955.
- "Morality Plays and Elizabethan Drama." *Shakespeare Quarterly* 1 (1950): 64–72.
- *Two Coventry Corpus Christi Plays*. London: Oxford University Press, 1957.
Craik, T.W. *The Tudor Interlude: Stage, Costume, and Acting*. Leicester: Leicester University Press, 1962.
Crouch, David J.F. "Paying to See the Play: The Stationholders of the York Corpus Christi Play in the Fifteenth Century." *Medieval English Theatre*, 1991, 13, 64–111.
Cunningham, J.V. *Collected Essays of J.V. Cunningham*. Chicago: Swallow Press, 1976.

Davidson, Clifford. *Technology Guilds and Early English Drama*. Kalamazoo: Medieval Institute Publications, 1996.

Davis, Norman, ed. *Non-Cycle Plays and Fragments*. London: Oxford University Press, 1969.

Davison, Peter. *"Hamlet": Text and Performance*. London: Macmillan, 1983.

Dekker, Thomas. *The Shoe Maker's Holiday*. Ed. D.J. Palmer. London: Benn, 1975.

Dessen, Alan, "Elizabethan Audiences and the Open Stage." *Yearbook of English Studies*, 10, 1980. 1–20.

– *Elizabethan Drama and the Viewer's Eye*. Chapel Hill: North Carolina University Press, 1977.

– *Elizabethan Stage Conventions and Modern Interpreters*. Cambridge: Cambridge University Press, 1984.

– *Recovering Shakespeare's Theatrical Vocabulary*. Cambridge: Cambridge University Press, 1995.

de Witt, Johannes. "The Interior of the Swan Theatre." *A Source Book in Theatrical History*. Ed. A.M. Nagler. New York: Dover, 1952. 116–17.

Dickens, Charles. *Great Expectations*. New York: Signet, 1963.

Diller, Hans-Jürgen. *The Middle English Mystery Play: A Study in Dramatic Speech and Form*. Cambridge: Cambridge University Press, 1992.

Dobson, R.B. "Urban Decline in Medieval England." *The Medieval Town: A Reader in English Urban History 1200–1540*. Eds Richard Holt and Gervase Rosser. London: Longman, 1990. 265–86.

Dollimore, Jonathan. *Radical Tragedy: Religion, Ideology and Power in the Drama of Shakespeare and his Contemporaries*. Chicago: Chicago University Press, 1984.

– and Alan Sinfield, eds. *Political Shakespeare: New Essays in Cultural Materialism*. Manchester: Manchester University Press, 1985.

Donaldson, E. Talbot. *The Swan at the Well: Shakespeare Reading Chaucer*. New Haven: Yale University Press, 1985.

Doran, Madeleine. *Endeavors of Art: A Study of Form in Elizabethan Drama*. Madison: University of Wisconsin Press, 1954.

Dorson, Richard M. *Folklore and Folklife: An Introduction*. Chicago: Chicago University Press, 1972. 159–91.

Drakakis, John, ed. *Shakespearean Tragedy*. London: Longman, 1992.

Dutton, Richard. *Modern Tragicomedy and the British Tradition*. Brighton: Harvester, 1986.

Eccles, Mark, ed. *The Macro Plays*. London: Oxford University Press, 1969.

Elam, Keir. *The Semantics of Theatre and Drama*. London: Routledge, 1991.

Elliott, John. "The Sacrifice of Isaac as Comedy and Tragedy." *Medieval English Drama: Essays Critical and Contextual*. Eds Jerome Taylor and Alan H. Nelson. Chicago: Chicago University Press, 1972. 157–77.

Empson, William. *Essays on Shakespeare*. Ed. David B. Pirie. Cambridge: Cambridge University Press, 1986.

– *Some Versions of Pastoral*. Harmondsworth: Penguin, 1966.

England, George, ed. *The Towneley Plays*. 1897. London: EETS, 1952.

Enough is as Good as a Feast. English Morality Plays and Moral Interludes. Eds Edgar T. Schell and J. D. Schuchter. New York: Holt, 1969. 367–418.

Erickson, Peter. *Rewriting Shakespeare, Rewriting Ourselves*. Berkeley: University of California Press, 1991.

Esslin, Martin. *An Anatomy of Drama*. New York: Hill and Wang, 1976.

Everyman. Medieval Drama. Ed. David Bevington. Boston: Houghton Mifflin, 1975. 939–63.

Farnham, Willard. *The Medieval Heritage of Elizabethan Tragedy*. Oxford: Oxford University Press, 1956.

– *The Shakespearean Grotesque: Its Genesis and Transformations*. Oxford: Oxford University Press, 1971.

Fish, Stanley E. *Is There a Text in this Class? The Authority of Interpretive Communication*. Cambridge: Harvard University Press, 1980.

Foakes, R.A. "Playhouses and Players." *The Cambridge Companion to English Renaissance Drama*. Eds A. R. Braunmuller and Michael Hattaway. Cambridge: Cambridge University Press, 1990. 1–52.

Four Elements. Three Rastell Plays. Ed. Richard Axton. Cambridge: D.S. Brewer, 1979. 29–68.

Frey, Charles. *Shakespeare's Last Romance*. Columbia: Missouri University Press, 1980.

Frow, Gerald. *"Oh, Yes It Is!": A History of Pantomime*. London: BBC, 1985.

Fulgens and Lucrece. Ed. G. Wyckham. *English Moral Interludes*. London: Dent, 1976.

Fulwell, Ulpian. *Like Will to Like Quoth the Devil to the Collier. Tudor Interludes*. Ed. Peter Happé. Harmondsworth: Penguin, 1972. 319–64.

Furnivall, F.J., ed. *The Digby Plays*. London: Oxford University Press, 1896.

Furrow, Melissa M. "Latin and Affect." *The Endless Knot: Essays on Old and Middle English in Honor of Marie Boroff*. Eds M. Teresa Tavormina and R.F. Yeager. Cambridge: D.S. Brewer, 1995.

– "Listening Reader and Impotent Speaker: The Role of Deixis in Literature." *Language and Style*. 1988. 21.4 365–78.

Galloway, David, ed. *Records of Early English Drama. Norwich 1540-1642*. Toronto: University of Toronto Press, 1981.

Gammer Gurton's Needle. Specimens of the Pre-Shakespearean Drama. Vol 11. Ed. John Matthews Manly. 1897. New York: Dover, 1967. 93–158.

Gardiner, H.C. *Mysteries' End: An Investigation of the Last Days of the Medieval Religious Stage*. Hamden, CT: Archon Books, 1967.

Gassner, John, ed. *Medieval and Tudor Drama*. New York: Bantam, 1963.

– *Medieval and Tudor Drama*. New York: Bantam, 1963.

Gibbons, Brian. *Jacobean City Comedy*. 2 ed. London: Methuen, 1980.

Goldman, Michael. *The Actor's Freedom: Toward a Theory of Drama*. New York: Viking, 1975.

– *Shakespeare and the Energies of Drama*. Princeton: Princeton University Press, 1972.

Goodman, Jennifer R. *British Drama before 1660*. Boston: Twayne Publishers, 1990.

Gorboduc; or Ferrex and Porrex. Specimens of the Pre-Shakespearean Drama. Vol. 2. Ed. John Matthews Manly. 1897. New york: Dover, 1967. 211–72.

Grantley, Darryll. "*The Winter's Tale* and Early Religious Drama." *Comparative Drama* 20 (1986): 17–37.

Greenblatt, Stephen. "Invisible Bullets: Renaissance Authority and its Subversion, *Henry IV* and *Henry V*." *Political Shakespeare: New Essays in Cultural Materialism*. Eds Jonathan Dollimore and Alan Sinfield. Ithaca: Cornell University Press, 1985. 18–47.

– *Renaissance Self-Fashioning from More to Shakespeare*. Chicago: University of Chicago Press, 1984.

– *Shakespearean Negotiations: The Circulation of Social Energy*. Berkeley: University of California Press, 1988.

Greene, Robert. *Friar Bacon and Friar Bungay*. Ed. W.W. Greg. Oxford: Oxford University Press, 1926.

Greenfield, Peter H. "'All for your delight / We are not': Amateur Players and the Nobility." *Research Opportunities in Renaissance Drama* 28 (1985): 173–9.

Greenfield, Thelma N. *The Induction in Elizabethan Drama*. Eugene: University of Oregon Press, 1969.

Gurevich, Aron Iakolevich. *Problems of Medieval Popular Culture*. Cambridge: Cambridge University Press, 1988.

Gurr, Andrew. *Playgoing in Shakespeare's London*. Cambridge: Cambridge University Press, 1987.

– "The Bear, the Statue, and Hysteria in *The Winter's Tale*." *Shakespeare Quarterly* 34 (1983): 420–5.

– *The Shakespearean Stage, 1574–1642*. Cambridge: Cambridge University Press, 1990.

– and John Orrell. *Rebuilding Shakespeare's Globe*. London: Weidenfield and Nicolson, 1989.

Hanning, Robert W. *The Individual in Twelfth-Century Romance*. New Haven: Yale University Press, 1977.

Happé, Peter, ed. *Tudor Interludes*. Harmondsworth: Penguin, 1972.

Harbage, Alfred. *Shakespeare's Audience*. New York: Columbia University Press, 1941.

Hardison, O.B. *Christian Rite and Christian Drama in the Middle Ages: Essays on the Origin and Early History of Modern Drama*. Baltimore: Johns Hopkins University Press, 1965.

Harris, William O. *Skelton's Magnyfycence and the Cardinal Virtue Tradition*. Chapel Hill: North Carolina University Press, 1965.

Hartnoll, Phyllis. *The Theatre. A Concise History*. London: Thames and Hudson, 1968.

Hartwig, J.L. *Shakespeare's Tragicomedy Vision*. Baton Rouge: Louisiana University Press, 1972.

Hattaway, Michael. *Elizabethan Popular Theatre: Plays in Performance*. London: Routledge, 1982.

– *Hamlet*. Atlantic Highlands, NJ: Humanities Press International, 1987.

Hawkes, Terence. *Meaning by Shakespeare*. London: Routledge, 1992.

Heinemann, Margot. "Political Drama." *The Cambridge Companion to English Renaissance Drama*. Eds A.R. Braunmuller and Michael Hattaway. Cambridge: Cambridge University Press, 1990. 161-206.

Helterman, Jeffrey. *Symbolic Action in the Plays of the Wakefield Master*. Athens: University of Georgia Press, 1981.

Henslowe, Philip. *The Diaries*. Eds R.A. Foakes and R.T. Rickert. Cambridge: Cambridge University Press, 1961.

Heywood, John. *A Mery Play Betwene Johan Johan the Husbande, Tib His Wife, and Sir Johan the Preest. Medieval Drama*. Ed. David Bevington. Boston: Houghton Mifflin, 1975. 970–89.

– *The Play of the Weather. Medieval Drama*. Ed. David Bevington. Boston: Houghton Mifflin, 1975. 990–1028.

Higgins, Anne. "Work and Play: Guild Casting in the Corpus Christi Drama." *Medieval and Renaissance Drama in England*. Vol. 7. Ed. Leeds Barroll. Madison: Fairleigh Dickinson University Press, 1995. 76–97.

Hilton, Rodney. "Women Traders in Medieval England." *Class Conflict and the Crisis of Feudalism*. London: Verso, 1990. 214–15.

Hodgdon, B. *The End Crowns All: Closure and Contradiction in Shakespeare's History*. Princeton: Princeton University Press, 1991.

Horestes, An Interlude of Vice. Three Tudor Classical Interludes: Thersites, Jacke-Jugeler, Horestes. Ed. Marie Axton. Cambridge: D.S. Brewer, 1982. 94–138.

Hosley, Richard. "Three Kinds of Outdoor Theatre Before Shakespeare." *Theatre Survey* 12 (1971): 1–33.

Howard, Jean E. *Shakespeare's Art of Orchestration: Stage Techniques and Audience Response*. Urbana: Illinois University Press, 1984.

– "Shakespeare's Creation of a Fit Audience for *The Tempest*." *Shakespeare: Contemporary Critical Approaches. Bucknall Review* 25 (1980): 142–53.

– *The Stage and Social Struggle in Early Modern England*. London: Routledge, 1994.

Impatient Poverty. Recently Recovered "Lost" Tudor Plays with Some Others. Ed. John S. Farmer. Guildford: Charles W. Traylen, 1966.

Ingram, R.W., ed. *Records of Early English Drama. Coventry*. Toronto: University of Toronto Press, 1981.

– *The Interlude of Wealth and Health*. London: Oxford University Press for Malone Society, 1907.

Ingram, William, ed. *The Business of Playing: The Beginnings of Adult Professional Theater in Elizabethan London*. Ithaca: Cornell University Press, 1992.

James, Mervyn. "Ritual, Drama and Social Body in the Late Medieval English Town." *Past and Present* 98 (1983): 3–29.

Jochum, Peter Klaus. *Discrepant Awareness: Studies in English Renaissance Drama*. Frankfurt am Main: Lang, 1979.

Johnston, Alexandra A. and Margaret Rogerson, eds. *Records of Early English Drama. York*. Toronto: University of Toronto Press, 1979.

Jones, Emrys. *The Origins of Shakespeare*. Oxford: Clarendon Press, 1977.

Jones, G.P. "*Henry V*: The Chorus and the Audience." *Shakespeare Survey* 31 (1978): 93–104.

Jones, Robert C. "Dangerous Sport: The Audience's Engagement with Vice in the Moral Interludes." *Renaissance Drama* ns 6 (1975, for 1973): 52.

– "The Stage World and the 'Real' World in Medwall's *Fulgens and Lucrece*." *Modern Language Quarterly* 32 (1971): 141–2.

Joseph, B.L. *Elizabethan Acting*. London: Oxford University Press, 1951.

Kahrl, S.J. *Traditions of Mediaeval English Drama*. London: Hutchinson, 1970.

– ed. *Records of Plays and Players in Lincolnshire, 1300-1585 Collections VIII*. Oxford: Oxford University Press for Malone Society, 1969.

Kastan, David Scott. *Shakespeare and the Shapes of Time*. Hanover: New England University Press, 1982.

– and Peter Stallybrass. "Introduction: Staging the Renaissance." *Staging the Renaissance*. Eds David Scott Kastan and Peter Stallybrass. London: Routledge, 1991. 1–17.

Kennedy, Dennis. "Shakespeare without His Language." *Shakespeare, Theory, and Performance*. Ed. James C. Bulman. London: Routledge, 1996. 133–48.

King Darius. Ed. John S. Farmer. London: Early English Drama Society, 1906.

King, Pamela M. "Spatial Semantics and the Medieval Theatre." *The Theatrical Space*. Ed. James Redmond. Cambridge: Cambridge University Press, 1987. 45–59.

King, T.J. *Shakespearean Staging: 1599-1642*. Cambridge, MA: Harvard University Press, 1971.

Kirsch, Arthur C. *Jacobean Dramatic Perspectives*. Charlottesville: University of Virginia Press, 1972.

Knight, G. Wilson. *The Wheel of Fire: Interpretations of Shakespearian Tragedy*. Oxford: Oxford University Press, 1954.

Kolve, V.A. *The Play Called Corpus Christi*. London: Arnold, 1966.

Kott, Jan. *Shakespeare Our Contemporary*. New York: Norton, 1974.

– *The Bottom Translation*. Evanston, IL: Northwestern University Press, 1987.

Kynge Johan. Specimens of the Pre-Shakespearean Drama. Vol. 1. Ed. John Matthews Manly. 1897. New York: Dover, 1967. 525–618.

Lancashire, Ian. *Dramatic Texts and Records of Britain: A Chronological Topography to 1558*. Toronto: University of Toronto Press, 1984.

– ed. *Two Tudor Interludes: "Youth" and "Hickscorner"*. Manchester: Manchester University Press, 1980. 157–238.

Levin, Richard. *The Multiple Plot in English Renaissance Drama*. Chicago: University of Chicago Press, 1971.

– *New Readings of Old Plays: Recent Trends in the Reinterpretation of English Renaissance Drama*. Chicago: University of Chicago Press, 1979.

Lomax, Marion. *Stage Images and Traditions: Shakespeare to Ford*. Cambridge: Cambridge University Press, 1987.

Luminiansky, R.M., and David Mills, eds. *The Chester Mystery Cycle*. London: Oxford University Press, 1974.

Lusty Juventus. Ed. J.M. Nosworthy. 1966. London: Oxford University Press for Malone Society, 1971.

Magnificence. Ed. Paula Neuss. Manchester: Manchester University Press, 1980.

Mankind. Medieval Drama. Ed. David Bevington. Boston: Houghton Mifflin, 1975. 901–38.

Marlowe, Christopher. *Christopher Marlowe: Complete Plays and Poems*. Ed. E.D. Pendry. London: Dent, 1976.

The Marriage of Wit and Wisdom. Five Anonymous Plays (Fourth Series). Ed. John S. Farmer. Guildford: Charles W. Traylen, 1966.

Mazer, Cary M. "Historicizing Alan Dessen: Scholarship, Stagecraft, and the 'Shakespeare Revolution'." *Shakespeare, Theory, and Performance*. Ed. James C. Bulman. London: Routledge, 1996. 149–67.

McGuire, Philip C. *Speechless Dialect: Shakespeare's Open Silences*. Berkeley: University of California Press, 1985.

– and David A. Samuelson, eds. *Shakespeare: The Theatrical Dimension*. New York: AMS Press, 1979.

McLuskie, Kathleen. "The Patriarchal Bard: Feminist Criticism and Shakespeare: *King Lear* and *Measure for Measure*." *Political Shakespeare*. Eds Jonathan Dollimore and Alan Sinfield. Ithaca: Cornell University Press, 1985. 88–108.

Medwall, Henry. *Fulgens and Lucrece. English Moral Interludes*. Ed. Glynne Wickham. London: Dent, 1976. 41–101.

Mehl, Dieter. *The Elizabethan Dumb Show: The History of a Dramatic Convention*. London: Methuen, 1965.

Meredith, Peter, and John E. Tailby, eds. *The Staging of Religious Drama in Europe in the Later Middle Ages: Texts and Documents in English Translation*. Kalamazoo: Medieval Institute Publications, 1983.

Mills, Howard. *Working with Shakespeare*. Hemel Hempstead: Harvester Wheatsheaf, 1993.

Mooney, Michael. *Shakespeare's Dramatic Transactions*. Durham, NC: Duke University Press, 1990.

Morgan, M.M. "'High Fraud': Paradox and Double-Plot in the English Shepherds' Plays." *Speculum* 39 (1964): 676–89.

Mullaney, Steven. *The Place of the Stage: License, Play and Power in Renaissance England*. Chicago: University of Chicago Press, 1988.

Mundus et Infans. Specimens of the Pre-Shakespearean Drama. Vol. 1. Ed. John Matthews Manly. 1897. New York: Dover, 1967. 353–85.

Nagler, A.M. *A Source Book in Theatrical History*. New York: Dover, 1952.

Nelson, Alan H. *The Mediaeval English Stage: Corpus Christi Pageants and Plays*. Chicago: University of Chicago Press, 1974.

– "Some Configurations of Staging in Medieval English Drama." *Medieval English Drama: Essays Critical and Contextual*. Eds Jerome Taylor and Alan H. Nelson. Chicago: University of Chicago Press, 1972. 116–48.

Nuttal, A.D. *A New Mimesis: Shakespeare and the Representation of Reality*. London: Methuen, 1983.

Owst, G.R. *Literature and Pulpit in Medieval England*. Oxford: Blackwell, 1961.

Palliser, D.M. "The Trade Guilds of Tudor York." *Crisis and Order in English Towns 1500–1700*. Eds Peter Clark and Peter Slack. Toronto: University of Toronto Press, 1972. 103–6.

Pasternak, Anne Slater. *Shakespeare, the Director*. Totowa, NJ: Barnes and Noble, 1982.

Patterson, A. *Shakespeare and the Popular Voice*. Oxford: Blackwell, 1984.

Pavis, Patrice. *Dictionary of the Theatre: Terms, Concepts, and Analysis*. Trans. Christine Shantz. Toronto: University of Toronto Press, 1998.

Pfister, Manfred. *The Theory and Analysis of Drama*. Cambridge: Cambridge University Press, 1991.

Pikeryng, John. *Horestes, An Interlude of Vice. Three Tudor Classical Interludes: Thersites, JackeJugeler, Horestes*. Ed. Marie Axton. Cambridge: D.S. Brewer, 1982. 94–138.

Platter, Thomas. "The Price of Admission." *A Source Book in Theatrical History*. Ed. A.M. Nagler. New York: Dover, 1952. 117–18.

Potter, Robert. *The English Morality Play: Origins, History and Influence of a Dramatic Tradition*. London: Routledge, 1975.

Power, Eileen. *Medieval People*. London: Harper, 1963.

Preston, Thomas. *Cambises. Specimens of the Pre-Shakespearean Drama*. Vol. 2. Ed. John Matthews Manly. 1897. New York: Dover, 1967. 159–210.

Price, Joseph, ed. *The Triple Bond: Plays Mainly Shakespearean in Performance*. London: Pennsylvania State University Press, 1975.

Pythian-Adams, C.V. "Ceremony and the Citizen: The Communal Year at Coventry 1450–1550." *The Medieval Town: A Reader in English Urban History 1200–1540*. Eds Richard Holt and Gervase Rosser. London: Longman, 1990. 238–64.

– *Desolation of a City: Coventry and the Urban Crisis of the Later Middle Ages*. Cambridge: Cambridge University Press, 1979.

– "Urban Decay in Late Medieval England." *Towns in Societies: Essays in Economic History and Historical Sociology*. Eds Philip Abrams and E.A. Wrigley. Cambridge: Cambridge University Press, 1978. 159–85.

Rabkin, Norman. *Shakespeare and the Common Understanding*. New York: The
    Free Press, 1967.

Rastell, John. *Four Elements*. *Three Rastell Plays*. Ed. Richard Axton.
    Cambridge: D.S. Brewer, 1979. 29–68.

Reed, A.W. *Early English Drama*. London: Methuen, 1926.

Rendell, Thomas. "Visual Typology in the Abraham and Isaac Play." *Modern
    Philology* 81 (1984): 221–32.

Respublica. Tudor Interludes. Ed. Peter Happé. Harmondsworth: Penguin,
    1972.

Ribner, Irving. *Tudor and Stuart Drama*. Arlington Heights: AHM Publishing,
    1978.

Righter, Anne. *Shakespeare and the Idea of the Play*. London: Chatto and
    Windus, 1962.

Rose, Jacqueline. "Sexuality in the Reading of Shakespeare: *Hamlet* and
    Measure for Measure." *Alternative Shakespeares*. Ed. John Drakakis. London:
    Routledge, 1988. 95–119.

Ross, Lawrence J. "Symbol and Structure in the Second Pastorum." *Medieval
    English Drama: Essays Critical and Contextual*. Eds Jerome Taylor and Alan
    H. Nelson. Chicago: University of Chicago Press, 1972. 180–98.

Rossiter, A.P. *English Drama from Early Times to the Elizabethans*. London:
    Hutchinson, 1950.

– *Shakespeare's Stagecraft*. Cambridge: Cambridge University Press, 1967.

Sackville, Thomas, and Thomas Norton. *Gorboduc; or Ferrex and Porrex*.
    Specimens of the Pre-Shakespearean Drama. Vol. 2. Ed. John Matthews Manly.
    1897. New York: Dover, 1967. 211–72.

Salter, F.M. *Medieval Drama in Chester*. Toronto: University of Toronto Press,
    1955.

Seltzer, David. "The Staging of the Last Plays." *Later Shakespeare*. Eds J.R.
    Brown and Bernard Harris. London: Edward Arnold, 1966. 127–66.

Serpieri, Alessandro. "Reading the Signs: Towards a Semiotics of
    Shakespearean Drama." *Alternative Shakespeares*. Ed. John Drakakis.
    London: Methuen, 1985. 119–43.

Shakespeare, William. *The Riverside Shakespeare*. Ed. G. Blakemore Evans.
    Boston: Houghton Mifflin, 1974.

Shapiro, Michael. "Annotated Bibliography on Original Staging in
    Elizabethan Plays." *Research Opportunities in Renaissance Drama* 24 (1981):
    23–49.

Skelton, John. *Magnificence*. Ed. Paula Neuss. Manchester: Manchester
    University Press, 1980.

Smith, Irwin. *Shakespeare's Blackfriars Playhouse: Its History and Design*. New
    York: New York University Press, 1966.

Southern, Richard. *The Making of the Middle Ages*. London, Hutchinson, 1953.

– *The Medieval Theatre in the Round*. London: Faber, 1957.

- *The Seven Ages of the Theatre*. London: Faber, 1968.
- *The Staging of Plays before Shakespeare*. London: Faber, 1973.
- *Western Society and the Church in the Middle Ages*. Harmondsworth: Penguin, 1970.

Spivack, Bernard. *Shakespeare and the Allegory of Evil: The History of a Metaphor in Relation to His Major Villains*. New York: Columbia University Press, 1958.

Squires, Lynn. "Law and Disorder in *Ludus Coventriae*." *Comparative Drama* 12 (1978): 207–11.

Stevens, Martin. *Four Middle English Mystery Cycles*. Princeton: Princeton University Press, 1987. 326–7.

Sticca, Sandro, ed. *Medieval Drama*. Albany: SUNY Press, 1972.

Streitberger, W.R. *Court Revels 1485–1550*. Toronto: University of Toronto Press, 1994.

Styan, J. L. *The Dark Comedy: The Development of Modern Comic Tragedy*. Cambridge: Cambridge University Press, 1962.

- *Drama, Stage and Audience*. London: Cambridge University Press, 1975.
- *Shakespeare's Stagecraft*. Cambridge: Cambridge University Press, 1967.

Swanson, Heather. "Artisans in the Urban Economy: The Documentary Evidence from York." *Work in Towns 850–1850*. Eds Penelope J. Corfield and Derek Keene. Leicester: Leicester University Press, 1990. 42–55.

Taylor, Jerome and Alan H. Nelson, eds. *Medieval English Drama: Essays Critical and Contextual*. Chicago: University of Chicago Press, 1972.

Teague, Frances. *Shakespeare's Speaking Properties*. London: Associated Universities Press, 1991.

Thomson, Peter. *Shakespeare's Professional Career*. Cambridge: Cambridge University Press, 1992.

- *Shakespeare's Theatre*. London: Routledge, 1983.

Tiddy, R.J.E. *The Mummers'Play*. Oxford: Oxford University Press, 1923.

Travis, Peter W. *Dramatic Design in the Chester Cycle*. Chicago: University of Chicago Press, 1982.

The Trial of Treasure. Ed. John S. Farmer. London: Tudor Facsimile Texts, 1967.

Twycross, Meg. "Places to Hear the Play: Pageant Stations at York, 1398-1572." *REED Newsletter* 2 (1978): 10–33.

- "The Theatricality of Medieval English Plays." *The Cambridge Companion to Medieval English Theatre*. Ed. Richard Beadle. Cambridge: Cambridge University Press, 1994. 38–64.

Tydeman, William. *The Theatre in the Middle Ages: 800–1576*. Cambridge: Cambridge University Press, 1978.

Tyler, Sharon. "Minding True Things: The Chorus, the Audience, and *Henry V*." *The Theatrical Space*. Ed. James Redmond. Cambridge: Cambridge University Press, 1987. 69–81.

Udall, Nicholas. *Respublica*. *Tudor Interludes*. Ed. Peter Happé. Harmondsworth: Penguin, 1972. 221–70.

Vickers, Brian. *Appropriating Shakespeare: Contemporary Critical Quarrels*. New Haven, CT: Yale University Press, 1993.

Wager, William. *The Longer Thou Livest the More Fool Thou Art*. Ed. R. Mark Benbow. Nebraska: University of Nebraska Press, 1967.

Warren, Roger. *Staging Shakespeare's Late Plays*. Oxford: Oxford University Press, 1990.

Weimann, Robert. *Shakespeare and the Popular Tradition in the Theatre*. Baltimore: Johns Hopkins University Press, 1978.

Wickham, Glynne. *Early English Stage 1300–1660*. 2 vols. London: Routledge, 1959.

- *The Medieval Theatre*. London: Weidenfeld, 1974.

- *Shakespeare's Dramatic Heritage: Collected Studies in Medieval, Tudor, and Shakespearean Drama*. London: Routledge, 1969.

- ed. *English Moral Interludes*. London: Dent, 1976.

Williams, Arnold. *The Drama of Medieval England*. East Lansing: Michigan State University Press, 1961.

Williams, Clifford John. *Theatres and Audiences: A Background to Dramatic Texts*. London: Longmans, 1970.

Withington, Robert. "Braggart, Devil, and 'Vice'." *Speculum* 11 (1936): 124–9.

Woolf, Rosemary. *The English Mystery Plays*. Berkeley: University of California Press, 1978.

Yachnin, Paul. *Stage-Wrights: Shakespeare, Jonson, Middleton, and the Making of Theatrical Value*. Philadelphia: University of Pennsylvania Press, 1997.

Youings, Joyce. *Sixteenth-Century England*. Harmondsworth: Penguin, 1988.

Young, Karl. *The Drama of the Medieval Church*. 2 vols. Oxford: Clarendon Press 1933.

Index